Kosher
Living

Kosher Living

It's More Than Just the Food

Rabbi Ron Isaacs

AN ARTHUR KURZWEIL BOOK

JOSSEY-BASS
A Wiley Imprint
www.josseybass.com

Library of Congress Cataloging-in-Publication Data

Isaacs, Ronald H.
Kosher living: it's more than just the food / Ron Isaacs.— 1st ed.
    p. cm.
"An Arthur Kurzweil book."
Includes bibliographical references and index.
    ISBN 0–7879–7642–3 (alk. paper)
    1. Judaism—Customs and practices—Miscellanea. 2. Jewish ethics—Miscellanea.
3. Jewish law—Miscellanea. 4. Jewish way of life—Miscellanea. I. Title.
    BM700.I7235 2005
    296.7—dc22   2004026727

Printed in the United States of America
FIRST EDITION
HB Printing   10 9 8 7 6 5 4 3 2 1

Contents

TOPIC 6

Celebrating a Wedding or Bar/Bat Mitzvah Party 21

TOPIC 9

Circumcision 38

TOPIC 10

Clothing and Care of the Body   42

What the Experts Say   59

Sources   61

TOPIC 13
Death and Dying   62

What's Kosher   62

TOPIC 14
Ecology 71

TOPIC 17
Food   86

What's Kosher   86

TOPIC 18

Friendship   *97*

TOPIC 19

Gossip and Speech   104

What's Kosher   104

What's Not Kosher   105

What the Experts Say   110

Sources   111

TOPIC 20
Hanukkah　112

TOPIC 21
Honesty and Truth 120

What's Kosher 120

What's Not Kosher 122

What the Experts Say 124

Sources 126

TOPIC 22
Hospitality 127

What's Kosher 127

TOPIC 23
Kindness to Animals 133

TOPIC 25
Mezuzah 146

TOPIC 26
Mitzvah 150

TOPIC 27
Office Work 159

TOPIC 28

Organ Transplants   163

TOPIC 31

Repentance   *183*

What's Kosher   183

TOPIC 32

Sabbath   *189*

TOPIC 33

Sex *198*

TOPIC 34
Shopping   207

TOPIC 37
Tallit 222

TOPIC 40

Torah Reading 238

What's Not Kosher 242

What the Experts Say 243

Source 243

TOPIC 41
Torah Study 244

What's Kosher 244

TOPIC 42

Visiting the Sick   250

For Elsie Fuerst,
who personifies kosher living

Foreword

One of my favorite stories is the one that is told about Professor Isaac Rabi, the distinguished physicist who taught at Columbia for many years. He said that he owed his achievements as a scientist to his mother because every day when he came back from school, she would say to him: "Did you ask a good question in school today?"

I love that story because Jews love questions even more than answers. The Bible is not a catechism to be memorized but a text to be examined and reexamined from every possible angle. And a student who asks questions of the text is not to be dismissed as a troublemaker but is to be honored as an inquiring mind.

Rabbi Ron Isaacs understands the centrality of the question and the respect for the questioner in the Jewish tradition, and therefore he has created this book of questions that are frequently asked or that ought to be asked about Judaism. It is kind of a continuation of the Four Questions with which the Passover Seder begins, for its purpose is to encourage the reader to ask more questions.

I think that this book comes at a good time in the Jewish spiritual story. I remember, not so many years ago, when people would stand after one of my lectures and ask me: "Why be Jewish?" That still happens on occasion, but much more often, people challenge me by asking: "How be Jewish?" It is for these people, for inquiring minds and searching souls, for people whose knowledge cannot be overestimated but whose intelligence cannot be underestimated, that Rabbi Isaacs has written this book.

I hope that those who read this book will be encouraged not necessarily to accept the answers that it contains but to continue to raise questions and to become part of the continuing conversation between the generations that is the Jewish story.

One more story and I will let you get on to the book itself. The story is told that the *New York Times* once heard about Professor Saul Lieberman of the Jewish Theological Seminary, one of the giants of Jewish scholarship, so they sent a reporter out to interview him. The reporter came into Professor Lieberman's office, and he saw a Talmud open on his desk. He pointed to the dark print in the middle of the page and asked him what that was. Dr. Lieberman said that that was the Mishnah, which is a second-century commentary on the Torah. The reporter then asked what the writing below the Mishnah was. Dr. Lieberman explained that that was the Gemara, which is a commentary on the Mishnah edited in the fifth century. The reporter then asked what the writing on the side of the page was. Dr. Lieberman explained that that was the commentary of Rashi, a sage who lived in France in the eleventh century. The reporter then asked what the writing in the column on the other side of the page was. Dr. Lieberman explained that that was the commentary of the Tosofists, who lived in Germany several generations after Rashi. And so it went, as the professor patiently explained what the commentaries in the back of the book were and where and when they were written.

Finally, the reporter said: "Now I get it! Judaism is a conversation between the generations!"

Dr. Lieberman said afterward that that was the shortest and the simplest definition of Judaism that he had ever heard and that he was especially impressed because it came from a non-Jew.

Ron Isaacs understands the need for this generation to listen in on and to continue this conversation between the generations, to add its questions, and perhaps even its own answers, and that is why he has written this book. May it be used.

—Rabbi Jack Riemer

Preface

The word *kosher* has come to mean that which is proper or fit, the correct way to do something according to Jewish law and tradition. That is why one can ask about a business dealing of questionable legality: "Is it kosher?" Similarly, one might say of parchment in a mezuzah whose written letters are beginning to fade due to excessive wear, "Is it kosher?" meaning: Is it fit to be used according to Jewish law?

When something is not kosher, we generally use the word *treif* or *pasul*. A Torah scroll, if improperly written or in disrepair, is considered nonkosher. Similarly, a tallit (prayer shawl) that is missing one of the four fringes on its corners is also considered nonkosher and therefore unacceptable to wear according to Jewish law. Food that is not kosher and by definition not permitted to be eaten according to Jewish law is called *treif* food.

Although the Hebrew word *kasher* (or kosher as we hear it in English) is generally associated in Judaism with food and dietary restrictions, the word appears only once in the entire Bible. In the Book of Esther, which is read on the festival of Purim, the word *kasher* appears in chapter 8, verse 5. Esther beseeches Ahasuerus to avert the evil that Haman has plotted against the Jews. "Esther said: 'If it pleases the king, and I have found favor in his sight, and the proposal seems proper [*kasher*], and if I am pleasing to you—let dispatches be written to revoke the letters concocted by Haman which he issued, ordering the destruction of the Jews in all the provinces." (All biblical quotations are my own paraphrasing of various printed versions.) In this context the word *kosher* undoubtedly means fit or proper.

Kosher Living: It's More Than Just the Food covers both topics of general interest and topics related to specific Jewish rituals and customs. Each topic is arranged alphabetically for easy access and reference and is presented in question-and-answer format. For Jews, asking questions is a national pastime; and the great sages of Jewish tradition ask every conceivable question about every conceivable topic.

Each chapter will begin with questions and answers related to the topic. These sections are divided into two parts: "What's Kosher" and "What's Not Kosher." Following the questions and answers is the section "What the Experts Say" (quotations from noteworthy Jewish sources, including Jewish folktales, proverbs, prayers, meditations, magazine articles, and quotations from famous Jews and non-Jews); another called "Sources" pinpoints the origin of the topic and concludes each chapter.

At the end of the book, I have included a discussion of the sources of Jewish law and a who's who of rabbinic sages and commentaries. This chapter is intended to explain how Jewish law develops over the ages and identify the major written and oral sources of legal opinion, from bygone years to the present time.

Remember that although you can use this book as a guide to kosher living, it is in no way a definitive code of Jewish law. There will surely be occasions when you will want to consult your own rabbi about a particular question or nuance of the law. I have, however, tried to present the modern traditional view of what is kosher and what is not for each entry; and on occasion I have also presented differing customs and views of the rabbis who make up the various branches of Judaism.

I truly hope that this book will help to answer your questions about what is proper and fit according to the Jewish law and help you in your quest to live a kosher life. With your additional knowledge, you might even choose to aspire to be even more caring and meticulous in your own observance, living each day and seeing it through Jewish eyes. I wish you happy reading and *l'chayim kesherim*—to a kosher life!

Acknowledgments

I want to thank my literary agent, Joan Parker, for bringing this volume to the attention of Jossey-Bass. Several friends and colleagues generously gave of their time to read drafts of this book. I feel blessed to have such good friends and colleagues and am pleased to acknowledge the contributions of Rabbi Jack Riemer; Dr. Arnie Dashevsky; Danny Siegel; Dr. Mark Gold; and my beloved wife and partner, Leora.

My appreciation goes to Alan Rinzler, who invited me to develop *Kosher Living* and whose keen editorial skills, vision, and knowledge are reflected in its pages. My thanks as well to Seth Schwartz (assistant editor), Andrea Flint (production editor), and Geneviève Duboscq (copy editor) for their help and guidance in enhancing this book. My sincere gratitude to Arthur Kurzweil for his many suggestions and insights that helped to shape this book and better structure its questions and answers.

I am grateful as well to my congregation, Temple Sholom, where I have served as rabbi since 1975. Its wonderful members and beloved supportive leadership have given me the forum to develop many of the ideas and questions in this volume.

Finally, much gratitude to a very special woman, Elsie Fuerst, who taught me and so many others the true meaning of kosher living at its finest.

Kosher Living

Topic 1

Abortion

❦ What's Kosher ❧

When is it kosher to have an abortion?

It depends on the case. Judaism is not against all abortion. Some rabbis would say that it's kosher to have an abortion if having the child would put the mother's life at risk or if the child's birth would cause mental anguish to the mother. Others would disagree.

Some would say it's kosher to have an abortion if the doctors are of the opinion that the child would be seriously deformed, thus causing severe anguish to the mother. Others would disagree.

Still other rabbinic authorities would permit abortion in cases in which the pregnancy is the result of rape. In recent years a number of prominent Orthodox rabbis have ruled that, even in cases of rape, the woman should not have the right to abort. These rabbis wish to restrict abortion solely to instances in which the mother's life is physically endangered. Others—more Reform and liberal rabbis—would disagree.

As with many Jewish things, there is a range of opinions about if and when an abortion is permissible.

When learning that you are going to have triplets, is it kosher to abort one of the fetuses?

When a woman is pregnant with three or more fetuses, either naturally or artificially, an abortion of one or more of them may be indicated in order to preserve both the life of the mother and the viability
and health of the remaining fetuses. Such abortions, according to
many rabbinic authorities, are permitted (and depending on the circumstances, even required). When it becomes possible to determine
through genetic testing which of the fetuses has a greater chance
to survive and be healthy, then it would be permissible selectively to
abort those less likely to survive.

✿ What's Not Kosher ❦

When is it not kosher to have an abortion?

Abortion may not be used as a form of birth control after the fact. In-
convenience would not be considered a kosher reason for allowing an
abortion. The Reform liberal position is that the mother (presumably
with input from the father) should make decisions concerning abortion and need not consult with a rabbi.

Is it kosher to consider a fetus a human being? Does Judaism see all abortion as murder?

According to Jewish law, a fetus is potential life and becomes human
life only when it is born. Therefore, equating abortion with murder
is not kosher, because biblical and rabbinic sources understand the
process of gestation developmentally.

Is it kosher to consider the health of the fetus when desiring an abortion?

Traditional Jewish sources show no justification for aborting a fetus for
reasons having to do with the health of the fetus; only the mother's

health is a consideration. As a result, some people object to performing an amniocentesis at all, even when the intent is to determine whether to abort a malformed fetus. Others reason in precisely the opposite direction. They justify abortion of a defective fetus on the basis of preserving the mother's mental health when it is clear that the mother is not able to cope with the prospect of bearing or raising such a child.

Many Conservative and Reform rabbis, and even a few contemporary Orthodox ones, have handled the matter in a completely different way. They reason that traditional sources recognize only threats to the mother's health as grounds for abortion because until recently it was not possible to know anything about the genetic makeup of the fetus before birth. Our new medical knowledge, they say, ought to establish the fetus's health as an independent consideration.

I agree with this last approach, although it is problematic. It raises the very difficult issue of determining what constitutes a sufficient defect to warrant abortion. Moreover, if families were to freely abort so-called defective children, one wonders about the degree to which society in the long run will tolerate imperfections and provide for people who have them. Thus, the very sensitivity of society to the sanctity of life is at stake.

❧ What the Experts Say ❧

If a woman suffers difficult labor in the process of giving birth, it is permitted to cut up the fetus in her womb, whether by drugs or by surgery, because the fetus is like one who is pursuing after her to kill her. But if it brings forth its head, it must not be harmed, for we do not set aside one life because of another. (Maimonides, Mishneh Torah, Commentary to Mishnah Oholot 7:6)

As long as the fetus has not emerged into the light of the world, it is not a human life (*nefesh*) and it is therefore permissible to take its life in order to save the life of its mother. (Rashi, commentary to Sanhedrin 72b)

When abortion is therapeutic, there can be no objection to it, because like any other surgery, we sacrifice the part for the whole. (Rabbi Isaac Klein, *A Guide to Jewish Religious Practice*, p. 416)

The embryo is considered to be mere water until the fortieth day of pregnancy. (Talmud, Yevamot 69b)

❦ Sources ❧

When men fight and one of them pushes a pregnant woman and a miscarriage results, but no other damage ensues, the one responsible shall be fined according as the woman's husband may exact from him, the payment to be based on reckoning. But if other damage ensues, the penalty shall be life for life. (Exodus 21:22–23)

If a woman is in hard travail [that is, she finds it very difficult to give birth to her child and there is consequently danger to her life], her child must be cut up while it is in her womb and brought out limb by limb, since the life of the mother has priority over the life of the child. But if the greater part has already emerged from the womb, it may not be touched, since the claim of one life cannot override the claim of another life. (Mishnah, Oholot 7:6)

❦ ❧

Applying for a Job

❦ What's Kosher ❧

If you must give a reference for a person applying for a job, is it kosher to tell the truth even if this will be detrimental to the applicant?

When answering questions about an employee who is searching for a new job and has given your name as a reference, one is bound to be truthful. Although Jewish law forbids saying negative things about a person (even if true), if the person to whom one is speaking has a legitimate need for this information, one must answer all questions truthfully. As a rabbi, I get many reference calls about teachers and employees of my temple. In addition to answering the questions I am asked as truthfully as possible (with regard to a candidate who had his or her share of deficiencies), I always try to find several positive things to say about the person. There are good traits to be found in everyone.

Is it kosher to apply for a job that you know you are unqualified for?

Yes, it is permissible to apply for a job for which you may feel underqualified. People do it all the time. By doing this, you are showing confidence in yourself and your abilities. Many employers may choose to hire a person who does not possess all of the necessary qualifications. It's up to the employer to decide whether he or she feels a person is qualified enough to at least start in the position. On meeting a person who is intelligent and eager to learn, employers are often willing to give the person a chance to show his or her worth and ability to grow with the job.

❦ What's Not Kosher ❧

If someone you know is applying for a job and seems to have a good chance of getting it, is it kosher to apply for the same job?

If someone you knew were pursuing a job opportunity and seemed to have a good chance of getting it, Judaism would view it as unfair for you to apply for the same job, even if you were more qualified.

Aware of how cutthroat some people can become, Jewish ethical teaching tries to condition them to rein in their more extreme competitive tendencies: "If a poor man is examining a cake for purposes of purchasing it and another knows of his intention and buys it for himself, the latter is called a wicked man" (Talmud, Kiddushin 59a). The story describes the purchaser as poor in order to underscore that he or she does not have the option of purchasing another cake, should one become available. Jewish law understands this principle as applying to more than just poor people.

It condemns as immoral the act of stepping in when one has finished a business deal and is about to sign the contract and trying to steal away the deal. This same principle would apply in the case of a worker seeking employment.

If someone you know solicits your advice on whether he should leave a job (and you are interested in applying for the position), is it kosher for you to offer advice?

Any time a person comes to you for advice and you have an interest in the matter at hand, you are obligated either to refrain from offering counsel or to inform the person of your interest in the case. Jewish law forbids a person to pretend to be helpful while framing the advice so as to help the advice giver pursue a hidden agenda.

If someone has a chronic disease that may keep him or her out of work for short periods, is it kosher to hide that information from a potential employer?

Judaism says that honesty is the best policy, with few exceptions. I believe it would be only fair for the person being interviewed to fully disclose the medical condition to the interviewer. Because the medical condition would entail asking for time off, I believe that an employer would need to be reassured that the prospective employee could do the job and that even with the medical condition, the work would get done in a timely fashion. Employers always appreciate honest workers, and it is quite possible that, having disclosed the medical condition, the candidate might well get the job based on his or her honesty.

❦ What the Experts Say ❧

If a person seeks your advice, do not give him counsel that is wrong for him. Do not say to him, "Leave early in the morning," so that thugs might mug him. Do not say to him, "Leave at noon," so that he might faint from heat. Do not say to him, "Sell your field and buy a donkey," so that you may circumvent him, and take the field away from him. (Sifra, on Leviticus 19:14)

Fifty productive people are better than two hundred who are not. (Jerusalem Talmud, Peah 8:8)

❦ Sources ❧

Six days you shall labor and do all your work. (Exodus 20:9)

You shall do what is right and good in the sight of God. (Deuteronomy 6:18)

Topic 3

Arguing with Others

❦ What's Kosher ❧

I am on my synagogue's board of trustees, and we fight all the time. Is this kosher?

With certainty it is kosher to argue, although excessive arguing is problematic. Much of the Talmud, the first rabbinic interpretation of the Bible, consists of arguments and disputes that various rabbis had in order to determine what would become the law of the land. Though the rabbis show regard for people of a peaceable nature, such as Aaron the priest, they never claimed that a person should shun controversy. On the contrary, controversy is sometimes necessary to sharpen the mind and produce constructive results. But remember, when arguing one should try to be kind and humble, making a point of always studying, understanding, and valuing all of the positions that are on the table.

Is there a kosher way to argue?

I have had my share of arguments with congregants in my thirty-year rabbinic career. Experience and study have taught me that some ways of arguing can be beneficial to both parties and make the experience a more fruitful and civil one. Here are my picks for kosher arguing:

- Be truthful.
- Be slow to anger.
- Never purposefully try to embarrass another person.
- Give the other person the benefit of the doubt.
- Argue with humility.
- Know your place.
- Be a good listener.
- Be open to the other person's opinions.
- Avoid petty squabbles.
- Try to end every discussion with shalom, in a peaceful manner.
- Never argue maliciously.
- Use words to advance your argument but not to hurt your adversary.
- Never use damaging information to invalidate your adversary's contentions.

Is it kosher to argue with God?

Judaism has a rich tradition of calling God to task over human suffering and injustice. Abraham is the first to do so in the Bible. When learning of God's intention to destroy Sodom and Gomorrah, he tries to change God's mind, asking: Because there are undoubtedly some good people in the cities, how can God destroy the innocent with the wicked? "Shall not the judge of all the earth act with justice?" (Genesis 18:25). Abraham also seems to be arguing on behalf of the evil people; otherwise he would have requested that the good people alone be spared. Instead he appeals to God to save all the people of Sodom and Gomorrah, provided some good people can be found within them.

Arguing with God is perfectly kosher. During the silent Amidah (daily petitionary prayer), I encourage my congregants to spend time in private prayer and meditation. Because the Amidah consists of numerous petitions, it is a perfect opportunity to add one's own.

I often argue for myself that God would reconsider certain circumstances or that He would make His path clearer to me as I seem sometimes to simply stumble along. Know that God doesn't always accede to our arguments. But arguing with Him (while respectfully recognizing God's authority) is a part of praying to God with fervor. It is being real with God, giving God a chance to hear and speak to our burdens and feelings, even if by His greater wisdom His path may already be set. Struggling with God in prayer may produce great blessing. Even when God says no, we can know that He has listened to us and considered what we have asked. As with a parent, that can make us love Him all the more.

I came across a wonderful poem that sums up this discussion. Here is an excerpt from Aaron Zeitlin's poem, "If You Look at the Stars" (in Sydney Greenberg and Jonathan Levine, editors, *Likrat Shabbat*):

> *Praise Me or curse Me says God,*
> *And I will know that you love Me.*
> *Raise your fist against Me and revile, says God.*
> *Sing out graces or revile,*
> *Reviling is also a kind of praise, says God.*
> *If you see suffering and don't cry out,*
> *Then I created you in vain, says God.*

❦ What's Not Kosher ❧

What kind of arguing is not kosher?

Arguing ethically is kosher, but arguing unfairly is not. In the Bible Korach was the prototype of controversy and argumentation that was not for the sake of heaven. Trying to wrest the leadership of the Israelites from Moses, he was a complainer, a grumbler, a power-hungry man who used the power of words as an opportunity to exalt himself above others (Numbers 16).

Like Korach, people who argue angrily and treat another unkindly or who are boastful and let their egos prevent them from acknowledging the truth that the other side states are practicing the nonkosher brand of argumentation. Pettiness and showing no care about another's views is also not proper arguing.

One must always keep one's words focused exclusively on the issue when quarrelling. Using damaging personal information to invalidate one's adversary, using obscenities and words that hurt, and showing lack of proper decorum is not only nonkosher but often transforms a moderate argument into a furious fight.

When arguing, is it kosher to say, "You don't know what you're talking about"?

According to Sefer Hasidim, a medieval ethical work that concerns everyday issues, if two people are debating an issue, one should never say to the other, "You don't know what you are talking about." One is cautioned that such language is nonkosher, even if the other person is way off the mark. The reason for this prohibition is that saying this phrase to another is tantamount to calling him a fool, which Judaism forbids.

✟ What the Experts Say ✥

Every dispute that is for a heavenly cause will ultimately endure. (Ethics of the Fathers 5:17)

The arrow maker is killed by his own shaft. (Talmud, Pesachim 28)

Whoever argues merely for the sake of argument is a boor. (She'aylot U'teshevot)

Disputes they may be, but they are God's living words. (Talmud, Eruvin 13)

When the purpose of the argument is not to contradict but to persuade others to accept the truth, that person's words will endure. (Maimonides)

For three years there was a dispute between the School of Shammai and the School of Hillel. Shammai asserted: "The law is according to our view," and the Hillel school asserted: "The law is according to our view." Then a voice issued from heaven and announced: "The teaching of both are the words of the living God, but the law is in agreement with the School of Hillel." But, it was asked, since both are the words of the living God, for what reason was the School of Hillel entitled to have the law decided according to its rulings? Because they were kind and humble, and because they studied their own rulings and those of the School of Shammai, and even mentioned the teachings of the School of Shammai before their own. (Talmud, Eruvin 13b)

Better an insincere peace than a sincere quarrel. (The Lubliner Rebbe)

When people start to argue, leave them and do not get caught in their snares. (Rav Hai Gaon)

❧ Source ☙

Every dispute that is for a heavenly cause will ultimately endure. (Ethics of the Fathers 5:17)

Topic 4

❧ ❧

Autopsies

❧ **What's Kosher** ❧

Is it kosher to demand an autopsy be performed?

On some occasions in the past, more Orthodox rabbinical authorities have said that autopsy might be permitted in these instances: to study anatomy, to determine the cause of a person's death, to save future patients who may have a similar disease (in the case of a genetic disorder), and to transplant an organ from a dead person to a living individual.

More liberal rabbis permit autopsies under all circumstances. The more traditional rabbis generally permit autopsy if it may directly contribute to saving the life of another patient at hand. In the case of hereditary diseases, the family or future offspring of the deceased are considered to represent patients at hand, and thus autopsies are allowed.

Is it kosher to have an autopsy in Israel?

A year after Israel became a state, Israeli Chief Rabbi Herzog enunciated a definitive position on autopsy in his 1949 agreement with Hadassah Hospital in Jerusalem. Under that agreement autopsies would be sanctioned only when one of the following conditions obtained:

The autopsy is legally required.

Three physicians agree that the cause of death cannot otherwise
be ascertained.

Three physicians attest that the autopsy might help save the lives of
others suffering from an illness similar to the one that caused
the patient's death.

In the case of a hereditary disease, performing the autopsy might
safeguard surviving relatives.

In each case Chief Rabbi Herzog mandated that those who perform
the autopsy do so with reverence for the dead and that they deliver the
corpse and all of its parts to the burial society for interment upon completion of the autopsy.

Today in Israel and elsewhere in the world, when autopsy is jus-
tified for legal or medical reasons, it is construed not as a dishonor to
the dead but as an honorable use of the body to help the living. Indeed, it is assumed that the dead person himself or herself would have
wanted the autopsy to take place if it could accomplish the legal or
medical end for which autopsy is intended.

In the last few years, there has been considerable controversy
over autopsies in Israel because they have become routine. New pro-
cedures, such as a needle biopsy or a peritoneoscopy with biopsy, may
soon accomplish most of the same medical objectives as autopsies
without invading the corpse to the same degree; and that would clearly
be preferable from the Jewish point of view.

Is it kosher to do stem cell research?

This question has at its core one's understanding of the moral status
of tiny human embryos no larger than a pinprick. In each of these
embryos are so-called stem cells, which can grow into any kind of
human tissue. Scientists have posited that use of these cells can help
researchers find a cure for severe illness. But harvesting them kills
the embryo, and therein lies the ethical issue and the questions of
when life begins and when a life is a life.

No single view can answer whether Jewish law permits stem cell research. A multitude of opinions exist on the subject. Reform rabbis, for example, posit that an isolated fertilized egg does not enjoy the full status of personhood. They wrote a letter to George W. Bush supporting federal funding for stem cell research, on the basis of the primary responsibility to save human life, a supreme Jewish value.

Many of my Conservative rabbinic colleagues posit that doing stem cell research that is funded under strict guidelines is kosher. Because an estimated 128 million Americans afflicted with conditions may benefit, stem cell research seems to me the right thing to do.

❦ What's Not Kosher ❧

When is it not kosher to do an autopsy?

The consensus of rabbinic opinion today seems to forbid doing an autopsy if it would not in any way directly contribute to saving the life of another patient at hand. I know some Orthodox Jews who believe that "in the end of days" God will resurrect the dead and that any kind of disfigurement of the body will interfere with the process.

❦ What the Experts Say ❧

According to Jewish law, autopsies may be performed if medicine is likely to be advanced thereby and if they lead to the saving of life. (*Jewish Post Weekly*, Mar. 27, 1967)

❦ Source ❧

It is forbidden to enjoy or derive benefit from anything belonging to the dead. (Yoreh Deah 349:1)

Topic 5

Business Practices

❦ **What's Kosher** ❧

Is it kosher to own a gun store?

I have not found a rabbinic answer that directly responds to this question. Centuries ago Maimonides prohibited Jews from selling weapons because they would inadvertently help their enemies procure weapons that could be the source of their own victimization. But in modern times, although selling guns to the wrong customer could be very dangerous, I can see no reason why a Jew would be forbidden to own a gun store. The owner, though, would clearly have the responsibility of being as certain as humanly possible that his customer was not a criminal or mentally deranged.

The Talmud offers a good piece of rabbinic advice that surely applies here: "Who is wise? One who foresees the future consequences of his acts" (Tamid 32). It seems to me that the right of a person to sell firearms to a customer is contingent on carefully checking into the purchaser's background. Without such a check, the seller shares in the moral responsibility for harm that might result from selling a gun to a person who shouldn't have one.

Is it kosher for a large business or corporation to make unlimited profits?

In his book *Capitalism and Freedom*, economist Milton Friedman states that a business's only social responsibility is to use its resources and engage in activities designed to increase profits, so long as it stays within the rules of the game. The Torah disagrees, saying that one must share one's profit with the needy. Thus, it teaches that "when you reap your harvest, you must leave the corners of your field uncut so that the poor can help themselves to the leftovers" (Leviticus 19:9). The very minimum that Jewish tradition says we must leave behind is one-sixtieth of the yield. The second mitzvah associated with this biblical verse is *leket*: the reaper lets grain stalks fall to the ground so that the poor can find them (Leviticus 19:10).

Believe it or not, some businesses apply these commandments to their work. Fred the Furrier is involved in more than thirty charities, most concerned with improving the quality of life and education in New York City.

Another is Ben and Jerry's, a Vermont-based ice cream company founded by best friends Ben Cohen and Jerry Greenfield. One of the largest purveyors of premium ice cream in the United States, Ben and Jerry's has worked tirelessly to harness its business power to improve the quality of life. For example, it has made a pitch for preserving the rainforest of Brazil on its pints of Rainforest Crunch ice cream. In addition, the company donates thirty-five cents from the sale of every pint of factory seconds to local causes. Furthermore, 7.5 percent of Ben and Jerry's pretax profits go the Ben and Jerry Foundation, which funds projects such as AIDS research and help for the homeless.

❦ What's Not Kosher ❧

After a stockbroker urged my cousin to buy shares in a company, its stock promptly fell precipitously. Rumors circulated that the broker's company had a large quantity to unload. Was the seller behaving in a kosher way?

The American credo says "let the buyer beware." However, in this case the brokerage firm did the nonkosher thing. It should have told its client that its representatives were trying to dispose of a large amount of stock due to its tenuous nature. According to the great eighteenth-century ethicist Moshe Chayim Luzzatto in his work *Path of the Just*, it is both good and honest to do everything possible to show the buyer the true value and beauty of the product. To cover and hide a defect is strictly forbidden. The stockbroker was wrong to withhold relevant information.

Honesty in business dealings is a high priority in Judaism. The rabbis remind us (Talmud, Shabbat 31a) that the first question we will be asked when we reach the world to come is whether or not we were honest in our business dealings.

Is it kosher for a liquor store owner to sell beer to a person whom he knows is an alcoholic?

The book of Leviticus (19:14) says that "one should not place a stumbling block before the blind." Thus, Jews are not permitted to take advantage of another's blindness (that is, one's inability to see clearly in a matter). Because alcoholics by definition lack the ability to say no to drinking, Jewish law forbids encouraging that addiction. It would thus be nonkosher to sell liquor or beer to someone whom one knows to be an alcoholic.

A Judaica store has decided to open a store directly across the street from another Judaica store. Is this kosher?

Jewish law would consider that opening a Judaica store in such close proximity to another would be unfair competition. The book of Deuteronomy (19:14) warns twice against the removal of a neighbor's landmarks, which were used to show where one person's property ended and the other's began. Removing a landmark was equivalent to stealing another's land. Before the introduction of land measurements, removing landmarks was a crime more difficult to combat than today.

Later this prohibition of unfair competition, known in Hebrew as *hasagat gevul*, was extended to include other areas of interference, especially in business affairs. Jewish law severely cautioned against unfair encroachment on another person's livelihood. For instance, if a woman held a position and another applied for the same position, this would be regarded as a violation of the biblical law. Any unfair cutting into another's territory was similarly forbidden.

Recently in a town in Northern New Jersey, a new kosher dairy restaurant opened across the street from another that had been in existence for many years. The more established restaurant protested and went to the rabbinic community, saying that the placement of a similar restaurant so close to its own was a violation of the Jewish prohibition of unfair encroachment. The case went to a Bet Din (a Jewish court of law), which ordered the new restaurant to relocate to a place that was far enough away so as not to encroach on the other's business.

If a non-Jew makes a monetary error in favor of a Jew in a business dealing, is it kosher for the Jew to keep the extra cash?

It is not kosher for a Jew to keep money that a non-Jew gave him in error during a business transaction. It is true that the Talmud once taught that a Jew was not required to correct a non-Jew's error in a business dealing. However, this ruling was issued in a society in which non-Jewish governments and laws discriminated against Jews. In such societies the rabbis of bygone years ruled that Jews were not required to practice a higher business morality toward non-Jews than non-Jews were required to practice toward them. The kosher way of doing business is to be honest in one's business dealings at all times.

☞ What the Experts Say ☜

Unfair competition is tantamount to committing adultery. (Talmud, Sanhedrin 81)

When the Chafetz Chayim was a young man, he opened a small store with his wife. He refused to keep in the store any goods that were not fresh. To make sure he was giving good value, he would always add a little to whatever was bought. Fearful that too many customers were buying at his store, thus depriving others of revenue, he would close his store at midday. Once, a Jewish customer left behind a herring he had bought and the Chafetz Chayim was unable to discover his identity. To make sure that he was not guilty of theft, he distributed a fresh herring to each one of his non-Jewish customers on the next market day when they came to buy. (Jewish folktale from Ellen Frankel, *The Classic Tales*)

If one is honest in his business dealings and people esteem him, it is accounted as though he had fulfilled the whole Torah. (Mechilta, Beshallach 1)

A person's drive for profit should be prompted by the desire to give charity. (Nachman of Bratslav)

❦ Sources ❧

Rava said: When a person is brought to judgment [at the time of death], when we must account for all our deeds before a heavenly court, the following questions will be asked: Did you negotiate in business with integrity? (Talmud, Shabbat 31a)

When you reap the harvest of your field, you shall not reap all the edges of your field, or gather the gleaning of your harvest. You shall not pick your vineyard bare, or gather the fallen fruit of your vineyard. Leave them for the poor and the stranger, for I am God. (Leviticus 19:10)

Celebrating a Wedding or Bar/Bat Mitzvah Party

❧ What's Kosher ❧

Is it kosher to have a Bar Mitzvah party that is not opulent?

Not only is it kosher to have a modest party, according to rabbinic consensus, it is highly desirable. The party is an integral part of the Bar/Bat Mitzvah ritual. There is an ethics to Jewish celebration, which in Hebrew is called a *simcha* (joyous occasion). The Code of Jewish Law (Orach Chayim 225:2) first mentions it by saying: "It is the religious obligation of the father to tender a festive meal in honor of his son's becoming a bar mitzvah."

Even in medieval times, there were excesses in celebration. In the sixteenth century Solomon Luria didn't like what he saw. In his commentary on the Talmud, he condemned Bar Mitzvah parties as "occasions for wild levity, just for the purpose of stuffing the gullet" (Yam Shel Shelomo, Baba Kamma, 7: 37). When Bar Mitzvah parties got to be excessively expensive, the seventeenth-century Jewish Polish communal leaders decided to impose a luxury tax in order to try to discourage such excesses and protect the dignity of the less wealthy.

Years ago Rabbi Gamaliel, a wealthy man and important communal leader, left orders that he be buried in a simple linen garment when he died. His example became so powerful that traditional Jewish funerals follow his lead, and simple white linen shrouds are used to dress the deceased.

Every Jew in the United States has a "Can you top this?" tale about the most opulent Bar/Bat Mitzvah party of the year. At these parties the first question is usually "What theme do you want?" The Jewish community needs people like Rabbi Gamaliel today to change the culture of Bar/Bat Mitzvah parties, which tend to run into the thirty, forty, and even fifty thousand–dollar range. A party can still be classy and celebratory without being lavish and garish.

Is there a kosher way to celebrate a Jewish party?

A Jewish celebration or a milestone is a sacred event. As such, the festivities should include religious activities. Here are some ideas to help you celebrate a *simcha* in a kosher manner:

Serve kosher food so that all your guests, whether traditionally observant of the dietary laws or not, can enjoy the meal.

Begin the meal with the *hamotzi* blessing over the bread and conclude it with the Birkat HaMazon, the blessing after the meal.

Select spirited Jewish and Israeli music for group dancing and rejoicing.

Arrange in advance to give the leftover food to a local food bank.

Give any flowers to a local nursing home or hospital after the *simcha* has ended.

In addition to giving friends of the Bar/Bat Mitzvah a souvenir favor, plant a tree in Israel in their honor and give each a tree certificate as a memento. A Jewish book is also a nice souvenir gift.

Ask guests to bring canned food, clothing, or toys to the party for subsequent distribution to the homeless.

Give a percentage of the cost of your *simcha* to a hunger fund (for example, MAZON, A Jewish Response to Hunger, 2940 West Boulevard, Suite 7, Los Angeles, California 90064).

Finally, be certain that your Jewish celebration emphasizes Jewish values. These include compassion, dignity, justice, learning, generosity, humility, and modesty. Plan your celebration around these values, and do not forget to put God on your guest list!

Is there a kosher time to arrive at the celebration?

Almost every *simcha* comes with an invitation announcing the celebration's starting time. Arriving on time is not only the polite thing to do but important to the hosts as well.

Because of the Jewish concept of *lifnim meshurat hadin* (going beyond the letter of the law), one could make a good case when an event is extremely important to the other person to try to come early. I can think of many times when members of the bridal party at a wedding in which I was officiating came just in the nick of time—causing the bride and groom concern, agitation, and worry. Judaism encourages a person to "hasten to perform a good deed" (Ethics of the Fathers 4:2). Better to be too early than too late.

❧ What's Not Kosher ❧

Only some guests at my daughter's wedding party are strictly kosher. Having an all-kosher party would be very expensive. Would it be kosher to provide kosher TV dinners for guests who keep kosher?

This is a question of conflicting values. Judaism would never want a person to spend more than he or she can afford. Therefore, serving a nonkosher and more affordable party as well as providing the strictly kosher guests with a separate meal would seem to make sense.

On the other hand, this is not just any wedding. It's a Jewish wedding—a *simcha*, a celebration of ultimate joy in which pleasure is to be sanctified. If the family can afford it, a kosher party is much more in keeping with a *simcha*. It allows all people to eat the same meal (including the rabbi!) and not be singled out with a special meal that is often not as tasty as what the rest of the guests are being served. Jewish celebrations ought to celebrate Jewish values, and keeping kosher is one of them.

What makes for a nonkosher party?

A *simcha* that includes excessive eating or drinking; the absence of blessings over food; excessive levity and irreverence; and lack of the values of generosity, dignity, and spirituality is often more a sham and a farce than a sacred celebration of ultimate joy.

In Talmudic times the story is told of Mar Rabina, a sage, who noticed his students becoming overly boisterous. Mar Rabina seized a costly glass dish and smashed it to the ground. It had a sobering effect on all of his disciples, who then realized that they were displaying excessive irreverence and acting in a nonkosher manner (Talmud, Berachot 31). It would be wise to remember this story when planning your next *simcha*.

⚜ What the Experts Say ⚜

Judaism says that we neither reject nor hoard pleasure. We sanctify pleasure. We sanctify what we eat through *kashrut* (the dietary laws), what we own through *tzedakah* (holy giving), what we drink by *kiddush* (blessing the wine) and by drinking moderately on Shabbat, on Pesach, or somewhat immoderately on Purim. (Jeffrey K. Salkin, *Putting God on the Guest List,* pp. 60–61)

Sukkot—season of our *simcha* [joy]. (Festival Kiddush)

Excess in absence of values is idolatry. (Rabbi Steven Z. Leder, *More Money Than God*)

The extravagant consumption, the conspicuous waste, and the crudity of many of these affairs are rapidly becoming a public Jewish scandal. The lowering of standards as reflected in many bar mitzvah celebrations is in direct violation of the teaching of the Torah. (Statement of Central Conference of Reform Rabbis, CCAR Response no. 33)

❦ Sources ❧

You shall rejoice in your feast. (Deuteronomy 16:13)

It is a religious obligation of the father to tender a festive meal in honor of his son's becoming a bar mitzvah, as he might do when the boy marries. (Code of Jewish Law, Orach Chayim 225:2)

Topic 7

❦ ❧

Charity: Righteous Giving

❦ **What's Kosher** ❧

When giving charity to your friend, is it kosher to inform him?

Concerned with showing love and concern to a friend in need, the rabbis advised that "if one gives a gift to a friend, one must inform him" (that is, let him know from whom the gift comes) (Talmud, Shabbat 10b). Although telling the friend the donor's identity may embarrass the friend, the rabbis surprisingly thought more about the importance of letting a friend know that one cares. As the rabbis understood it, what matters more to the recipient of a gift is the thoughtful intent behind it. That is why when most people receive a gift, they will open the card before even opening the gift.

Is it kosher to give to non-Jewish charities?

Yes, there is nothing wrong with giving money to needy people who are not Jewish. Jewish law even mandates that the non-Jew not be forgotten: "One is required to feed and clothe the non-Jewish poor together with the poor of Israel, this for the sake of the ways of peace" (Maimonides, Mishneh Torah, Laws of Tzedakah 7:7).

Tzedakah (charity) is meant to help all who are in need, regardless of race, religion, or color. The Jewish community has a record of giving extending through the millennia: Jews give to all in need.

Is it kosher to make giving to a poor relative a priority before considering giving to the poor within one's own town?

Maimonides, in Mishneh Torah (Laws of Tzedakah 7:13), prioritizes who comes first when it comes to giving *tzedakah*: "A poor person who is your relative should receive your charity before all others; and likewise the poor of your own household have priority over the poor of your city; and the poor of your city have priority over the poor of another city, as it is stated in the Torah, 'To poor and needy brothers in your land'" (Deuteronomy 15:11).

The proof text from Deuteronomy refers to your "needy brother" "in your land." Maimonides takes this as a warrant that it is kosher to help the poor nearby before turning to the poor in distant places. Because in our own setting "poor" stands for the needs of the Jewish community at large, the message is not difficult to translate.

The law is clear and unequivocal. Help the poor nearby before the poor far away: relative, household, city, and outward from there. This principle is less obvious than it seems. Often a person may feel sympathy for starving people somewhere else and forget about those in need on the home front. Judaism says: start by taking care of those near home, and then work to help others outside of the community.

Is it kosher to solicit *tzedakah* from others to help one's own community?

Most people dislike having to ask others to give. Doing so makes them feel uncomfortable. Judaism says that one has the obligation to do so and that is an honor to do so: "In every city in which the Israelites have settled, they are required to appoint from among their number, well-known and trustworthy persons to act as collectors of charity funds, to go around collecting from the people each Friday. These collectors should demand from each person what is proper for that one to give and what amount has been assessed to that person. And they should distribute the money each Friday" (Maimonides, Mishneh Torah, Laws of Tzedakah 9:1–3).

Individuals become a community through the shared labor of *tzedakah*. It is an honor to them and an honor to the community. To people active in Jewish Federation and Jewish communal work, this comes as no surprise. The workers are to be trustworthy and well known. This is because others must accept their demands. These positions rest on honor, and they enhance the honor of the ones who fill them.

Is it kosher for a poor person who lives on charity to give *tzedakah*?

Surprisingly, the answer is yes: a poor person must give some *tzedakah*. The idea here is that giving to others helps preserve the poor person's dignity. The giving is what most matters, as this statement attests: "At no time should one permit oneself to give less than one-third of a *shekel* per year. One who gives less has not fulfilled the commandment of *tzedakah* at all. Even a poor person who lives entirely on *tzedakah* must give *tzedakah*" (Maimonides, Mishneh Torah, Laws of Tzedakah, 7:5).

Is it kosher for a person to give *tzedakah* and want it publicized?

Although rabbinic consensus approves of charity that is given privately and anonymously whenever possible, a number of rabbinic thinkers have suggested that if giving in public will help inspire others to do so, then it would be kosher to announce the nature of the gift and the name of the donor as well.

We had this very same issue in our congregation with regard to our Kol Nidre appeal, where each year on Yom Kippur we ask congregants to give to the synagogue. For years the board of trustees did not publicize the gifts and their amounts in the synagogue bulletin, for fear that doing so might offend some people and cause others embarrassment. Recently, however, we, as well as many other synagogues, have rethought the issue and have decided (based on the reasoning that it might inspire others to give) to publicize the names of those who gave, set up under categories that had displayed a range of gift amounts. Although at first this caused some discussion and a few complaints, the congregation has accepted it as what we now do. The results have been magnificent. Gift giving in our congregation has tripled, due in part (I believe) to people seeing others of similar means giving substantial gifts and then wanting to do the same.

✶ What's Not Kosher ✻

Is it kosher to be overly generous?

Jewish law teaches that there is such a thing as being too beneficent. With 10 percent of one's gross income the norm, the sages passed a law saying that no one should give away more than 20 percent of his or her income (Talmud, Ketubot 50a).

Clearly, the rationale for capping one's generosity had to do with the rabbis' concern that one who got carried away with his or her righteous giving might in turn become impoverished. The rabbinic ruling of not giving more than 20 percent is a nice reminder that Judaism respects a life of moderation. Give charity, and do it with an open heart, but you don't have to give away everything that you have.

If a beggar approaches you for money, is it kosher to question him or her to be certain that he or she is really in need?

Jewish law distinguishes two kinds of needs: immediate and long-term. Here is the primary text on which this law is based: "If a poor stranger appears and says, 'I am hungry, give me something to eat,' do not question whether or not the stranger is an imposter—provide food immediately. If, however, the stranger has no clothing and says, 'Give me clothing,' then question to see if it is a case of possible fraud. If the person is known, provide clothing immediately in the style best suited to the person's dignity, without further questioning" (Mishneh Torah, Laws of Tzedakah 6:6).

An immediate need is a case of hunger. Here it is kosher to supply what is needed without asking questions. You can never be sure that someone who says "I am hungry" really is hungry. You must take people at face value—when it comes to an emergency. If someone is cold, you provide heating and then look into the matter. So much for emergencies.

For a long-term need, which is less urgent and might be able to be postponed, you have the obligation to make certain that the need is real. Obviously, if you know the poor person, you provide clothing without further inquiry. The main point comes at the outset, therefore, and stresses that in matters of *tzedakah*, you give first and ask questions later. Asking questions is proof positive that Jewish law is concerned that one not waste money set aside for *tzedakah*.

Is it kosher to throw away clothing that you no longer wear?

Many people simply throw away old clothing, furniture, or appliances, without ever making inquiries as to whether someone else might be able to use them. Withholding goods from others who might benefit from them is nonkosher. All of us have been guilty of doing this, not because of stinginess but because of laziness. Doing good for others often requires making that extra effort. Next time you are about to trash something, think about whether someone might be able to use it.

❧ What the Experts Say ❧

The person who gives to the poor shall not lack. (Proverbs 28:27)

Worthless charity is when a woman acquires money dishonestly and then distributes it to the poor and the ill. (Midrash, Exodus Rabbah 31)

Charity is equal in importance to all the other commandments combined. (Talmud, Baba Batra 9b)

A person who secretly gives is greater than Moses. (Talmud, Baba Batra 9b)

A person should be more concerned with spiritual than with material matters, but another person's material welfare is his own spiritual concern. (Rabbi Israel Salanter, quoted in Immanuel Etkes and Jonathan Chipman, translator, *Rabbi Israel Salanter and the Mussar Movement*)

You can always give something, even if it is only kindness. (Anne Frank, *The Diary of a Young Girl*, March 1944)

It is good to give charity before praying. (Code of Jewish Law, Orach Chayim 92:10)

One who increases *tzedakah* increases peace. (Ethics of the Fathers 2:8)

If you have done the mitzvah of charity, you will be privileged to be wealthy. And if you are privileged to be wealthy, do the mitzvah of *tzedakah* with your wealth. (Talmud, Derech Eretz Zutah 4)

Rabbi Yossi said: "I would rather be a *tzedakah* collector than a *tzedakah* distributor." (Talmud, Shabbat 118b)

Whoever does deeds of charity and justice is considered as having filled the entire world with loving-kindness. (Talmud, Sukkah 49b)

Maimonides' Eight Degrees of *Tzedakah*

　　The person who gives reluctantly with regret.
　　The person who gives graciously, but less than he should.
　　The person who gives what he should, but only after being asked.
　　The person who gives before being asked.
　　The person who gives without knowing to whom he gives,
　　　　although the recipient knows the identity of the donor.

The person who gives without making his or her identity known.
The person who gives without knowing to whom he or she gives.
    The recipient does not know from whom he receives.
The person who helps another to support himself by a gift or finding
    employment for that person, thus helping him to become self-
    supporting. (Mishneh Torah, Laws of Gifts to the Poor 10:7–14)

Especially great is the sin of those who pledge money to charity in
public but do not give it. (Talmud, Taanit 8b)

There was a secret chamber in the Temple where pious people
would leave money in secret, and those who had been well-to-do
would come and take in secret. (Mishnah, Shekalim 5:6)

A generous person who gives charity beyond what that person can afford, or denies oneself in order to give to the collector of alms so that
the person would not be embarrassed, should not be asked to contribute charity. (Maimonides, Mishneh Torah, Laws of Tzedakah 7:11)

❦ Sources ❧

You shall open your hand to your brother, and to the needy.
(Deuteronomy 15:9–11)

Charity is equal in importance to all the other commandments
combined. (Talmud, Baba Batra 9b)

You shall surely tithe all the increases of your seed, that which is
brought in the field year by year. (Deuteronomy 14:22)

❧ ❧

Children's Obligations to Their Families

❧ What's Kosher ❧

When a parent disapproves of a child's relationship, what's the kosher way for a child to respond?

Does the commandment to honor one's parents mean that a child should break off a relationship that parents do not sanction? Rabbinic consensus says that it's kosher for a child to ignore a parent's opposition in such a case. As one medieval rabbi reasoned, if a child breaks off a relationship with a person he loves and then marries a partner whom his parents force upon him, he will end up abhorring that spouse. Forcing the child to marry someone he or she will hate is tantamount to the parents demanding that the child violate the law of "love your neighbor as yourself" (Leviticus 19:18).

Is it kosher for a child to call a parent by his or her first name?

Years ago the Code of Jewish Law (Yoreh Deah, chap. 240) advised that "one should not call his father by his first name," neither during nor after his lifetime, except to identify him to others. In those days calling a parent by a first name showed a lack of respect.

Times have changed, and today I would suggest that there is nothing nonkosher about a child calling a parent by his or her first name. Although it is probably more common for a child to call one's parents Mom and Dad, Mother and Father, or *Eema* and *Abba*, in no way do I think that modern rabbinic consensus would see this as a sign of disrespect or reverence. Interestingly, when explaining the biblical verse "let each of you revere his mother and father" (Leviticus 19:3), the Talmud says that *revere* means "that a child must neither stand nor sit in his father's place, nor contradict his words, nor tip the scales against him" (that is, side with a parent's opponent in a dispute).

When I was growing up, my father, of blessed memory, always took his special seat on a rocking chair in our living room before he read the newspaper. Neither of my brothers would have ever considered taking his seat, even though I doubt now that he would have minded. Nor did we ever call Dad by his first name!

❦ What's Not Kosher ❧

Is it kosher to expect a child always to follow his parent's advice?

Although a child is obligated to show love and respect to his parents, there will be instances when a parent tells the child something that he must ignore. Here is one of the earliest rabbinic cases of such an instance: "Everything which your father says to you, you are obliged to obey. But, if he says to you: 'Let us bow down to idols,' you must not obey him, lest you become an apostate" (Yalkut, Proverbs 960). From this example we learn that a father cannot demand an action by his son that would be contrary to Jewish law, namely the heinous crime of idolatry.

Two more examples illustrate that a child does not owe his parents control over his own conscience. "When a child is admonished by his father not to return a lost object [which is a great *mitzvah* in Jewish law], a child should not listen to him" (Talmud, Baba Metzia 32a). Finally, the Code of Jewish law rules that "if a child is told by his father not to speak to, or to forgive, a certain person with whom the child wishes to be reconciled, he should disregard his father's command" (Kitzur Shulchan Aruch 143:11). The father's command would only be justifiable if the person was a particularly malevolent sinner. Otherwise, it is wrong for a father to command his son to act in such a hateful manner.

Is it kosher not to be your brother or sister's best friend?

It is not necessary for a child to be his sibling's best friend. Siblings often have different personalities, interests, and talents. What interests one may not interest another. In fact, it might even be boring to the other.

It is a kosher expectation, though, to expect siblings to love and honor each other, be respectful of each other, and come to the assistance of the other in time of need. Therefore, it's a kosher expectation that we need to be our brother's and sister's keeper.

Is it kosher for a child to have to be afraid of his parents?

It is not kosher for a child to have to be fearful of a parent. The Talmud (Sotah 3) says that "anger in a home is like rottenness in fruit." A parent's uncontrolled temper can easily lead to a physically and verbally abused child, or a spouse for that matter. Putting any kind of excessive pressure on a child (such as to succeed in school or in a particular sport) is deleterious to a child's mental well-being. Therefore, the parent who realizes that he or she is causing undue fear is morally obligated to seek professional help immediately.

Is it kosher for a child to say to a parent: "I hate you"?

From Judaism's perspective, a statement such as "I hate you" or even "I don't give a damn what you want; I'll do what I want" constitutes parental abuse and is strictly nonkosher and forbidden. Many times children will need to express disagreement with their parents. Even when disagreeing, though, a child must always do so in a respectful and fair manner.

❦ What the Experts Say ❧

Both one's mother and one's father should be treated equally with respect, and a child ought not to show favoritism of one over the other. (Mechilta of Rabbi Ishmael, 1)

Whether you have wealth or not, honor your parents. (Jerusalem Talmud, Peah 1:1)

To honor parents is more important even than to honor God. (Jerusalem Talmud, Peah 1:1)

If a parent unwittingly transgresses a law of the Torah, his child shall not reprimand him, "Father, you have transgressed a law." Rather, he should say, "Father, is that what it says in the Torah?" But in the end, aren't both expressions equally insulting? Yes, what he should really say is, "Father, the Torah says such-and-such." (Talmud, Sanhedrin 81a)

When Rabbi Joseph heard his mother's footsteps he would say, "I will rise before the approaching Shechinah." (Talmud, Kiddushin 31b)

To what length should the duty of honoring parents go? Even were they to take a purse of his, full of gold, and cast it in his presence into the sea, he must not shame them, manifest grief in their presence, but accept the Divine decree without demurral. (Shulchan Aruch, Yoreh Deah, chap. 240)

If a child's parents became mentally ill, he should try his best to help them according to their needs until improvement is vouchsafed. If their condition becomes impossible to him, he should place them in the hands of those who can properly care for them. (Shulchan Aruch, Yoreh Deah, chap. 20)

If a child wants to make aliyah [immigrate] to Israel, and the father says "no," the child need not listen. (Rabbi Moses Trani)

If the son wants to marry a certain woman but the father is not pleased, the son need not listen. (Gloss of the Rama to Code of Jewish Law, Yoreh Deah 240:25)

It was asked of Rabbi Ulla: "How far must a child go in respecting one's parents?" Rabbi Ulla replied: "Consider what a certain pagan named Dama, the son of Nathina, did in the city of Ashkelon. The sages once desired merchandise from him from which he would make a 600,000 gold dinarim profit. But the key to the room in which the merchandise was kept was lying under Dama's sleeping father. Dama would not trouble his father in order to complete the transaction." (Talmud, Kiddushin 31b)

Our rabbis taught: What is *mora* ("fear") and what is *kavod* ("honor")? "Fear" means that a son must neither stand in his father's place nor sit in his place, contradict his words, nor tip the scales against him.

"Honor" means that he must give him food and drink, clothe and cover him, and lead him in and out.

The rabbis asked: "At whose expense?"

Rabbi Judah said: "At the son's expense."

Rabbi Nachman ben Oshiah said: "At the father's expense."

The rabbis ruled that it must be at the father's expense. (Talmud, Kiddushin 31b-32a)

Honor your father and mother just as you honor God, for all three have been partners in your creation. (Zohar 3:93a)

❧ Sources ☙

Honor your father and mother. (Exodus 20:12)

A person should revere his mother and father. (Leviticus 19:3)

Topic 9

Circumcision

❧ What's Kosher ❧

What are the kosher guidelines regarding the person who can perform a circumcision?

According to Jewish law, only three persons can perform a circumcision. In the order of preference, the first is the father of the baby boy. It is incumbent upon every father to fulfill the biblical precept to circumcise his son on the eighth day or to designate a qualified representative to do so on his behalf. The person usually designated is called a mohel. This person should be a pious Jew who has been properly trained to perform the circumcision. When there is no possibility of attaining the services of a mohel, a Jewish physician who is well versed in the ritual may perform the circumcision.

Is it kosher to light candles in the home on the day of a circumcision?

The Yaavetz commentator says that many lights should be lit when a circumcision takes place. This is based on the verse in the book of Esther 8:16: "The Jews had light, gladness and joy." "Joy" refers to circumcision, as it is written, "I rejoice at Your pronouncements."

Is it kosher to have a circumcision on the Sabbath or on Yom Kippur?

A circumcision must be performed on the eighth day, regardless of whether the eighth day is the Sabbath or the Day of Atonement. My son had his Brit Milah (circumcision) on Rosh Hashanah. It turned out to be the perfect day, for I didn't have to send out a special invitation to my congregants—they were all there in honor of the new year.

Is it kosher for a woman to be a mohel?

Although few females do circumcisions in the United States, it is kosher by Jewish law (Yoreh Deah 264:1) for a female to be a mohel. I met a former student of mine only a few months ago who told me that she was now a family pediatrician and a *mohelet* (female mohel). She told me how much she enjoyed doing God's work and found her work to be spiritually uplifting.

Are there any kosher reasons to postpone a circumcision beyond the eighth day?

If the child is ill and the physician advises postponement, the circumcision is postponed for as long as the physician deems necessary. Often a physician will advise that a child born prematurely not be circumcised on the eighth day. The Talmud and codes speak of cases in which two brothers of the child have died as a result of circumcision. In such cases circumcision is not permitted until it is certain that the child will not be similarly affected. This situation has been interpreted as referring to cases of hemophilia.

If a baby is circumcised before the eighth day, can any kind of kosher procedure rectify the situation?

Opinions vary. Some authorities maintain that an early circumcision is valid if it was done properly (Yoreh Deah 262:1). Others hold that it must be validated by drawing a drop of blood on the eighth day.

Nowadays, through ignorance or for convenience, babies are often circumcised before the eighth day because doctor and parents want the circumcision to be done in the hospital before the baby is taken home. In order to discourage this practice, the Conservative and Orthodox branches of Judaism insist that such circumcisions are valid only if a drop of blood is drawn on the eighth day.

❦ What's Not Kosher ❧

Someone explained to me that a baby has to be circumcised to become Jewish. Is this a kosher explanation?

According to halacha (traditional Jewish law) a baby born to a Jewish mother is considered a Jew whether or not he is circumcised. Failure of the parents to perform the mitzvah of circumcision does not alter the child's identity as a Jew.

Is it kosher to have a baby boy circumcised and to have the baby named several days later when more family members can attend?

No, separating the circumcision from the baby naming is not kosher. Unlike baby naming for girls, which has no time restriction, the naming of a baby boy must be performed immediately following the circumcision. The naming of the boy is part and parcel of the circumcision service and must not be postponed for reasons of convenience.

Is it kosher for an adult male who has never been circumcised and wishes to convert to Judaism not to have a circumcision?

In contradistinction to a child born to a Jewish mother, a male candidate for conversion cannot be considered Jewish until he is circumcised according to Jewish law.

Is it kosher for a baby to be circumcised at night?

The whole day, beginning with sunrise, is permissible, but Jewish law prefers the morning so as to show zeal in the performance of the mitzvah. Some rabbinic authorities (such as the Rama) say that a circumcision must not be performed at night; if it was, it is necessary to draw an additional drop of blood from the penis during the day.

I was once at a circumcision that took place in the summer at a 6:30 A.M. Shacharit service—the earliest circumcision that I ever attended. The family was eager to have it, and the father and mother of the baby had an *aliyah* (they were called to recite Torah blessings) during services.

❧ What the Experts Say ❧

Behold, how gladsome is circumcision that not even the Sabbath defers. (Tosefta)

One who circumcises his son is as though he offered all the sacrifices to God. (Zohar, Genesis 17:10)

❧ Source ❧

You shall keep My covenant, you and your descendants after you throughout their generations. Every male among you shall be circumcised, and it shall be a sign of the covenant between Me and you. He that is eight days old shall be circumcised. (Genesis 17:11–12)

Clothing and Care of the Body

❧ What's Kosher ❧

Is it kosher for a man to go to synagogue in casual clothing, or must he always wear a jacket and tie?

Jewish law does not require a man to wear a jacket and tie to synagogue on a holy day. The requirement on the Sabbath regarding dress is that the clothing be clean and look more festive than weekday clothes, in order to distinguish the holy day from the regular days of the week. When Yom Kippur falls on the Sabbath, the wearing of white clothing (including a white robe (*kittel*) and a white *kippa* (yarmulke) is a time-honored custom to recall the white shrouds in which the dead are clothed in preparation for burial, serving to mellow the heart of the worshipper. White also symbolizes purity and freshness.

Much of kosher Sabbath dress depends on the synagogue's culture. Some congregations get dressed up, with men expected to wear jackets and ties and women to wear dresses; other congregations are more casual. Generalizations are difficult, as each Jewish community has its own character. A jacket and tie for a man and a long skirt for a woman should be a safe bet at most synagogues. If you haven't been someplace before, it never hurts to err on the side of formality.

The Code of Jewish Law (chapter on deportment) recommends that a Jew ought to avoid wearing costly garments, for this is conducive to pride. Nor should a Jew wear clothes that are too cheap or soiled. Rather, one should wear moderately priced and clean clothes.

My rule of thumb for kosher synagogue dress would be that clothes ought to be clean and festive (in order to distinguish a holy day from the regular days of the week) and cover enough body parts to express modesty in dress. This would mean that men and women have their shoulders covered and a neckline that is not so low cut as to draw other worshippers' attention. Rashi, the great medieval commentator, states that modesty and morality are synonymous. He observes that God made garments for Adam and Eve, for they were not ashamed of their nakedness and did not know the ways of modesty.

With frankness and realism, the rabbinic authorities were vitally concerned with dangers of immodesty in dress. Every attempt was made to discourage seductiveness that might lead to intimacy before marriage or an adulterous relationship after marriage.

Is it kosher for a man not to wear a *kippa*? And what about a woman?

Wearing a *kippa* is a custom, not a law. Nowhere does the Torah mandate that a Jewish man wear a head covering. The head covering has come to symbolize a sign of respect and acknowledgment that there is a God in the universe. As for the size of a *kippa*, my rabbi always taught me that if you take a *kippa*, fold it in quarters, and it covers three knuckles, then it will cover enough of your head to be considered kosher.

Orthodox men wear the *kippa* at all times. Men in the Conservative movement always wear them while in synagogue and sometimes when eating, because a blessing is recited before and after the meal. Reform and Reconstructionist Jews are less likely to wear them while eating but do often wear them in synagogue.

In Orthodox circles the custom for women is to cover their hair with a handkerchief or a wig. Once a woman is married, her husband is the only person who is supposed to see her hair.

Many Orthodox women wear wigs. Is it kosher for a married woman to choose not to wear one?

Although some Conservative synagogues require head coverings for women while in synagogue, there is certainly no requirement for them to wear wigs. For Reform and Reconstructionist Jewish women, the issue of wearing wigs is moot.

The Bible describes the sensuous hair of a woman as a mark of beauty: "You are beautiful my love. . . . your hair is like a flock of goats, trailing down from Mount Gilead" (Song of Songs 4:1). Both in Bible times and Talmudic times, a woman covered her head as a sign of modesty. Exposing a woman's hair was considered a disgrace.

Toward the end of the eighteenth century, the *shaytl* (Yiddish for "wig") was introduced as a head covering. Today only strictly Orthodox married women wear a head covering at all times. The reason generally given is that they should not appear attractive to men. In some cases Orthodox women shave their hair or cut it very short before covering it with a wig. Many Orthodox and Hasidic women today also wear a *shaytl*, but they use a kerchief (known as a *tichel*) as a head covering.

I want to get my nose pierced. Is this kosher?

Although contemporary Jewish law does not prohibit body piercing, I continue to have questions about whether or not it challenges the value of "in God's image" (Genesis 1:26). At all times Jews should remember that they are created in God's image and that they are called to incorporate this understanding into all of their decisions.

You may be interested to know that ear piercing is not exclusively a contemporary phenomenon. It was known even in Biblical and Talmudic times. In the Torah a pierced ear is the sign of a slave who had earned freedom but chose to remain enslaved. The Talmud tells of various Jewish artisans who wore earrings to indicate the specific nature of their trades. The rabbis make no negative comment about those ancient examples of widespread piercing.

Not long ago the Law Committee of the Conservative Rabbinical Assembly issued a permissive ruling with regard to body piercing.

If body piercing was acceptable to the rabbis of the Talmud, we have no Jewish cause to object.

There are, however, two exceptions. Judaism prohibits body piercings that interfere with personal hygiene and can therefore threaten our health. We are not permitted to imperil our good health for the benefits of fashion. Piercing of the genitals is also prohibited, both on hygienic grounds and because of the Jewish value of *tzniut* (modesty). Our tradition teaches us to treat our private parts as just that, private. Only in our most intimate relationships, and to obtain necessary health care, are we permitted to expose ourselves. Out of respect for those parts of our bodies most directly involved with the highest of human acts, the creation of a new generation of life, we must not treat our genitals as display cases for jewels.

As a woman, I've always felt more comfortable wearing pants. Is this kosher?

Yes, rabbinic authorities in the non-Orthodox world would say that it's kosher for a woman to wear pants if she chooses. We have come very close to the interchange of apparel with the emergence of unisex clothing. Thus, rabbinic authorities posit that the biblical prohibition (Deuteronomy 22:5) that forbids a woman from cross-dressing (that is, wearing that which pertains to a man) no longer applies today.

Other more traditional rabbinic authorities have decided that cross-dressing is prohibited in all instances, even on Purim, when men customarily dress like women. Others would say that women can wear pants when they're appropriate to the activity at hand—such as skiing or horseback riding. Still others say it is prohibited only when the intention is to create illicit sexual opportunity through deception. Thus, a drag queen is clearly in violation of this prohibition.

Is it kosher to wear a fur coat?

In recent years scores of animal activists have strongly protested stores in the fur business. A number of parameters would render some furs kosher for wear and others forbidden. If the wearing of furs provides for a legitimate need (that is, the fur will keep a person warmer than other materials), then it would be permissible. The reality today, though, is that artificial materials would keep a person equally warm.

Many women choose to buy fur coats to display their wealth and make a fashion statement. In such a case, this would not be a legitimate need, thus rendering the fur coat nonkosher.

❧ What's Not Kosher ❧

Is tattooing kosher? Does it preclude taking part in synagogue rituals or being buried in a Jewish cemetery?

The prohibition of tattooing is found in the Torah: "You shall not make gashes in your flesh for the dead, or incise any marks on your-selves: I am the Lord" (Leviticus 19:28). Maimonides clearly sees the origin of this prohibition as an act of idolatry, stating that pagans would mark themselves for idolatry. In our day most traditional rabbis maintain that the prohibition against all forms of tattooing, regardless of their intent, should be maintained. In addition to the fact that Judaism has a long history of distaste for tattoos, tattooing becomes even more distasteful in a contemporary secular society that is constantly challenging the Jewish concept that we are created in God's image and that our bodies are to be viewed as a precious gift on loan from God, to be entrusted into our care and not our personal property to do with as we choose. Voluntary tattooing, even if not done for idolatrous purposes, expresses a negation of this fundamental Jewish perspective.

However distasteful we may find the practice of tattooing, there is no real basis for restricting burial to Jews who violate this prohibition or even limiting their participation in synagogue ritual. The fact that someone may have violated the laws of keeping kosher at some point in his or her life would not merit such sanctions. The prohibition against tattooing is certainly no worse.

New laser technology has raised the possibility of removing what was once irremovable. It will likely not be long before such technology is affordable and less painful than it currently is. When this occurs, the more traditional branches of Judaism may then choose to consider whether removal of tattoos should become a requirement for conversion or burial.

Is it kosher to bathe only once a week?

Although Judaism does not specify how often a person must bathe, it has always recognized the fact that the body is imbued with sanctity. It is a gift from God, who lends it to us for the duration of our lives, and we return it only upon our deaths. Because of the underlying principle that our bodies belong to God, many responsibilities related to the body emerge. First, we must take reasonable care of our bodies. Such obligations clearly include proper hygiene such as daily bathing, in addition to proper amounts of sleep, exercise, and proper diet. Bathing before the Sabbath has always been a widely kept Jewish custom.

Here's a Talmudic tale that not only sums up Judaism's concern for proper hygiene and body care but suggests that it is a mitzvah to do so:

> When Hillel had finished a lesson with his students, he accompanied them part of the way. They said to him, "Master, where are you going?" He answered, "To perform a religious duty." They asked, "Which religious duty?" He responded, To bathe in the bath house." They questioned, "Is this a religious obligation?" He replied, "If somebody is appointed to scrape the statues of the king that are set up in the theaters and circuses, and is paid to do the work, and furthermore associates with the nobility, how much more so should I, who am created in the divine image and likeness, take care of my body." (Leviticus Rabbah 34:3)

Is cigarette smoking kosher?

The rabbis in Talmudic times were unaware of tobacco—its use for smoking developed much later. There are no classical Jewish statements specifically on this matter. Modern scholars concerned about the issue are somewhat divided. Some have unequivocally indicated that smoking is not consistent with Jewish law, on the grounds that it is injurious to health. Some authorities who accept this view even prohibit offering a friend a cigarette, because we are not permitted to "put a stumbling block in front of the blind" (Leviticus 19:14).

Others do not feel that Jewish law forbids smoking. They cite two principles that they feel exclude smoking from the prohibition of harming oneself. The first is that human beings may rely on God to preserve them from dangers that are normally part of life and that "many people have tread upon" (Talmud, Shabbat 129b), that is, that are part of many people's practice. The second principle regards the immediacy of the danger. Even some who agree that "one must not place himself in danger" (Talmud, Shabbat 32a) draw a distinction between immediate danger—which must be avoided—and a potential or future danger—which is not necessarily prohibited. They apply cigarette smoking to the "potential" category and thus do not prohibit smoking, but they do not recommend it either.

Being created in God's image, we are commanded to care for our bodies and respect them. Therefore, to the extent that they contribute to harming the body, any external substances, such as tobacco, alcohol, or drugs, other than those that physicians prescribe for specific symptoms, must be avoided.

With all the statistics relative to cigarette smoking, one can no longer argue that the hazard involved in the practice is unsubstantiated. On the contrary, the peril involved has been totally exposed.

If a drug is illegal but could provide benefit, would using it be kosher?

In Jewish law anything that is dangerous to life and limb must be avoided. Because we are made in God's image, we must protect our bodies. Classical Jewish sources make many references to the use of drugs as medicine or as a painkiller. All of the drugs, of course, were legal in the communities where they were authorized for use. If certain drugs that are now illegal were made legal, rabbinic authorities might allow their use under some circumstances.

A good example would be marijuana: it is illegal in most states but in some cases can be used under a doctor's supervision to help alleviate the pain of a life-threatening illness or for another medical application. The bottom line is that if a particular drug were deemed to be noninjurious to one's health and had a physician's approval, using it would surely be permissible according to most rabbinic authorities.

❦ What the Experts Say ⁂

Let your garments always be clean. (Ecclesiastes 9:8)

How much toil had Adam to spend until he found a shirt to wear. (Talmud, Berachot 9)

A person's honor is his garment. (Exodus Rabbah 96)

The glory of men is the clothes that they wear. (Talmud, Derech Eretz Zuta 10)

A scholar should always wear modest garb, not too costly or ornate, so that people should not stare at him, and not too shabby, lest he be mocked. (Menorat HaMaor)

A man's clothes are the index of his character. (Nachman of Bratslav)

We do not tolerate people passing through our streets immodestly dressed. (Sign in Mea Shearim, a Hasidic section of Jerusalem)

Every person has outer clothes and inner clothes. The outer clothes are his material garments and the inner clothes are his character traits and mannerisms. (Nachum Chaimovitz, *Timeless Fashion*).

You shall not make any tattoo marks on you. (Leviticus 19:28)

One's sleep is service of the Almighty. (Maimonides, Mishneh Torah, Laws of Ethics 3:3)

The prohibition of women wearing men's clothes or of men wearing women's clothes is not violated unless a man or woman wears trousers distinctly designed for the opposite sex. If however, a certain type of trousers are meant for both men and women, no prohibition will apply. (Responsa Yaskil Avdi, vol. 5, Yoreh Deah 20)

❧ Sources ❧

God made garments of skin for Adam and Eve, and God clothed them. (Genesis 3:22)

A person should maintain physical health and vigor in order that his soul may be upright. (Maimonides, Mishneh Torah, Laws of Ethics 3:3)

Since it is the will of the Almighty that man's body be kept healthy and strong, it is therefore his duty to shun anything that may waste his body, and strive to acquire habits that will help him to become healthy. (Code of Jewish Law, Condensed Version, chap. 32)

In the image of God did God make humankind. (Genesis 9:6)

Take good care of yourselves. (Deuteronomy 2:4)

Topic 11

Commitments

❧ **What's Kosher** ❧

Is it kosher to break a promise?

We are expected to carry out everything we say, unless we specify that it is not a solemn promise but a mere thought expressed in words. Nevertheless, many people do make promises, often regretting them soon afterward. The Torah allowed a way out of a vow through *hattarat nedarim*, a release from vows and oaths. In this procedure a learned sage or three ordinary people can absolve a person from his vow by asking him whether he would have made it had he known beforehand what the consequences of the vow would have been.

The best-known statement about promises and vows occurs on the eve of Yom Kippur, the Day of Atonement, at the Kol Nidre service. This declaration specifies that all the promises that one has made to God but not fulfilled are null and void.

One of the worst blunders in biblical history was that of Jephthah the judge. On the eve of his battle with the Ammonites, archenemy of the Israelites, he vows that if he returns safe and victorious he will offer to God as a burnt offering "whatever comes out of the door of my house to meet me" (Judges 11:31). The conclusion of that chapter relates the personal disaster when Jephthah's own daughter is first to come out to meet him and he declares that he cannot retract his vow.

This is one of the many reasons that rabbinic advice cautions a person to think twice before making a vow. The popular Hebrew expression *blee neder* (without vow), which accompanies any statement concerning some future action the speaker contemplates, is in keeping with that idea.

Is it kosher to make a promise in the name of God?

It is best to resort to swearing in God's name only when required to do so, for example, in court, when taking an oath in God's name with one's hand on the Bible.

Exodus 20:7 commands that "one should not swear falsely by the name of God." This law demands that we neither swear falsely in court nor use God's name in vain. This means refraining from using the traditional names for God in secular writings or conversation, much less in voicing profanities.

There are various rabbinic interpretations of this prohibition. Some say that one must not resort to using God's name to make one's lies more plausible. The twelfth-century Spanish commentator Ibn Ezra says not keeping one's word is tantamount to repudiating the name of God. Thus, it is especially important for a religiously committed Jew not to bring God's name into disrepute by false dealings. Once misusing God's name becomes a habit, it will proliferate until one uses God's name before every assertion. Other scholars interpret this verse to prohibit linking God's name to anything false, such as sorcery or fortune-telling.

On the whole, Jewish tradition treats the prohibition of false oaths in God's name with utmost regard. It frowns on all secular or self-serving uses of the name, in conversation, writing, and judicial proceedings. An oath was to be avoided at all costs, for God's name was too holy to be pronounced in matters affecting nothing more than one's material welfare. Today the Jewish custom to bury every parchment or paper on which God's name is inscribed is only occasionally applied.

It is unfortunate that people today need to be certain that another's statement is truthful only when the person swears to it, often in God's name. A much better standard would be the Talmud's: "Let your 'yes' be 'yes,' let your 'no' be no" (Baba Metzia 49a).

❧ What's Not Kosher ❧

Is it kosher to make a promise to God while asking for something in return?

Although Jewish prayer is predominantly about thanking and praising God for what we have, Judaism is not so otherworldly as to be embarrassed by prayers for material sustenance.

One of the first instances of someone making a promise to God in return for God's blessings is Jacob's vow: "If God remains with me, if He protects me on this journey that I am making, and gives me bread to eat and clothing to wear, and if I return safely to my father's house—the Lord shall be my God. And this stone, which I have set up as a pillar, shall be God's abode; and of all that You give me, I will set aside a tithe for You" (Genesis 28:20–22). Jewish commentators have questioned whether this vow represents a posture of gratitude or is simply an attempt to manipulate God with promises of worship and generosity. Is Jacob excessive in his demands, asking that God give him everything he will ever need; or is he simply asking for food, clothing, and safety, the minimum he needs to survive?

At first reading, Jacob's vow sounded to me as if he was trying to make a commercial deal with God, offering something in exchange for something else. Many of the commentators, trying to "protect" Jacob, posit that all that Jacob's vow implied was to give him the possibility of serving God; the vow is simply a petition for God's help in granting Jacob the opportunity to give of himself, his life, and his soul to God.

If this is the true intention of Jacob's vow, then it is a valid one. However, if Jacob was intending to make a deal with God, then it would not be a proper vow. In Judaism, when one performs a good deed, one is not to do so with the expectation of reward. As the Ethics of the Fathers (1:3) rightly states: "Do not be like slaves who minister to the master for the sake or receiving reward, but be like slaves who minister to the master not for the sake of receiving a reward."

I once made a promise that if I won a million dollars I would become a religious Jew. Is this kosher?

Everybody should recognize the importance of not making statements indiscreetly or rashly. One should weigh his words and should abide by them after uttering them. This includes making a vow and fulfilling it.

Jewish law calls some vows invalid from the beginning. Among these is the *neder zerizim*, an oath taken for purposes of convenience but never taken seriously. We often find this kind of vow in business dealings. Another invalid vow is the *neder havai*, an exaggerated oath, for example, a vow to do something if one sees a million people or a flying camel or wins a million dollars.

An invalid vow could also be a *neder shegagah*, a vow made unintentionally. For example, one thinks that he ate yesterday and takes an oath on that condition, when in truth he did not eat then.

Finally, there is a *neder onesim*—when illness prohibits the fulfillment of a vow, where we assume that the vow would not have been made under such circumstances.

❦ What the Experts Say ❧

The making of vows is the doorway to folly. (Talmud, Kallah Rabbati 5)

A person who utters a vow places a burden on his neck. (Jerusalem Talmud, Nedarim 9:1)

Any person who breaks his oath denies God without hope of pardon. (Talmud, Shevuot 39)

Rabbi Eliezer said: "Yes is an oath and no is an oath." (Talmud, Shevuot 36a)

Vows are a fence for abstinence. (Ethics of the Fathers 3:13)

✷ Source ✷

A person who makes a promise to God or takes an oath to do something must carry it out. (Numbers 30:3)

Topic 12

Criticizing Others

❧ **What's Kosher** ❧

Is it kosher to criticize God?

The Torah reminds us that it is not only possible but permissible to criticize or complain to God when we think that God has done something wrong. Of course, it takes a great deal of audacity to think that we can challenge God. Abraham was the first to do so. In the book of Genesis, God decides that he is going to destroy Sodom and Gomorrah. Abraham intercedes and asks if God will sweep away the innocent along with the guilty. He rebukes God by further saying: "Far be it from You to do such a thing and bring death upon the innocent as well as the guilty; shall not the Judge of all the earth deal justly?" (Genesis 18:25).

There are going to be lots of occurrences in life in which you and God will disagree. Having a relationship with God means being willing and able to tell God when something is wrong. Doing so is a mitzvah.

A hockey team plays poorly and is harshly admonished by its usually soft-spoken coach. Is this kosher?

Although most coaches might tend to use profanity and raise their voices, trying to embarrass and humiliate their players, others might choose a different approach. In this case the coach used a perfectly kosher approach in criticizing members of his team. Realizing that his players were already embarrassed and upset with their perform-ance, the coach used reassuring words that offered specific ways for the team to improve its play. The criticism was fair and constructive and got the players' attention.

❦ What's Not Kosher ❧

My history teacher is extremely critical of students who answer questions incorrectly. Is this kosher?

The answer depends on the nature of the teacher's criticism. If his criticism was exaggerated and said in a way that was obviously meant to hurt and embarrass, then it was not kosher. This kind of criticism often gives the one who offers it great pleasure. Even if the teacher felt the need to offer a public critique in order to teach the rest of the class a lesson, he likely could have done so without making the student feel like a total failure.

Kosher criticism is that which uses words that are nonthreat-ening and reassuring. This kind of criticism is much more likely to induce change rather than simply hurting or embarrassing the per-son criticized.

Maimonides offers this advice: "He who rebukes another should administer the rebuke in private, speak to the offender gently and ten-derly, and point out that he is only speaking for the wrongdoer's own good." (Laws of Personality Development, 6:7)

A mother has long criticized her son for a very bad habit. The son rejects her criticism and says he has no intention of changing his behavior. Is it kosher for his mother to stop criticizing him?

According to Jewish tradition, if a person is known to reject all criticism or to respond to it with great outrage and hostility, you're under no ob-ligation to continue to offer it. It's sad for anyone to have to conclude that they can't do anything to change a bad trait and that it's a waste of time to even try.

But change is simply impossible for some; and when this is apparent, it's better to move on and apply your energies where they can be of use to someone.

When restaurant food is served late, is it kosher to admonish the waiter and not leave a tip?

Because it is not the waitress's fault that the food took so long to be prepared, blaming and rebuking her is not appropriate. Even though a tip generally reflects good service, withholding it does not in this case seem to be fair, because the waitress did nothing wrong and had no control regarding the speed of food preparation. To blame her will likely only hurt her feelings and will not change the fact that your food arrived in an untimely manner.

A better and more kosher approach would be to speak to the restaurant manager and let him or her know how you feel about having to wait so long for your food. The manager is in a better position to get the chef's attention and perhaps improve the service in the future.

Is it kosher for a person overly compelled by a sense of justice to chastise others for even a minor offense?

We need to realize that it is impossible to change everything. Therefore, it's not kosher to feel that you need to correct every misdemeanor or wrong that you perceive. That's simply an impossible goal. Save your energy for the more major ones.

Is it kosher for a woman to criticize her next-door neighbor for leaving her two dogs in a kennel and going on a trip?

Not everything that bothers you about what another person does needs to be said. The words that this woman said to her neighbor were not helpful at the time and likely had the effect of putting a damper on her intended trip. Obviously, the woman was concerned for the welfare of her neighbor's dogs. It would have been more appropriate for her to discuss her feelings well in advance of her neighbor's trip or upon her return. The timing of one's criticism can be important, and one should always be cognizant of this as well.

☙ What the Experts Say ☙

Rabbi Tarfon said: I wonder if there is anyone in this generation capable of accepting reproof. Rabbi Eleazar ben Azaryah said: I wonder whether there is anyone in this generation who knows how to reprove without humiliating the one being criticized. (Talmud, Arachin 16b)

Love unaccompanied by criticism is not love. Peace accompanied by reproof is not peace. (Genesis Rabbah 54:3)

Whoever can prevent members of his household from committing a sin, but does not, is punished for the sins of his household. If he can stop the people of his city from sinning, but does not, he is responsible for the sins of the people of his city. If he can stop the whole world from sinning, and does not, he is held responsible for the sins of the whole world. (Talmud, Shabbat 54b)

One is obligated to continue admonishing until the sinner assaults the admonisher and says to him, "I refuse to listen." (Maimonides, Mishneh Torah, Laws of Personality Development 6:7)

It is the duty of every Jew to correct the wrongdoings of his fellow Jews, so that he himself may not eventually fall under the influence of sin. (Recanti)

Rabbi Judah the Prince says: Which way should a person choose? Let a person love rebuke since as long as there is rebuke in the world, ease of mind comes to the world, good and blessing come to the world, and evil departs from it, as it is taught in Proverbs 24:25: Those who rebuke find favor with God and a good blessing comes to them. (Talmud, Tamid 28a)

How often does a person rebuke sinners at the wrong time or place, so that they pay no attention to what is being said? This can make the rebuker the cause of their becoming more confirmed in their wickedness, and of their desecrating the name of God by adding rebellion to their sin. In a case like this, it is better to remain silent. "As it is our duty to criticize when we are likely to be heard, it is our duty to withhold rebuke when we are not likely to be heard." (Talmud, Yevamot 65)

A Model Biblical Rebuke

Background: King David has sexual relations with the beautiful Bathsheba, wife of Uriah the Hittite. David then decides to have Uriah stationed in the front line where fighting is fiercest. Uriah is killed, and David proceeds to take Bathsheba as his wife. God is displeased with David's behavior and sends Nathan the prophet to David to let him know so. Following is Nathan's rebuke of David:

> "There were two men in the same city. One was rich and one was poor. The rich man had very large flocks and herds, but the poor man had only one little ewe lamb that he had bought. He tended it and it grew up together with him and his children. It used to share his morsel of bread, drink from his cup and cuddle with him. It was like a daughter to him. One day, a traveler came to the rich man, but he didn't want to take anything from his own flocks or herds to prepare a meal for the guest who had come. So he took the poor man's lamb and prepared it for the man who had come to him."
>
> David flew into a rage against the man and said to Nathan, "As God lives, the man who did this deserves to die. He shall pay for the lamb four times over, because he did such a thing and showed no pity."
>
> And Nathan said, "That man is you." (2 Samuel 12:1–7)

Just as one is commanded to say that which will be heeded, so one is commanded not to say that which will not be heeded. (Talmud, Yevamot 65b)

❧ Sources ❧

You shall not hate your fellow man in your heart. Reprove your kinsman and incur no guilt because of him. (Leviticus 19:17)

One who rebukes another will in the end find more favor than one who flatters that person. (Proverbs 28:23)

Topic 13

Death and Dying

❧ **What's Kosher** ❧

Is it kosher to have a funeral in a synagogue?

Historically, Jewish funerals took place at the home of the deceased or at the cemetery. Synagogues were used very rarely and only for people of extraordinary distinction and stature in the community. Today some communities do permit funeral services to be held in the synagogue. Many allow it only for rabbis, cantors, and those who have served the synagogue as its president.

Is it kosher to bring children to a funeral?

Yes, children should be provided with the opportunity to grieve in their own way. It is permissible to bring a child to a funeral. One must take one's cue from the child. If a child is frightened, it would be best to arrange appropriate child care. In any case, the wise thing to do would be to have the rabbi who is officiating sit down with the child prior to the funeral and explain what will be taking place.

Is it kosher to bring flowers to a Jewish funeral?

The Sephardic custom allows for flowers, although there is no real proscription against them in Ashkenazic practice. Today well-wishers are encouraged to give *tzedakah* (charity) as a more lasting memorial.

Must I cut my clothing during the rending-of-the-garment ceremony?

Keriah is the tear made on the mourner's clothing as an outward sign of grief. If one chooses not to have one's clothing cut, one may attach a black ribbon to one's clothing and have it cut instead. Cutting *keriah* is the ceremony that takes place before the funeral. It is an opportunity for psychological relief, allowing the mourner to express anguish and anger by means of an act of destruction made sacred by Jewish tradition.

What makes a casket kosher?

In Jewish tradition we follow the Bible's lead: "for you are dust, and unto dust you shall return" (Genesis 3:19). In other words, whatever prevents the process of returning to dust is considered inconsistent with traditional Jewish practice. Thus, a kosher casket must be made entirely of wood, including its wooden pegs and handles.

Reform and Reconstructionist rabbis, because they have more personal autonomy, will often permit the use of caskets not made entirely of wood.

What is the kosher procedure of a mourner during shivah?

It is customary for the mourner to refrain from work and commerce during shivah, unless there is a clearly articulated public need or the mourners are very poor. More traditional Jews avoid shaving (or haircutting of any sort), as they do personal grooming (but not hygienic practices). One is not to wear new clothes and should refrain from conjugal marital relations. The formal study of Torah is prohibited as well, but mourners are encouraged to reflect on books of the Bible such as Psalms and Job.

During shivah mourners sit lower than others, usually on low stools, and traditionally do not wear leather shoes. Both practices are signs of mourning. In addition, mirrors in the house (a sign of vanity) are covered. Very often, a minyan of worshippers will assemble in the mourner's home in order for the mourner to have the opportunity of saying the Mourner's Kaddish during shivah. Finally, a seven-day shivah candle is lit and kept in the house throughout the week of shivah.

What are some kosher guidelines for one who pays a shivah call to a mourner?

The most important Jewish law related to a visitor to a shivah home is not to speak to the mourner until the mourner speaks first. Mourners are there to support the bereaved, even in silence. It is also customary for mourners to bring meals to the bereaved. And of course, sharing reflections about the bereaved's beloved is often a nice way of helping to comfort the bereaved and assuaging them of some of their pain.

Are there kosher guidelines regarding the words to be written on the tombstone of the deceased?

The name of the deceased in English, and often in Hebrew too, appears on the tombstone, along with the date of death according to both the Hebrew and secular calendar. Sometimes above the inscription, among Ashkenazic Jews, one finds two Hebrew letters, *pey* and *nun*, which are the initials of *po nach*, here rests. The Sephardic Jews often use the Hebrew letters *mem* and *kuf*, standing for *matzevet kevurah*, meaning monument of the grave of. Underneath the inscription one often finds the Hebrew letters *tav, nun, tzadee, bet,* and *hey,* standing for *tehi nishmato tzerurah betzror hachayim,* "may his soul be bound up in the bond of eternal life."

The tombstone of a Levite (an assistant to the Kohanim, Jewish priests, descended from Aaron) often has a ewer carved out over the inscriptions as a symbol of his office, because in bygone years the Levite washed the priest's hands before the priest gave the Priestly Benediction. The tombstones of Kohanim are often marked by a carving of the hands raised in the Priestly Benediction.

Occasionally there will be a verse from the Bible or rabbinic literature, often related to the person's life. A tombstone of one of my congregants who was a professional baseball player had a baseball bat and ball on it.

When is it kosher to have an unveiling?

In Eastern European countries and in the United States, it has become customary to consecrate the tombstone with a brief service. Because the stone is covered with a cloth that the family removes during the service, the ritual is called the unveiling.

The unveiling generally takes place within a year after the death. It can take place anytime after thirty days. Unveilings may take place whenever grave visitations in general are permissible. The most kosher days for grave visitation are the day that concludes the *sheloshim* (thirty-day period after the death); the day of the *yahrzeit* (anniversary of the death); and days before holidays such as Passover, Rosh Hashanah, Sukkot, and Shavuot. Visitation ought not to be made on the Sabbath or on Passover, Sukkot, and Shavuot.

Is it kosher to be buried in a mausoleum?

Because the requirement to inter the deceased refers specifically to burial in the earth, a mausoleum built over a burial plot is permissible. Mausoleums in which the casket is kept above the earth are contrary to the biblical directive that emphasizes earthly burial, but liberal Jews permit them.

What's the kosher procedure regarding what to do with amputated limbs?

If an individual dies with severed limbs, then those limbs are to be buried with the deceased. Previously amputated limbs should have been buried in the future plot of the individual or in a family plot nearby.

Is it kosher for a Jew to attend a funeral of a non-Jewish friend or colleague?

Absolutely. Attending a funeral is a sign of respect, and there is no reason to prevent a Jew from paying his or her respects to the deceased.

May non-Jews serve as pallbearers at a Jewish funeral?

Although it is traditional for members of the family or close Jewish friends to carry the deceased to his or her final resting place, Jewish law does not prohibit non-Jews from acting as pallbearers.

May one recite the Mourner's Kaddish for a parent who abandoned the Jewish faith?

I have had several cases of congregants whose parents abandoned Judaism and passed away. Authorities differ as to whether it is kosher for a child to recite the Kaddish for deceased parents who were apostates and severed all ties with the Jewish community. Rabbi Moses Isserles says in the Code of Jewish Law (Laws of Mourning) that a son may recite Kaddish for an apostate father who was murdered by idolaters because it is presumed that through his death the father has made atonement for his sin and that in all probability the man repented just before he died. Other authorities follow the lead of Rabbi Akiba Eger, an eighteenth-century major Polish authority, who held that a son is permitted to mourn and say Kaddish for an apostate parent even if the death was natural.

Is it kosher for a woman to say Kaddish for a loved one?

Most Orthodox rabbis would suggest that a male member of the family assume the responsibility of saying Kaddish, because by Jewish law it is a male's obligation to do so. In the other branches of Judaism, women are encouraged to say the Kaddish for their loved one.

Is embalming kosher?

Jews in Bible times practiced embalming, preserving the remains of the deceased. (Both Jacob and Joseph were embalmed, as described in Genesis 50:2, 26.) This practice, however, has been abandoned because the Talmudic rabbis considered it disrespectful of the deceased.

Today for sanitary reasons and by requirement of civil law, embalming a body sometimes becomes necessary. Examples include when a burial must be delayed because a person dies at sea or a body is flown out of the country to be buried abroad. The only kosher method of embalming in those cases, however, is one that leaves the body intact.

✠ What's Not Kosher ✠

If a grandchild loses his grandfather, is it kosher for him to consider himself a mourner?

Jewish tradition requires only seven relatives to observe the traditional laws of mourning: father, mother, spouse, son, daughter, sister, and brother. Anyone can say the Mourner's Kaddish as well, including a grandchild, but a grandchild is not required or expected to follow the traditional laws and customs relating to Jewish mourning practices.

Is it kosher to bury a Jewish man in his favorite suit and tie?

Jewish law says that every person must be buried in *tachrichim*, simple white linen shrouds. They are all alike in order to ensure that everyone, regardless of socioeconomic status, is equal at death. A deceased male (and any female whose family elects to do so) is also wrapped in a tallit (prayer shawl), with one tzitzit (ritual fringe) cut. Once again, more liberal rabbis, who have more personal autonomy, will permit the deceased to be dressed in regular clothing.

Is it kosher to sit shivah for less than the traditional seven days?

According to Jewish tradition, shivah, the seven-day period of mourning, begins once the deceased is buried and lasts for seven days. Most Reform and Reconstructionist rabbis have abbreviated shivah to a three-day period.

Is cremation kosher?

Although liberal Judaism allows for cremation, it is traditionally prohibited because it does not allow for the body to naturally return to the earth. According to this perspective, if a cremation does take place, the ashes would not be buried in a Jewish cemetery. Some cemeteries will allow for burial of ashes, however, and in this way one preserves some attachment to the Jewish community by allowing for burial in Jewishly consecrated soil.

Is it kosher for a Jew to be buried in a non-Jewish cemetery?

Because in bygone years idolatry was prevalent among non-Jews, all heathens—and by extension, all non-Jews—were placed in the same category. This is likely the rabbinic foundation for insisting that Jews be buried in their own cemeteries. In theory and in emergencies, however, the law does permit a Jew to be buried next to a non-Jew.

Must a funeral be conducted by a rabbi to be kosher?

A rabbi is not required to officiate at a funeral. A layperson may recite the appropriate prayers. Nor must a rabbi deliver the eulogy for that matter. A member of the family or a friend of the deceased may do so, and many rabbis encourage this. Today most funeral services are conducted by both rabbis and cantors because of their experience and professional skill, not because Jewish law requires them to lead the service.

Is it a kosher requirement for the family of the deceased to dress in black for a funeral?

No law requires Jews to wear black clothing at the funeral or during the week of mourning. Even the wearing of dark clothes is not required of mourners, although being clothed in subdued colors seems appropriate.

Is it a kosher requirement for mourners to sit on boxes during the period of shivah?

There is no truth that requires mourners to sit on boxes. True, many funeral homes and synagogues provide boxes for the family of the bereaved, and thus it is quite possible that you may recall seeing boxes in a house of shivah. The law does require mourners to sit in a lower position than usual. One explanation is that mourners are expected to sit closer to the earth in which the deceased is buried, a symbolic gesture of feeling spiritually united with a loved one in spite of physical separation.

❦ What the Experts Say ❧

Silence is meritorious in a house of mourning. (Talmud, Berachot 6b)

The duty of comforting mourners takes precedence over the duty of visiting the sick, because comforting mourners is an act of benevolence toward the living and the dead. (Maimonides, Mishneh Torah, Laws of Mourning 14:7)

When a person sheds tears at the death of a virtuous man, the Holy One counts them and places them in His treasure house. (Talmud, Shabbat 105a)

The dust returns to the earth as it was, but the spirit returned to God who gave it. (Ecclesiastes 3:2)

When a person dies, all that accompanies him are Torah and good deeds. (Ethics of the Fathers 6:9)

We have been taught: Even as the deceased are requited, so are eulogizers who are untruthful and they who echo the falsehoods spoken by them. (Talmud, Berachot 62a)

❦ Sources ❧

His body shall not remain all night. You shall surely bury him the same day. (Deuteronomy 21:23)

They sat down on the ground with him for seven days and nights. (Job 2:13)

Topic 14

❦ ❧

Ecology

❦ What's Kosher ❧

Recycling every scrap of paper, can, and piece of plastic is a nuisance. Is it kosher to throw stuff away occasionally?

No one is perfect, and of course it's permissible every so often to throw a recyclable object into the regular trash. However, it is important not to get into the habit of doing this, because habituation brings routine. The Bible warned against needless destruction of the environment even in wartime. One should therefore be careful when it comes to the weekly task of recycling. Although one may sometimes have to forgo showing the usual care to recycle (due to illness, for example), laziness cannot be used as a kosher excuse.

Is it kosher for a group of homeowners to complain about the smells from a chicken farm a mile away?

According to the Mishnah Baba Batra 2:9, graveyards and tanneries that emit foul odors are to be located at least fifty cubits (seventy-five feet) outside a city. A tannery can only be operated on the east side of a city (that is, the side of town that will carry the bad odor from the residential area).

Centuries ago traditional Jewish law recognized the desirability of proper zoning in communities, where business and residences would be separated: "If a person wishes to open a shop in the courtyard, his neighbor may stop him because he will be kept awake by the noise of people going in an out of the shop" (Talmud, Baba Batra 20b).

In 1565 Rabbi Joseph Karo completed his Code of Jewish Law, known as the Shulchan Aruch. In this volume we learn that if one builds a threshing floor on one's own property, digs a latrine, or does work that makes for dust or dirt, he must situate it so that the dirt or smell of the latrine does not reach a neighbor and cause damage. Even if the dust is carried by the wind, such a case is analogous to causing damage with an arrow. Therefore, those who cause airborne pollution are guilty and must make restitution to those they harm. The chicken farmer was guilty as charged!

I want to cut down an apple tree growing close to my house. Is this kosher?

The biblical prohibition "do not destroy fruit trees" (Deuteronomy 20:19) does not apply if a thing was destroyed for constructive purposes. Thus, if a fruit-bearing tree causes damage to other trees or if the value of its wood for fuel is greater than the value of the fruit it produces, it may be cut down (Talmud, Baba Kamma 91b-92a). In addition, if the fruit tree's roots were causing damage to the house's foundation, one could remove it.

An interesting midrash (Exodus 34) observed that the wood used for building the tabernacle in the wilderness was not from fruit-bearing trees. This was to teach us that our own houses should be built with wood from other than fruit-bearing trees.

Is it kosher for me not to refrain from planting my vegetable garden every seventh year, as the Torah ordains?

You are correct that the Torah provides for a special Sabbath for the land, to be observed every seventh year. However, the laws of the sabbatical year apply only to Jews living in the land of Israel. One way for a U.S. Jew to symbolically observe the sabbatical year would be to offer all of the fruits of that year to the needy. Exodus 23:10 says: "Six years you shall sow your land and in the seventh let it rest. Let the needy among your people eat of it." Offering the fruit of your harvest to the needy would surely be a kosher way of symbolically observing the sabbatical year.

❦ What's Not Kosher ❧

I remember counselors at a Jewish camp allowing kids to have food fights. Is this kosher?

A Jewish principle known as *bal taschit* forbids unnecessary destruction. Deuteronomy 20:19 says that "when you besiege a city, you shall not destroy its fruit. . . . You may eat of them, but not cut them down, for man's life depends on the trees." In wartime people are prone to ignore ecological issues, but even war does not justify needless destruction of the environment.

The principle of "do not destroy" is broadened in rabbinic law to include any gratuitous act of destruction: "Not only one who cuts down fruit trees, but also who smashes household goods, tears clothes, demolishes a building, stops up a spring, or destroys food, violates the command, 'You must not destroy'" (Maimonides, Mishneh Torah, Laws of Kings 6:1).

This law in Maimonides' authoritative code clearly lets us know that wasting food in a food fight is a violation. I have always taught my students of the importance of not wasting food, with millions of people starving in the world. In fact, when we celebrated our children's Bar and Bat Mitzvah, we donated a huge amount of leftover food to a local food pantry. We encourage others to do the same. Similarly, we also regularly donate clothing that we no longer use to a clothing bank. I believe that throwing out clothing without making an effort to give it away to the needy is in violation of the principle of avoiding needless destruction.

I love to take long showers. Is this kosher?

When putting the principle of *bal taschit* into action, Jewish tradition requires us to show respect for the environment and to be ecologically minded. The rabbis applied the principle of not destroying to three areas of concern:

There is a general principle of not being wasteful. For example, in the Talmud, Shabbat 67b, we learn that one should not adjust a lamp to burn too quickly. Using water-saving shower faucets and environmentally correct toilets would help to save our most important natural resource—water. Taking shorter showers would also be less wasteful.

Never be excessively wasteful. Even when commanded by the Torah to destroy, we are warned not to exceed what is commanded. For example, although one is required to tear one's garment when hearing of the death of a loved one, one should not tear the garment too much because that would violate the commandment of "do not destroy" (Talmud, Baba Kamma 91b).

It is not proper to demean food. Food fighting is strictly prohibited. This area was singled out for special attention. For example, one is not allowed to throw bread, because bread is symbolic of the essence of all food (Talmud, Berachot 50b).

Is it kosher to throw a candy wrapper out my car window?

Jewish law forbids a person to be aloof and indifferent to environmental concerns. I have always been concerned about the trash that lines the many streets in communities all over the country. Every single cigarette butt and candy wrapper that is thrown from a car window adds to the pollution of the earth. It is clearly not kosher to throw trash out your car window.

Here's an idea for something kosher you can do to help clean up the environment. Just recently our congregation "adopted" the street on which our synagogue is located. With special arrangements made through the mayor, members of the congregation spent an entire day cleaning the street and its refuse. As a reward for our efforts, which will continue several times throughout the year, we received a street sign that said: Temple Sholom, Adopt a Street Program.

A small business owner with fifty workers is unable to observe all environmental regulations concerning smoke emissions. Is it kosher for him to make full compensation to his workers a higher priority?

This question pits one important Jewish value against another. Jewish law obligates an owner to pay his workers fairly and in a timely fashion while at the same time ensuring that the operation of the business is respectful to the environment. The kosher approach for the owner here would be to discuss with all of the employees the dilemma that he is facing with regard to the issue and see whether perhaps they would be willing to make some concessions so that the business could function in an environmentally sound way. It would not be kosher for the owner simply to disregard smoke pollution because of lack of funds to do anything about it.

❦ What the Experts Say ❧

It is forbidden to live in a town that does not have a green garden. (Jerusalem Talmud, Kiddushin 4:12)

Care is to be taken that bits of broken glass should not be scattered on public land where they may cause injury. (Talmud, Baba Kamma 30a)

A tannery must not be set up in such a way that the prevailing winds can send their unpleasant odor to the town. (Jerusalem Talmud, Baba Batra 2:9)

Not only one who cuts down fruit trees, but also who smashes household goods, tears clothes, demolishes a building, stops up a spring, or destroys food, violates the command, "You must not destroy." (Maimonides, Mishneh Torah, Laws of Kings 6:1)

Rabbi Yochanan ben Zakkai used to say: If you see a sapling in your hand and someone should say to you that the Messiah has come, stay and complete the planting, and then go to greet the Messiah. (Talmud, Fathers of Rabbi Natan 31b)

A Jewish ecology is not based on the assumption that we are no different from other living creatures. It begins with the opposite idea: We have a special responsibility precisely because we are different, because we know what we are doing. (Rabbi Harold Kushner, *To Life*, p. 59)

Rabbi Simeon ben Yochai said: Three things are of equal importance: earth, humans and rain. (Midrash, Genesis Rabbah 13:3)

❦ Sources ❧

Six years you may sow your fields and gather in the yield. But in the seventh year the land shall have a Sabbath of complete rest. (Leviticus 25:2–7)

When in your war against a city, you have to besiege it a long time in order to capture it, you must not destroy trees, wielding the ax against them. (Deuteronomy 20:19)

The earth is the Lord's and the fullness thereof. (Psalms 24:1)

⅍ ⅍

The Elderly

⅍ **What's Kosher** ⅍

Is it kosher to expect older people to fulfill all of their religious obligations?

Older Jews, like others, are commanded to carry out all religious obligations that they are capable of fulfilling. There is no retirement age when it comes to carrying out commandments. A high proportion of retired people in our community attend daily morning services and adult education classes. They seem more eager than ever, now that they are free from the regular demands of a workday, to participate in synagogue-related activities.

The one exception regarding fulfillment of a religious obligation relates to the issue of health. If an elderly person (or any person for that matter) is physically unable to carry out the fulfillment of a religious obligation, Jewish law would afford that person a total exemption.

Is it kosher to put my aging mother in a nursing home?

Although most adult children would prefer to have a parent who can no longer take care of himself in a home care situation, sometimes it is simply not possible.

According to the Code of Jewish Law (Yoreh Deah, chap. 240), if a child's parents become mentally ill, he should try his best to help them according to their needs until improvement is vouchsafed. If their condition becomes impossible to him, he places them in the hands of those who can properly care for them.

In modern times this ruling would suggest that children first try to care for parents on their own and if necessary with outside help. When that is not possible, they should hire others to serve as primary caretakers. Sending a parent to live in an old age home should be only the final step, never the first one. Very often, depending on the health of the elderly parent, a nursing home is much better equipped to care for his or her needs.

The real problem regarding an aged parent who needs more extreme health care is having adequate insurance and being able to afford it. Once a parent is placed in the care of a nursing home, it is important to follow through to be sure that he or she is getting the proper medical, social, and psychological care. This requires, as you know, being attentive, being an advocate, intervening frequently, supervising, and just taking the time and energy to make sure that everything is OK.

What is the kosher way of providing for the best interests of treating the elderly?

The Jewish people from the outset have paid particular attention to the welfare of the aged. In many passages in the Bible, the "elders" are the wise men, the judges of the people. We read in the book of Leviticus 19:32: "You shall rise up before the hoary head, and honor the face of the old man, and you shall fear your God." The rabbis understood this literally, that whenever an old man passes by, one should rise to one's feet as a token of respect.

In general, the Bible honored and respected the elderly. They were the persons to whom people went for life advice. Unlike biblical times, today old people are often perceived as socially, psychologically, and physically isolated, restricted, and deteriorated. My wife, Leora, wrote her doctoral dissertation, titled "The Development of Children's Attitudes Toward the Aged," on this subject. The study sought to determine whether young children already hold and demonstrate the negative stereotypes and attitudes common among older children, adolescents, and adults. Subjects in the study were children ages four through eight. The results of her study indicated that by ages six and eight, children begin to demonstrate negative beliefs and feelings about the aged.

What we owe the elderly is reverence, but all they ask for, as Abraham Joshua Heschel writes in *The Insecurities of Freedom* (p. 70), is "consideration, attention, not to be discarded" or embarrassed. The whole philosophy of care for the aged is expressed in the psalmist's poignant cry (71:9): "Cast me not off in the time of old age. When my strength fails, do not forsake me!"

It is undoubtedly true that care of aged parents can be a severe burden, but in return God promises longevity to those who shoulder the burden: "Honor your father and mother, that your days may be long upon the land which God gives you" (Deuteronomy 5:16).

✴ What's Not Kosher ✴

Is it kosher for me to remain seated when an elderly person passes me by?

The book of Leviticus 19:32 states: "Rise before the aged and show respect to the elderly." One does not have to take this verse literally and stand (if seated) when an older person passes by. The verse is to be understood metaphorically, meaning to show respect in all ways to an elderly person.

This passage brings to mind my very first trip to Israel in 1970. Riding on a public bus in Jerusalem, I was intrigued to see the verse "rise before the aged" on a sign among the other advertising signs in Hebrew. The obvious intention of the sign was to remind passengers to relinquish their seats to an older person who needed a seat. Today, many years later, many public buses and subway trains have a special seating area for the disabled and the elderly. Unfortunately, however, not all people observe or honor these notices.

Is it kosher not to hire a person because of his age?

Ageism, discrimination based on a person's age, happens all the time in business and industry. The prejudice toward old age and the elderly is underscored by the desperate need of so many of us to look and feel younger. Know that it is unequivocally nonkosher not to give equal respect and employment opportunity to a person because of his or her age. Judaism has always suggested that a person be judged on his or her merits. In traditional societies elders are respected for their ties to the past and for the wisdom they transmit. It is unfortunate that today we are prone to view the wisdom of the old as out-of-date or out of touch and an older person as not being able to do the job. My teacher the late Abraham Joshua Heschel was right when he wrote: "What they [the elderly] deserve is preference, yet we do not even grant them equality" (*The Insecurities of Freedom*, p. 70).

❧ What the Experts Say ❧

How welcome is old age. The aged are beloved by God. (Midrash, Exodus 5:12)

Rabbi Joshua ben Levi said: Honor and respect the elderly and saintly scholar, whose physical powers are broken, equally with the young and vigorous one. For the stone tablets that were broken, no less than the whole ones, had a place in the Ark of the Covenant. (Talmud, Berachot 8b)

Rabbi Jose the Galilean said: To honor the aged means that one should not sit in the seat of an elderly person, nor speak before he has spoken nor contradict him. (Talmud, Kiddushin 32b)

What we owe the old is reverence, but all they ask for is consideration, attention, not to be discarded and forgotten. What they deserve is preference, yet we do not even grant them equality. (Abraham Joshua Heschel, *The Insecurities of Freedom*, p. 70)

❦ Sources ❧

The property of a country is in accordance with the treatment of its aged. (Nachman of Bratslav)

Even in old age they shall bear fruit, they shall be full of vigor and strength. (Psalms 92:15)

You shall rise up before the hoary head, and honor the face of the old man, and you shall fear your God. (Leviticus 19:32)

Topic 16

Employer-Employee Relations

❦ **What's Kosher** ❧

Is it kosher for a worker to ask for time during the day to say his prayers?

According to the Code of Jewish Law (Orach Chayim 100:191), it is obligatory for an employer to set aside time for his employees to eat, pray, and say the Grace after the meal. Therefore, it is kosher for a worker to ask for time during the day to say prayers.

Is it kosher for a person who observes the Sabbath to ask for time off on Jewish holidays without being penalized?

Is it certainly kosher if one is observant to let his or her employer know at the outset that he or she is an observant Jew and will need to observe a number of Jewish holidays during the year. However, it is not a kosher expectation to think that the employer will acquiesce to giving him or her all these days off with pay or with no obligation to make up the missed work.

Many observant Jews who choose not to work on the Jewish holidays will often come in to work on a Sunday, work at home, or work late into the night to be sure to finish all that is part of his or her responsibility. This is the fair and kosher thing to do, for when an employer hires a worker, the employer should reasonably expect that the employee will do the job as agreed in the contract.

❧ What's Not Kosher ❧

I always receive my paycheck late. Is this kosher?

The rabbis were most concerned about the rights of the workers, which include such items as the employer's treatment of a worker, the frequency of payment, and even the permissibility of food as compensation. It is not kosher for an employer to delay payment to a worker. The Torah teaches, "You shall not abuse a needy and destitute laborer, whether a fellow countryman or a stranger in one of the communities of your land. You must pay him his wages on the same day, before the sun sets" (Deuteronomy 24:15).

In modern times, with regard to workers who are compensated by the week or month, Jewish law requires the employers to pay them no later than nightfall on the last day of the week or month unless the employers have entered into a previous arrangement.

I have a teacher who continually arrives late. Is this kosher?

Common sense would posit that an employer would have certain basic obligations to its employees. In Judaism a worker has numerous obligations to the employer. For example, workers are expected to be punctual and work diligently for their employers. According to Maimonides (Mishneh Torah, Laws of Hiring 13:7), just as the employer is enjoined not to deprive the poor worker of wages or withhold it when it is due, so is the worker enjoined not to deprive the employer of the benefit of the work by idling away his or her time, a little here and a little there, thus wasting the whole day deceitfully. The worker must be very punctual.

Is it kosher to call in sick to your employer when you simply want the day off?

Employers can expect to get a full and complete effort from their workers. Certainly employers would expect their workers to be honest and trustworthy. Jewish law demands that an employee act fairly and truthfully. It would therefore not be kosher to call in sick when in reality you simply wanted the day off. Most jobs include personal days, which allow one to take off work for any reason, with no questions asked. It would be preferable that an employee simply take a personal day rather than resort to telling a lie.

Is it kosher for a person to come late to work with a hangover or groggy from lack of sleep?

Honesty requires that a worker who expects to be paid normal wages perform the workload of a normal employee. Thus, to arrive late in a condition that prevents you from completing your duties on a professional level is a form of thievery from one's employer.

Is it kosher for an employee to follow his boss's orders when he knows they are wrong?

Because every person is endowed with free will, even if a superior orders you to perform an evil act, Jewish law forbids your following the order. If you do carry out the order, you cannot then blame the person who issued it, for you should not have listened to it.

At the trials of the Nazi war criminals held after World War II, most Nazis offered the defense that they were only following orders. From the standpoint of Jewish law, this is no defense.

Quite simply, according to Jewish law, a person given an unethical order is obligated not to carry it out. If one does, he or she is no less blameworthy than the person who gave the order. In the Talmud this principle is known as *ain shaliach le-davar aveirah*, "there is no messenger in a case of sin" (Talmud, Kiddushin 42b). This means that all the blame must not be directed at the one who sent the message.

❦ What the Experts Say ❧

Whoever wants to be saintly should live according to the tractates of the Talmud dealing with commerce and finance. (Talmud, Baba Kamma 30a)

There is a general tendency for a worker to labor faithfully for his employer throughout a period of two or three hours and then to become lazy at his job. (Midrash, Genesis Rabbah 70:18)

The unfaithful worker is a robber. Such a person does God's work deceitfully. (Talmud, Baba Metzia 78a)

It is obligatory for an employer to set aside time for the workers to eat and say the Grace after Meals and prayers. (Code of Jewish Law, Orach Chayim 100:191)

Whoever holds an employees wage's, it is as though he has taken the person's life from him. (Talmud, Baba Metzia 112a)

He who shares with a thief is the enemy of his own soul. (Proverbs 29:24)

❦ Source ❧

Do not oppress a hired servant that is poor and needy. (Deuteronomy 24:14)

Topic 17

Food

❦ What's Kosher ❧

Is it kosher to be a vegetarian?

I've always felt that the ideal Jewish diet is vegetarian. After all, human beings were permitted to eat meat only after the flood. Adam and Eve, in the ideal garden of Eden, were permitted to eat only the produce of the fruit trees. However, the advent of the dietary laws of keeping kosher has created a good working compromise, allowing us to eat animal flesh while creating limits that spare the animal undue pain and refining our sense of compassion.

Is eating veal kosher?

Veal comes from a calf, and if slaughtered in a kosher manner, is entirely acceptable. But some people who call themselves eco-kosher consider eating veal to be *treif* (nonkosher). When calves are factory farmed, the animals are often kept in cramped, despicable conditions. To ensure the meat's tenderness, factory-farmed calves are often immobilized in a contraption that does not permit them to graze, and they are force-fed. So-called eco-kosher Jews refrain from eating any kind of meat when they know that the animal from which the meat is produced is treated without true concern for its welfare. These same people are also not likely to buy vegetables treated with pesticides.

As the greening of Judaism takes root across the country, eco-kosher is just one of the many earth-friendly trends that seems to be gaining momentum. Synagogues of all denominations are beginning to look for more ways to integrate ideas coming from the eco-kosher movement. To give a small example, in our synagogue we try to use cloth table coverings instead of the disposable variety.

If you are interested in more information about this fast-growing eco-kosher movement, you can contact the Coalition on the Environment and Jewish Life, 443 Park Avenue, 11th Floor, New York, NY 10016.

At a kosher restaurant, my friends learned that the restaurant was not *glatt* kosher and refused to order. Is this kosher?

Although I would have no problem eating in a kosher restaurant (without it having to be *glatt*), some people adhere only to the *glatt* standard. The word *glatt* is Yiddish and means smooth. Originally in Talmudic law it referred to an animal's lung. If a slaughtered animal's lung was found to be damaged or in some way scarred, the meat of that animal was considered nonkosher. *Glatt* kosher restaurants adhere to the standards of smoothness of the animal's lungs, and some people posit that only this standard is acceptable to them. Others who keep kosher are not so concerned with whether the meat is *glatt* kosher as long as the restaurant is deemed kosher and has acceptable rabbinic supervision.

Misconceptions about the meaning of *glatt* are widespread. If I were to ask members of my congregation the meaning of *glatt* kosher, many would answer that it means extra kosher or super kosher, holding to a higher standard. But it is common to find fish, candy, and even dairy products with the stamp of *glatt* on them. It is technically inaccurate to do this, because *glatt* specifically relates to animal foods.

If I keep kosher, can I eat at a nonkosher restaurant and just have fish or salad?

Some Jews do not eat in a restaurant even if there is a kosher sign on the window (they may not have faith in the rabbinic supervision), whereas other Jews may say they keep kosher and eat only certain foods, such as broiled fish and salad, in a nonkosher establishment. It all depends on the level of observance.

Jews who are extremely careful about their dietary observance do not eat in a restaurant unless they are certain the owner is an observant Jew. They also require the restaurant to be closed on the Sabbath and Jewish holidays. Others may choose to eat in a kosher restaurant even if it stays open on the Sabbath.

Owing to the relatively small number of kosher restaurants in most of the United States and Canada, situations frequently require relaxing the strict standards of kashruth observed in the home. When in such a predicament, consider the following principles:

Make a thorough investigation to ascertain whether kosher facilities are available within a reasonable distance. This might be a vegetarian or dairy restaurant. As a Conservative rabbi, I would always prefer a kosher facility even if a nonkosher one appears more appealing.

If it is necessary and desirable to dine in a restaurant that does not have a *mashgiach* (rabbinic supervisor), those who keep kosher at home do not eat meat and dishes containing meat. Some kashruth observers sanction the eating of cold foods only, such as salads, if these contain no forbidden ingredients. Some approve of eating permitted fish and other foods, even if cooked.

When my students who observe the kosher laws are beginning the application process to college, I am usually able to advise them about the availability of kosher food or facilities for doing one's own cooking. All national and international airlines provide kosher or vegetarian meals if passengers request them ahead of time. This is also true of many hospitals, hotels, and resorts.

Are some kosher symbols on food products more kosher than others?

Various organizations, generally in cooperation with well-trained Orthodox rabbis, supervise the manufacture of and processing of kosher foods. A company wishing to have its food certified kosher must apply to one of these organizations. They carefully investigate manufacturing techniques and ingredients to determine whether they meet the kashruth standards of the kosher-certifying organization. Currently these organizations certify more than ten thousand food products.

More than one hundred organizations nationwide offer rabbinic certification, and each has a specially designed symbol that appears on the food product. The larger organizations that offer rabbinic certification are likely to be the ones that a person can better trust, because they have more employees and more checks and balances in their work. One of the most popular and largest is the Union of Orthodox Congregations, which certifies thousands of products manufactured by more than one thousand firms. It is known as the OU; its symbol is a letter U with a circle around it. One of the smallest operations is an individual rabbi in Pittsburgh who certifies a brand of soft drink.

Some kosher products simply carry the letter K on their packaging to indicate that they are under rabbinic supervision but not necessarily Orthodox supervision. Write directly to the manufacturer to determine the certifying agent's name.

When I was first ordained, I took on the responsibility of giving a local Jewish-owned bakery its kosher supervision. Each week I would make spot checks to examine the ingredients of its breads and cakes and the fillings in its pastries. I designed my own rubber stamp with my name on it, which I used to stamp the baked goods as either dairy or pareve (nondairy). What was even more fun was getting and eating the Danish pastries right out of the oven. This was the reward for my services!

Is swordfish kosher?

Jews are permitted to eat only fish that have fins and scales. The problem with swordfish is that they are born with fins and scales but shed their scales after a year. Although Orthodox Jews do not consider swordfish kosher, the Conservative movement's Committee on Law and Standards studied the issue and several decades ago wrote a legal responsum that said that indeed, swordfish was kosher and may be eaten.

Is it kosher to eat fish and meat on the same dish?

In the Code of Jewish Law (Yoreh Deah 116), we find a series of pro-
hibitions, all related to the issue of *sakanah* (things that are dangerous
to one's health). Paragraph 2 specifically prohibits eating meat and fish
together, because it states "it could lead to leprosy." The entire chapter
deals with other cases of danger, such as the prohibition of putting
coins in one's mouth, drinking from uncovered beverages, and the like.

Historically, when a specific danger ceased to exist, the rabbis
had the power to end the prohibition. Today we know that there is no
danger of contracting leprosy by eating fish and meat together. The
Conservative movement's Law Committee studied the issue and now
permits not only putting fish and meat on the same plate but allowing
them to be consumed together. Some Orthodox rabbis would certainly disagree and would not allow the commingling of fish and meat.
But there really is no reason to avoid mixing these.

Is eating a rare steak kosher?

Although it is kosher to eat a rare steak, most traditional Jews, when
ordering a steak in a kosher restaurant or barbecuing one on their own
grill, prefer to have their steaks on the more well-done side. First of all,
a well-cooked steak is less likely to cause injury due to bacteria in meat
that is not well cooked. But more importantly, it is because the Torah
imposes an absolute prohibition against consuming blood. Blood is
viewed as a symbol of life, and man has a right to nourishment, not to
life. Hence, in Jewish law the blood must be drained and returned
to the universe, to God. The removal of blood is one of the most powerful means of making us constantly aware of the concession and compromise that the whole act of eating meat, in reality, is. It teaches
reverence for life.

Based on this enactment, traditional Jews do not even like the
thought of having to look at a steak that exudes red juice (a reminder
of blood). And hence they like to eat their steaks well done. In addition, the only way to eat liver, which contains an excessive amount
of blood, in a kosher way would be to broil it.

What makes a kitchen kosher?

In a nutshell the basic requirements for a kosher kitchen are twofold: it should contain nothing nonkosher, and it should provide for separation of meat and dairy foods and utensils.

If it has been a nonkosher kitchen, all traces of nonkosher food must be removed. Then, following a thorough cleaning, everything possible must go through the process known as *kashering*, which involves both immersing utensils in boiling water and exposing them to an open flame.

Are all raw vegetables kosher?

I always thought they were but now have some additional thoughts. A *mashgiach* of a local kosher Chinese restaurant told me that a large part of his job is to check for small bugs that often lodge themselves in the heads of cauliflower and broccoli. These bugs are nonkosher and, if not removed, would render the broccoli nonkosher for eating, according to his superiors and other Orthodox rabbinic authorities. Some people, I am told, go to the trouble of washing their broccoli in a dishwasher before eating it, to be sure that all of the bugs are removed.

What makes an animal kosher?

Chapter 11 of the book of Leviticus and chapter 14 of the book of Deuteronomy list the characteristics of a kosher animal: it must have hooves that are fully split, and it must chew its cud. If only one of these characteristics is present in an animal, it is not kosher. Thus, animals such as horses and rabbits, which chew their cud but do not have genuine split hooves, are not kosher; nor are pigs, which have split hooves but do not chew their cud. On the other hand, oxen, sheep, deer, and goats fulfill both requirements and are therefore kosher.

What is kosher slaughtering?

For meat to be considered kosher, a kosher animal must be slaughtered by a *shochet*, a ritual slaughterer whose knowledge, skill, and personal piety are attested to by rabbinic authority. The entire process demands rigid inspection.

If the animal to be slaughtered is identified as kosher, the hindquarters are separated from the forequarters, because the forbidden sciatic nerve is deeply imbedded in the muscle tissue of the hindquarters and can be removed only with great difficulty. For this reason, hindquarters are set aside and are sold as nonkosher. (That is why real sirloin or T-bone steaks are not kosher.)

Is there such a thing as kosher milk?

No. All milk that you would buy in any reputable store or supermarket would be perfectly permissible to drink and use, unless you are an Orthodox Jew who keeps to a "higher" standard of kashruth. Many Orthodox Jews use only milk that has been under careful surveillance by a Jew from the moment of milking to the time of bottling. Such close supervision offers assurance that at no time during processing was the milk of a nonkosher animal or some other prohibited ingredient mixed with it. Milk carefully guarded in this manner is called *chalav yisrael*, milk of Israel.

Does medicine have to have a kosher label?

Some companies produce medicine that has been rabbinically supervised. However, pharmaceuticals, even if they contain an animal derivative, may be used according to most rabbinic authorities, because the laws of kashruth apply only to food products. However, vitamins and other food supplements are not considered medicine; and here more observant Jews will want to be certain that they have rabbinic supervision.

Can you give me some tips for buying kosher food?

When buying kosher products, you are paying a premium price for special preparation and handling. You can help ensure that you are getting your money's worth by taking a few simple precautions while shopping:

When buying packaged goods, look for kosher certification on the label.

All poultry must be tagged with a *plumba* (metal tag) stating under whose authority the bird was slaughtered.

Supermarkets or other stores that sell both kosher and nonkosher prepared meats, fish, baked goods, cheeses, or other foods must keep the kosher products in separate display sections.

Kosher foods require their own slicers or knives, and kosher meats must be sliced separately from kosher dairy products.

Retail stores are not permitted to affix or even process labels bearing the words *kosher* or *kosher for Passover.* If you are suspicious, do not hesitate to ask the store manager to tell you who added the label.

You must note whether or not the meat you are buying has been soaked and salted. Once meat is ground, it can no longer, according to Jewish law, be soaked and salted.

If you have doubts about a product, ask about the source and supervision of the food and its preparation and handling. If you are still in doubt, don't buy it.

Is it kosher to serve your pet nonkosher dog food?

Today some Jewish companies make kosher pet food, and I am told that many Orthodox Jews who own pets serve them only kosher food. However, because the laws of kashruth were intended for humans and not for animals, I see no reason why not to serve a dog or cat the regular pet food available in the store. My dog eats it and loves it, although occasionally on Friday night she will get a scrap of challah, one of her favorites.

❧ **What's Not Kosher** ❧

Is it kosher to eat like a pig?

Although the Torah does not place a limit on food intake ("you may eat to your heart's content," Deuteronomy 12:21), most of the post-biblical rabbinic views suggest that being a glutton, even if the food is kosher, is unacceptable. Ben Sirah says, "Eat, as it becomes a man, those things that are set before you, and be not insatiable. When you sit among many people, do not be the first to reach out your hands."

Maimonides, who always advocates moderation as a philosophical and practical principle, cautions: "Gluttonous eating is comparable to consuming poison." To Maimonides, causing harm to one's body is also a moral violation against God.

Is it kosher to believe that killing animals the kosher way is painful for the animal?

On the contrary! Judaism has a distinguished record on the issue of proper treatment of animals. We may use animals for our benefit and are even permitted to kill them for food, but at the same time Jewish law absolutely requires us to minimize their pain and suffering. Thus, we must be meticulous in seeing that the sharpness of the knife used in kosher slaughtering causes as speedy and painless a death to an animal as possible.

Adding to the animal's agony of death renders its meat *treif*, strictly forbidden. Jewish ritual slaughter thus has both an economic and moral incentive to hasten the animal's death. Concern for animal welfare is as a result cited as one good reason to keep kosher. In fact, the laws of kashruth are traditionally cited as yielding the most humane methods of slaughter.

Is it kosher for Jews to hunt for sport?

The laws of keeping kosher guaranteed that an animal be permitted as food only if slaughtered quickly and painlessly. Any prolonging of an animal's death renders the animal *treif*. All animals killed through hunting are nonkosher. The Talmud permitted the slaying of wild animals when they invaded human settlements but not simply for sport. Thus, Jews partake in many sports but not hunting. Rabbinic consensus continues to posit that the shooting of an animal for no reason other than sport is an utter abhorrence.

What makes an egg nonkosher for eating?

Only eggs of kosher fowl may be eaten. A blood spot found on the yolk or the albumen (white) renders the entire egg nonkosher. Therefore, it is important to remember to examine each egg individually after cracking to determine whether it contains any blood spots.

Is there such a thing as kosher style?

Often restaurants use the term *kosher style*, misleading people into thinking that the food being served is kosher. Some states, such as New York, prohibit the use of such terminology in restaurant advertising. Beware: a kosher-style restaurant is not kosher!

❦ What the Experts Say ❧

A man should not eat meat unless he has a special craving for it. (Talmud, Hullin 84a)

The laws of *kashrut* come to teach us that a Jew's first preference should be a vegetarian meal. If, however, one cannot control a craving for meat, it should be kosher meat, which would serve as a reminder that the animal being eaten is a creature of God, that the death of such a creature cannot be taken lightly, that hunting for sport is forbidden, that we cannot treat any living thing callously, and that we are responsible for what happens to other human beings even if we did not personally come into contact with them. (Pinchas Peli, *Torah Today,* p. 118)

The dietary laws are intended to teach us compassion and lead us gently into vegetarianism. (Rabbi Shlomo Riskin, *Jewish Week*, p. 21)

A person should not say, "I loathe pig's meat . . . " but he should say, "I do desire it, but what can I do since my Father in heaven has decreed that it is forbidden." (Sifra, Leviticus)

❦ Sources ❧

Every creature that lives shall be yours to eat. . . . You must not, however, eat flesh with its blood in it. (Genesis 9:3–4)

You shall not cook a kid in its mother's milk. (Exodus 34:26)

Whatever parts the hoof and is completely cloven-footed, you may eat. (Leviticus 11:3)

You shall not eat anything that dies a natural death. (Deuteronomy 14:21)

Topic 18

❦ ❧

Friendship

❦ **What's Kosher** ❧

Is it kosher for me to have non-Jewish friends?

Of course it is. Jews have lived with non-Jews for centuries, often eager to be a part of the larger society. There is certainly no Jewish prohibition of a Jewish person having non-Jewish friends. One of my closest friends and colleagues is the local United Methodist minister, with whom I have had a long and important friendship. Our friendship has forged a friendship and bond between our respective synagogue and church members. Each year on Thanksgiving eve, we gather together (alternating synagogue and church) for a joint Thanksgiving commemoration.

The concern about non-Jewish friends is often with parents who worry about whom their children will fall in love with and eventually marry. With the high rate of marriage out of the faith, I know many Jewish parents who would prefer their unmarried children to "hang out" with Jewish kids as opposed to non-Jewish ones. To that end they encourage them to join exclusively Jewish youth groups and go to Jewish summer camps.

My good friend is never afraid to criticize me. Is this kosher?

Rabbinic advice regarding friendships suggests that we choose friends who are not afraid to offer constructive criticism and speak honestly when we have done something wrong. One of the ethical demands of friendship is to keep one's friend on track when he or she has gone astray.

One of the most surprising stories in the Bible is in chapter 11 of the second book of Samuel. David sees beautiful Bathsheba, a married woman, from his palace room, and asks his servants to bring her to him. After sleeping with the woman and getting her pregnant, he arranges to have her husband, Uriah, an officer in his army, killed in battle. Subsequent to Uriah's death David marries Bathsheba.

There were clearly servants in David's court who knew about David's transgression, but no one said anything to the king. Finally, Nathan the prophet, the king's friend and confidant, confronted and censured David for his bad behavior. Mastering the art of rebuking is a virtue, requiring sensitivity to others' feelings and conviction in our belief. Nathan's words to David are a model of how to rebuke another. They resulted in David repenting, saying to Nathan, "I stand guilty before the Lord" (2 Samuel 12:13).

A true friend is one who will speak openly and honestly with you and who will offer you constructive criticism. "The person who sharply criticizes a friend destroys the friendship" (Ecclesiasticus 22:20). The key to rebuke and criticism is that it be done sensitively and privately, so that we do not publicly disgrace or embarrass the friend. Giving constructive criticism with a softer tone in my words has worked well for me when dealing with members of my congregations with whom I have a disagreement.

My friend and I want to compete for the same scholarship. Is this kosher?

Yes, there is nothing wrong with two friends competing for the same award. One of the values of having a good friend is being able to do things together and share things in common. Competing with each other for the same award is certainly kosher and often even a good test of the friendship.

The midrash teaches: "On the day of your friend's success, participate in his or her joy" (Ecclesiastes Rabbah 7:22). I knew two people who were once good friends in high school. Both were academically gifted and realized as graduation approached that a small differential in grade point average would ultimately determine who would become the class speaker. When one learned that her friend had been chosen the class valedictorian, jealousy ensued and the friendship dissipated. A good friend loves nothing better than to hear good news about his or her friend and desires to participate in the joy of the event.

Your friend is about to consult a physician whom you have heard is incompetent. Is it kosher to warn him of the situation?

Jewish law in most situations forbids transmitting rumors. Some will argue that when one does not know for a fact that the negative details that one has heard are true, one ought to refrain from saying anything. To me saying nothing does not seem morally right. I would therefore opt for what I think would be the kosher position here, namely to have a person warn the friend of what he or she has heard while at the same time claiming that it is not an established fact and suggesting that the friend explore it further on his or her own.

Is it kosher to pass on a gift that you received?

Yes, it is permissible to give someone else a gift that your friend gave you. It rightfully belongs to you, and you may do with it as you wish. Very often we receive gifts that are not really useful to us. My son, for instance, received several duplicate gifts at his Bar Mitzvah. When giving away a gift that you received, you must make certain that there would be no chance of the person who gave it to you ever finding out. The last thing you would want to do is hurt another's feelings.

❦ What's Not Kosher ❧

Is it kosher for me to end my friendship with my best friend just because his mother does not like me?

If there is no justifiable reason for one's friend's mother not liking the friend, then there is no reason to end the relationship with the friend. Jewish law does not require a child to honor the parent's desire if it is whimsical or unjustifiable.

This question reminds me of the friendship of David and Jonathan in the Bible. It is a unique one in that each man gives totally of himself while making no demands on the other. After David's victory against the powerful giant, Goliath, Jonathan's father, King Saul, becomes suspicious and jealous of David's rising popularity. Although Jonathan was the presumed heir to his father's throne, David was the people's choice to become king. Jonathan remains completely loyal to his best friend, David, who goes into hiding after realizing that his life is in danger (1 Samuel, 20:18–42). The biblical passage concludes with a description of a prearranged code by which Jonathan informs his best friend to flee for his life. The story clearly shows the deep loyalty that each of the two friends shows to the other. Jonathan risked his father's anger and his life to protect David from Jonathan's father's efforts to kill him.

My friends house-sat for me while I went on vacation. When I returned, I found an array of untidy rooms. Is this kosher?

No, it's not kosher, for there are ethical demands on a friend. Your friends had the responsibility of taking care of your home, seeing that it remained clean and tidy. Ethics of the Fathers 2:17 says: "Let the property of your friend be as precious to you as your own." What they did in leaving your home in an unkempt manner is unacceptable and simply not kosher.

Is it kosher to barge in on a friend unexpectedly?

Jewish tradition opposes people entering another's home without knocking or announcing yourself in advance. The Talmud (Pesachim 112a) enjoins "Do not enter a house suddenly."

The book of Genesis provides the ultimate proof text that tells us that intruding on friends unannounced is not kosher. After Adam and Eve sin against God's command and eat of the forbidden fruit, God calls out first to them and says, "Where are you?" (3:9). From this the rabbis deduce that a person should not enter another's house suddenly. Obviously, God knew all along where Adam and Eve were, but not wanting to startle them, God had the courtesy to give them advance warning. Jewish etiquette tells us to do the same.

Is it kosher to do anything for a friend, no questions asked?

We all would like to think that our best friend is one who would do anything for us. Although loyalty is important to a friendship, one must be certain that when a friend asks us to do something that sounds suspicious, we be certain that the action does not violate the law. Jewish law forbids a person to break the law by being an accomplice to an illegal act. Therefore, it would behoove a good friend to be careful here and voice concern if skeptical of the request.

A midrashic folktale tells the story of a dying father who calls his son to his bedside and asks him how many friends he has. The son replies, one hundred. The father then tells his son that he has only half a friend and proceeds to tell his son that perhaps if he were to test them, he would discover that he had fewer than he thought.

The son agrees, and his father tells him to kill a calf and take its pieces in a bag to his friends and ask them to bury it, without asking any questions. The son agrees and brings the bloodstained bag to his closest friend. But when his friend sees the blood, he fears that his friend has committed a murder and refuses to bury the bag.

And so it goes with all his friends. Chastened, the son returns to his father's bed and tells him what happened. The father then instructs his son to take the bag to the father's so-called half-friend and ask him to bury the bag. The son does so, and the man buries the bag in his garden without asking so much as a single question. Only then does the son reveal to him that it has all been a test.

When the son again stands before his dying father, he says to him, "Now I understand how rare true friends are. But tell me, if this friend was only a half-friend, have you ever had a whole friend?"

All lasting friendships will bring with them opportunities, as well as tests. When tested by your friend to do something for him with no questions asked, it is always better to err on the side of caution, if the request seems to be dubious.

❦ What the Experts Say ❧

Let the property of your friend be as precious to you as your own. (Ethics of the Fathers 2:17)

If one is aware that one's friends always greet him when they meet, he should first anticipate his friend's greeting and greet him first. (Talmud, Berachot 6a)

On the day of your friend's success, participate in his joy. (Midrash, Ecclesiastes Rabbah 7:22)

One who elevates himself at the expense of his friend's shame has no share in the World to Come. (Jerusalem Talmud, Hagigah 2:1)

Do not make friends with a person who is given to anger. (Proverbs 22:24)

Who is a leader? Any person who can turn an enemy into one's friend. (Avot de Rabbi Natan, chap. 23)

Your good conduct will make you friends, but your evil conduct will make you enemies. (Mishnah, Eduyot 5:7)

Do not judge your friend until you put yourself in his position. (Ethics of the Fathers 2:5)

Choose a true friend to whom you can confess your failings and who would help you to tread the road to self-perfection. (Elimelech of Lyzhansk)

If you want to lose a friend, lend him money. (Jewish proverb)

❧ Sources ❧

Get yourself a companion. (Ethics of the Fathers 1:6)

Let the honor of your friend be as dear to you as your honor. (Ethics of the Fathers 2:15)

Topic 19

❧ ❧

Gossip and Speech

❧ **What's Kosher** ❧

Is it ever kosher to use language that would shame another?

Although Jewish law in most circumstances strictly forbids embarrassing a person, there are always exceptions to the rule. Many of the exceptions deal with validating the competency of a person regarding the performance of a Jewish ritual on behalf of another. For example, in the Talmud (Chullin 3b) is a discussion concerning a kosher slaughterer. Because of the importance to the Jewish people of keeping the kosher dietary laws, the rabbis remark that if the person who slaughtered the animal is present, it is permissible to examine him and ask him whether or not he is knowledgeable in the laws of ritual slaughtering. If he does not know the laws, there is no concern about embarrassing him, and it is permitted to ask him outright: "Why did you slaughter the animal? You had no right to slaughter an animal before being examined by a rabbi about the laws of ritual slaughter."

Is it kosher to call someone by a nickname rather than that person's given name?

It is perfectly kosher to call a person by his or her nickname. Nicknames are often used as terms of endearment, reflecting a special relationship that one has with the other. Most of my close friends and others who know me well call me by the nickname my grandmother gave me: with her Eastern European accent, she turned my Hebrew name, Reuven, into Reeven, which then was shortened to Reeve.

It is, however, not kosher to call someone by a cruel nickname. Children often have to endure years of being called by a nickname they dislike, a name that is often both hurtful and humiliating. I myself was surprised to learn that calling a person by a cruel nickname is a serious offense in Jewish tradition. According to the Talmud: "All who descend to *Gehenna* [hell] will ascend except three who descend, never to return: One who sleeps with a married woman, one who shames his friend in public, and one who calls his friend by a cruel nickname" (Talmud, Baba Metzia 58b).

Is it ever kosher to pass on a rumor to others?

Unless there is an ethically compelling reason to pass on a rumor, it is best to simply let it die. However, every once in a while an occasion might arise that morally obligates a person to pass on a rumor privately. For example, if you were to hear that a certain physician in town was practicing medicine that was harmful to patients, rabbinic consensus would be that one has a moral obligation to pass the information on to others. When disclosing the rumor, though, you must report it as a rumor that requires further investigation. Don't say that it's definitely true, for it may well not be and may cause devastating damage that likely will be irrevocable. Rather, the prudent thing to say is that it is well worth checking into the matter.

❧ What's Not Kosher ❧

I know a person who doesn't stop talking about some person she dislikes. Is this kosher?

As children we are all taught, "If you have nothing nice to say, don't say anything at all." Jewish tradition goes one step further: don't say anything about anyone; that way, there's no chance of saying something bad.

Words are powerful and unyielding. Once uttered, they live a life of their own. And words do many things, including desecrate, attack, and tear down. Too often we hurl words without bothering to see where they land or what effect they have. And once words leave our mouths, retrieving them is impossible. A famous rabbi graphically illustrated this point. Assembling his followers, he ripped open a pillow and waved it in the air. The feathers floated upward in all directions. Catching them was impossible. The feathers, the rabbi explained, are the unthinking, often inadvertent evil words we speak. There is no way to retrieve them. So you have to make sure not to utter them in the first place.

Here are a number of pieces of advice from Jewish sources that I have found useful in helping control the words that we speak.

Do not speak too much. As the book of Proverbs (10:19) rightly suggests, "one who holds one's tongue acts wisely." The Menorat HaMaor suggests that a person should try to discipline himself not to speak too much so that he should not come to the point of uttering slander or indecent words and should not become a constant complainer. He should rather stress silence. Rabbi Joshua ben Levi once said: "A word is worth a sela [small coin], but silence is worth two." (Leviticus Rabbah 16:5)

Keep silent. Martin Buber, in his book *Tales of the Hasidim: The Later Masters*, describes Rabbi Mendel, who teaches the art of silence by practicing it. When Reb Mendel was in Kotzk, that town's rabbi asked him, "Where did you learn the art of silence?" He was on the verge of answering the question, but then he changed his mind and practiced his art!

Keep a civil tongue. The Menorat HaMaor also advises each person to try to keep a civil tongue in his head, whether he is engaged in the study of Torah or discussing affairs of the world. Especially learn to restrain your tongue when you are with a person who is in the heat of anger. Many people become enraged when provoked. It is better to wait for them to calm down before trying to appease their anger.

Study Torah. A midrash to the book of Psalms advises that if one's tongue turns to uttering slander, it would be best for that person to go and study the words of Torah.

Put your hands in your ears. This suggestion, one of my favorites, comes from the Talmud (Ketubot 5a-b), which advises that if one hears something unseemly, one should simply put one's hands in one's ears and not listen.

Minimize small talk. In the Ethics of the Fathers (6:6), we learn that the Torah is acquired through forty-eight virtues. Minimizing small talk is one of them. It is difficult to learn and contemplate righteousness if one is chattering away. It's not that talking and conversation are wrong. Rather, it's just that getting caught up in trivialities can often cause one to lose focus on what is truly important. An excess of small talk takes away focus from learning and personal involvement and can often lead to inappropriate use of language.

Is it kosher to talk behind a person's back?

Talking about someone behind his back is a form of *lashon hara*, evil talk, and strictly forbidden. *Lashon hara* is the subject of a famous book by Rabbi Israel Mayer Kagan, *Chafetz Chayim: Shemirat Lashon.* Rabbi Kagan believed that the ability to express our thoughts is one of God's greatest gifts to us. Speech, he said, is not inherently evil, but everything we say must be guarded, guided, and well intended. Taking care about what we say is not popular in the modern United States. Instead, we try to be spontaneous, using free-flowing words, which often get us into trouble.

A group of people in Jerusalem continually study the teachings about *lashon hara* and for two hours each day refrain from saying anything that might harm anyone else. One of their leaders is Rebbetzin Samet, who is quoted as saying: "If we care very much about someone else, we become creative in finding ways to avoid speaking *lashon hara.*"

Jewish tradition and law has three categories of evil speech that we are to avoid. The first category, *lashon hara* (literally the "evil tongue"), includes making unfavorable, damaging, or false comments about someone or something. Sharing ethnic jokes, spreading negative gossip or rumors, or even telling a true story that places a person in a bad light are all harmful.

The second category, *motzi shem ra* (giving someone a bad name), includes even inadvertently spreading gossip that is untrue. People must learn that they cannot repeat negative stories, especially because they cannot be sure that such stories are even true. They must also learn that it's nonkosher to embarrass or humiliate someone deliberately, even a person they dislike, by telling lies. Exodus (23:1) teaches, "Do not carry rumors that are untrue."

The final category, *rechilut*, involves telling our friends the negative gossip about them that we heard from someone else. Nothing is gained by reporting such gossip—except hurt feelings and disruption of the peace. One of the most important lessons that we can give ourselves is to realize that we cannot ever know the ultimate outcome of such unfavorable speech. As the Talmud says, "What is spoken in Rome may kill in Syria" (Genesis Rabbah 98:23).

A person I know continually interrupts me when I speak. Is this kosher?

It is not proper to interrupt a person when he or she is speaking to you. Listening is a virtue in Judaism, and it is best to allow a person to finish speaking before responding. The Ethics of the Fathers (5:9) offers details and suggestions relating to how a wise person uses speech:

> There are seven characteristics which typify the fool, and seven the wise person:
> Wise people do not speak in the presence of those who are wiser than they are;
> They do not interrupt their friend's words;
> They do not reply in haste;
> They ask what is relevant, they answer to the point;
> They reply to questions in an orderly sequence;
> Of what they have not heard, they say, "I have not heard";
> The opposite of these typify the fool.

My son loves to listen to a particular radio show, known for its use of profanity. Is this kosher?

Although the use of vulgar and obscene language has certain protection by the First Amendment, Jewish tradition demonstrates and holds other values. For Judaism using profanity in speech is inappropriate and improper. The Talmud (Pesachim 3a) says that "one should not utter a gross expression." Jewish tradition also suggests that we try to avoid hearing foul language from others: "If one hears something improper, he should put his fingers in his ears" (Talmud, Ketubot 5a). Rephrased today this would mean turning off the radio show.

Because Judaism values purity of speech, we have a responsibility openly and unapologetically to point out what we find offensive and vulgar. We may not be able to do anything about vulgarity on T-shirts, bumper stickers, or even radio shows known for their obscene language; but we can write letters to radio stations and advertisers, when the material they have presented has offended us.

A Hasidic teaching states that "human beings are God's language." I think this teaching says it all.

Is it nonkosher to complain that you never received a thank-you note?

Everyone enjoys receiving thanks for something that one does well or gives to another. Thanking someone is the gracious and proper thing to do. However, if one failed to receive a thank-you note, complaining and making an issue of it would be improper. Complaining would likely only serve the purpose of making the person feel bad. It is entirely possible that a person unintentionally forgot.

Is it kosher to speak badly of yourself?

Although humility is a virtue in Judaism, being modest does not mean that a person has to deny one's own virtues. The book of Leviticus (19:18) commands us to "love your neighbor as yourself." Just as you would not wish to hear other people speaking badly of someone you love, so too it would not be kosher for you to speak ill of someone you are supposed to love, namely yourself.

❧ What the Experts Say ❧

Whoever dirties his mouth, even though it had been decreed in heaven that he should live seventy years, causes the decree to be reversed. (Talmud, Ketubot 8b)

Whoever tells tales about someone secretly has no place in the World to Come. (Pirke de Rabbi Eliezer, 53)

The person who utters foul language commits a great transgression and becomes despised in the eyes of others, for that person has abandoned the traits of decency and modesty that are the distinguishing marks of his people Israel, and walks the path of an insolent and defiant person. (Menorat HaMaor, chap. on gossip)

The speech of a person should always be clean and his words polite. (Talmud, Pesachim 3a)

The person who is vulgar of speech descends to the deepest region of the netherworld. (Talmud, Shabbat 33a)

A person should try to discipline himself not to speak too much so that he should not come to the point of uttering *lashon hara* or indecent words and should not become a chronic complainer. He should, rather, stress silence. (Menorat HaMaor, chap. on gossip)

The Holy One hates the person who says one thing in his mouth and another in his heart. (Talmud, Pesachim 113b)

Just as one is commanded to say that which will be listened to, so is one commanded not to say that which will not be heeded. (Talmud, Yevamot 65b)

If you say of a rabbi that he does not have a good voice, and of a cantor that he is not a scholar, you are a gossip. But, if you say of a rabbi that he is no scholar and of a cantor that he has no voice, you are a murderer. (Rabbi Israel Salanter)

Have you heard something? Let it die with you. (Apocrypha, Ecclesiasticus 19:10)

I can retract what I did not say, but I cannot retract what I already have said. (Solomon ibn Gabirol, *Pearls of Wisdom*)

❧ Sources ❧

Do not go about as a gossipmonger among your people. (Leviticus 19:16)

Who is the person that desires life and loves days, that he may see the good therein? Keep your tongue from evil, and your lips from speaking guile. (Psalms 34:12–13)

A person who guards his tongue and lips is worthy to be clothed with the spirit of holiness. (Zohar 4:183b)

Topic 20

✦ ✦

Hanukkah

✦ **What's Kosher** ✦

When I was a child, we always used to call the Hanukkah candelabrum a menorah. Is this kosher?

A menorah refers to the seven-branched candelabrum in the Jerusalem Temple. Today it is more proper to call the Hanukkah candelabrum either a Hanukkah menorah or *hanukkiah*. *Hanukkiah* is preferable. The word was actually created, combining the words *menorah* and *Hanukkah*. The *hanukkiah* is an adaptation of the ancient seven-branched menorah of the Holy Temple. When Judah Maccabee decreed an eight-day holiday to commemorate the rededication of the Temple, our ancestors began to kindle the eight lights of the festival. At first people would simply line up ordinary clay lamps. But since multiple lamps of this type were required, the need for a single lamp with multiple wicks became evident, giving birth to the eight-branched *hanukkiah*.

Is it kosher for every family member to have his or her own *hanukkiah* to use during Hanukkah?

For most Jews, other than the Orthodox, the prevailing custom would be to have one *hanukkiah* for the entire family. Among the more devout, the Code of Jewish Law (Condensed Version, Laws of Hanukkah, Chap. 139) suggests that each member of the family light his or her own Hanukkah candles.

Is it kosher to exchange gifts on Hanukkah?

No one is quite sure when and where the custom of gift exchange originated. Because Western Jews live in a predominantly Christian society, and because of Hanukkah's usual proximity to Christmas, many parents do give their children gifts (some a different gift each of the eight nights). Although it is perfectly kosher to exchange gifts on Hanukkah, one ought not to feel obliged to do so.

Many families in my congregation have a new tradition of dedicating each night of Hanukkah to a type of gift. For example, on one night children might choose to give to their grandparents. On another night everyone recites an original poem. On the last night of Hanukkah, everyone bestows a gift to a charity of his or her choosing, with the parents matching the children's gifts.

Is there a kosher time to light the *hanukkiah*?

The Talmud says the proper time for kindling Hanukkah lights is "from the time the sun sets" (Code of Jewish Law, Laws of Hanukkah, chap. 139). What the Talmud means by this varies according to whom one asks. Some authorities prefer lighting immediately at the beginning of sunset. Others prescribe thirteen to forty minutes after sunset. Because there is no prohibition against kindling lights on the holiday itself, the exact minute of candlelighting is not terribly important. If one is not able to kindle lights after sunset, it is kosher to light them before sunset, but only if the lights themselves will last the half hour after sunset. If one forgets to light them at the proper time, lights may be kindled anytime during the evening.

What is the kosher procedure for lighting the *hanukkiah*?

The placement of the candles in the Hanukkah menorah and the proper procedure for kindling the lights is one of the most misunderstood aspects of the ritual. Actually, it is quite simple if you remember the following guideline: set to the left; light to the right.

The basic pattern of placing the candles is this:

1. Set the *shammash* (candle used to light the others) in its holder.
2. On the first night of Hannukah, place the candle for the first night in the far right holder.
3. On the second night, repeat steps 1 and 2, and add a candle in the next holder toward the left of the first night's candle.
4. On each subsequent night, continue to add one candle toward the left until on the eighth night, all holders are filled.

The procedure for kindling the lights is this:

1. Light the *shammash*.
2. Say or chant the Hanukkah blessings (On the first night three blessings are chanted: *l'hadlik ner shel Hanukkah, she'asah nissim la'avoteinu, she-he-cheyanu.* On the second and subsequent nights of Hanukkah, only the first two blessings are recited, and the *she-he-cheyanu* is omitted.
3. Using the *shammash*, light the newest candle first. (Option: some begin to kindle the lights while reciting *she'asah nissim.*)
4. When all the lights are kindled, place the *shammash* in its holder.
5. Say or chant "*Ma'oz Tzur*" and other Hanukkah songs.

(Note: According to the School of Shammai, instead of adding a candle each night, Shammai argued that all eight lights should be kindled on the first night and that on each subsequent night one light should be taken away.)

Is there a kosher place in the house to place the *hanukkiah* while the candles are burning?

If one interprets the dictum "publicize the miracle" (Laws of Hanukkah, chap. 139) to refer to the outside world, you may decide to place the *hanukkiah* in a windowsill or even outdoors. This is the preferred practice. It is a good idea to place sheets of aluminum foil or a tray under the *hanukkiah* in order to catch dripping wax or even to prevent the spread of fire.

Is it kosher to go to work during Hanukkah?

Except when Hanukkah falls on a Saturday, it is permissible to go to work during Hanukkah. Women, though, are given a dispensation from work during Hanukkah while the candles are burning. (I know some women who put their candles in the freezer before loading them into the *hanukkiah* each night, so that they burn twice as long!) The reason that the rabbis give for this special women's dispensation is that the miracle of deliverance was brought about through Judith, the daughter of Yochanan the high priest. She succeeded in intoxicating the king; when he fell asleep, she beheaded him (Judith 13:8).

Is it kosher to light the *hanukkiah* in my hotel room if I am traveling without my family?

According to the Code of Jewish Law (Laws of Hanukkah, chap. 139), one who is out of town and knows that his family lights the *hanukkiah* at his house should light candles wherever he is without saying the blessings.

My Hebrew school teacher told me that the Hanukkah miracle (the jug of oil burning for eight days) never really happened. Is this kosher?

Although there is a brief mention of Hanukkah in the Talmud (Shabbat 21b), there is no miracle story in the book of the Maccabees, written some forty years after the first Hanukkah. Historians now believe that the first Hanukkah celebration and rededication of the Temple functioned as a "makeup" Sukkot, just as the second book of Maccabees suggests. In those days Sukkot was one of the most important holidays of the year. Hanukkah as Sukkot explains a lot of things. It gives us eight days, because Sukkot was an eight-day festival; and it gives us a sense of the dedication of the original Temple. The real meaning of the Hanukkah story was the defeat of the Syrian Greeks by the undermatched Maccabees.

I once spent a winter vacation in Israel during Hanukkah, and all they served there were jelly donuts. Is this kosher?

The latke or potato pancake is the food that most U.S. Jews associate with Hanukkah. Because the Hanukkah miracle concerned oil, all the preferred Hanukkah foods are fried in oil. In Israel the most popular Hanukkah delicacy is the *sufganiyah*, a fried jelly donut.

❧ What's Not Kosher ❧

Are there special kosher candles that one must use for Hanukkah?

Interestingly, Jewish law prefers that you use oil, not candles, for your *hanukkiah*. Actually, the codes mention olive oil as the most preferred of all oils, because the miracle in the Temple was also brought about with the use of olive oil. Many people, of course, use Hanukkah candles. The legal requirement for candles to burn is "until the time that people cease to walk about in the street" (Talmud, Shabbat 21b). Before the advent of street lighting, people did not usually walk about at night long after nightfall. In fact, it was somewhat dangerous to do so. Because people's practice was to be in their homes within one-half hour after nightfall, and the primary mitzvah was "publicizing the mitzvah of Hanukkah," the practice of displaying the Hanukkah lights was designed for pedestrian traffic. Therefore, the rabbis decided that the Hanukkah lights should last a half hour after three stars appear. Using birthday candles in a miniature *hanukkiah* is not acceptable practice.

Is it kosher to use candles of different lengths and colors in the *hanukkiah*?

All candles should be the same height, although the *shammash* is usually placed higher (although it could be lower too) in order to distinguish it from the other eight candles. Most *hanukkiot* allow for this design. There is no requirement regarding the candles' color. A person can mix and match colors if he or she chooses.

Is it kosher to use an electric menorah as a *hanukkiah*?

According to nearly all authorities, an electrified menorah may not be used to fulfill the mitzvah of kindling the Hanukkah lights. Although electric bulbs undoubtedly give off light, the filaments are not considered a flame. Moreover, a requisite amount of fuel must be available when the lights are kindled. An electric menorah depends on continuous generation of power to remain lit. Thus, the act of kindling in itself is insufficient to cause the lamp to burn for the prescribed period of time. Because the legal principle governing the *hanukkiah* is "kindling constitutes the performance of the mitzvah" (Laws of Hanukkah, chap. 139), turning on an electric light would not fulfill the commandment.

It would be acceptable, however, in places such as a hospital or nursing home room in which lit candles are not permitted, to use an electrified menorah.

Is it kosher to blow the candles out?

No, the lights are to be left alone to burn out. Each night, new candles should be used. If, however, there is more oil than needed for the minimum half hour of burning, one may extinguish the wicks in an oil-burning *hanukkiah* after the required half hour and relight them the next evening.

Is it kosher to light the *hanukkiah* after lighting the Shabbat candles on Friday evening?

With the prohibition against lighting fire on Shabbat, Hanukkah lights are to be lit immediately before the Sabbath candles on Friday evening. So the procedure would be to first set up the Hanukkah candles, recite the Hanukkah blessings, and then light the Shabbat candles. Because we light Shabbat candles at least eighteen minutes before sunset, some people use extra long candles for the *hanukkiah* so that they last at least thirty minutes after sunset.

❧ What the Experts Say ❧

On Hanukkah we are given part of the primordial light that has
been hidden away since creation and is preserved for righteous
people in the World to Come. With this light, you can see from one
end of the earth to the other. With this light, we are not allowed to
kindle mundane light but only other holy lights, the souls within
each other. (Bnei Yissacher)

In order to recall the miracles and wonders that You performed for
our ancestors through the agency of holy priests, we kindle these
lights. We hold these flames sacred throughout the eight-day Hanukkah period. We shall not make any profane use of them. Indeed, we
will simply look at them so that we may recall Your reputation as a
God who makes miracles, does wonders, and delivers our people.
(Prayer Hanerot Hallalu)

The sanctuary was purified on the twenty-fifth of Kislev. This
joyous celebration went on for eight days and it was like Sukkot,
for they recalled how only a short time before they had kept the
festival while living like animals in the mountains, and so they
carried *lulavim* and *etrogim* and they chanted hymns to God.
(2 Maccabees 10:3–7)

One should place the Hanukkah lamp by the door of the house,
on the outside. (Talmud, Shabbat 21b)

❧ Source ❧

The rabbis taught: The laws of Hanukkah require that one light for
a person and household; those who want to be more careful may
use one light for each member of the household. For those who
want to be even more careful, the school of Shammai suggested
that on the first day of the festival, eight candles are lit and we

light one fewer each progressive night. Hillel suggested that on the first day, one candle is lit and one candle is added each night. Shammai reasoned that the number of candles corresponds to the number of days to come. Hillel reasoned that the number of candles corresponds to the days already passed. (Talmud, Shabbat 21b)

Topic 21

Honesty and Truth

❦ **What's Kosher** ❧

Is it ever kosher to tell a lie?

From various Talmudic sources, we see the value the rabbis place on telling the truth. "Do not speak what you do not mean in your heart." The rabbis did believe however, that occasionally a "white lie" is permissible, especially where the intention is to promote peace and harmony (Talmud, Yevamot 65b).

They note that on occasion even God modifies the truth for the sake of peace and harmony. They cite the story in Genesis, chapter 18, when three angels visit the ninety-one-year-old Abraham to inform him that his eighty-nine-year-old wife, Sarah, will give birth to a child in a year. Standing in a nearby tent, Sarah overhears the comment and laughs to herself, saying, "Now that I am withered, am I to have enjoyment with my husband so old?" A verse later, God appears to Abraham and says, "Why did Sarah laugh, saying, 'Shall I in truth bear a child, old as I am?'" (vv. 12–13).

God repeated only part of Sarah's original comment, omitting the words in which she spoke of Abraham as being "so old." That comment could have hurt Abraham or made him angry at Sarah. On the basis of this biblical story, the Talmud (Yevamot 65b) concludes, "Great is peace, seeing that for its sake, even God modified the truth."

Yes, there are occasions when a white lie is permissible. Rabbi Judah says in the name of Samuel (Talmud, Baba Metzia 23b-24a) that learned men may conceal the truth regarding the following three matters: tractate, bed, and hospitality.

Rabbinic commentators explain "tractate" to mean that a modest scholar is permitted to declare that he is unfamiliar with a tractate of the Mishnah in order not to flaunt his learning. The intent here is for the scholar to preserve a sense of modesty and humility.

"Bed" is understood to mean that if a man is asked intimate questions regarding his marital life, he need not answer truthfully. Such a question is an embarrassing one and does not deserve a response.

Finally, "hospitality" is understood to mean that a man who has been generously treated by his host may decide not to tell the truth about his reception if he feels that the host will be barraged by unwelcome guests.

If someone asks how he or she looks in new clothing, is it kosher to compliment if the compliment is insincere?

Jewish thought generally forbids truths that tend to inflict hurt without achieving a great good. Thus, according to the School of Hillel, when asked what words one says about a bride, Hillel answered: "Every bride is described as beautiful and a graceful bride" (Talmud, Ketubot 16b). Hillel's position is accepted as Jewish law. One is required to praise the beauty of all brides. All brides are likely to appear beautiful in the eyes of their grooms, and that is all that matters.

In general, modifying the truth when it can only inflict pain and harm without benefit would be the kosher thing to do. Feelings do count in Judaism, so always be sensitive to the other person's emotions.

Is it kosher to give a person the benefit of the doubt?

Refraining from hasty judgment and giving a person the benefit of the doubt is a Jewish virtue. Its origin is based on a verse in Ethics of the Fathers 1:6: "Judge all people on the scale of merit." "Give the benefit of the doubt" is a more idiomatic way of understanding the verse.

You call a friend, and she is not home, so you leave a message. Several days pass, and your friend does not call back. You call again— no answer. When the same thing happens a third time, you begin to feel irritated, believing that your friend is now rude and inconsiderate. Finally, after a week your friend calls. She has been away on a family emergency and just now returned home to get your message. And she calls immediately.

There are many ways in which we can heighten our willingness to give the benefit of doubt. Hillel offers some relevant advice: "Judge not your fellow until you have been in that person's place" (Ethics of the Fathers 2:5).

Giving someone the benefit of the doubt, expecting honesty and forthrightness, is a kosher way of looking at the world that can become a self-fulfilling prophecy. If you are generous in judgment, tend to see others in the best possible light, give people a break, look for the good in others, don't jump to conclusions, and wait until all the facts are in, you are well on your way to mastering the virtue.

If a person finds a dollar bill on a busy street, is it kosher to keep it?

In an instance when an item has no specific signs, such as a dollar bill, one may assume that the loser has given up hope of having it returned. In such a case, when it is reasonable to assume that the loser despairs of ever finding it, Jewish law permits the finder to keep it.

❧ What's Not Kosher ❧

Is it kosher for a doctor or a close family member to always tell the truth to a person who has a life-threatening illness?

Telling the truth to a person who has a serious illness can have a devastating impact on his psyche. The Bible tells us that when the king of Aram became ill, he sent a messenger to inquire of the prophet Elisha if he would recover. Elisha told the messenger that the king was dying but that the messenger should tell him, "You shall surely recover" (2 Kings 8:7–10).

The Talmud (Moed Katan 26b) teaches that one who is ill should not be informed of the death of a close relative lest it hasten his or her demise. Because Judaism forbids a person to do something to another that hastens another's demise, one does not have to be truthful to a patient who is dying. It is advisable, however, to instruct the patient to take care of his affairs and make appropriate arrangements, while at the same time reminding him or her not to take such advice as meaning that death is imminent.

When it is obvious to everyone, including the person dying, that the end is near, then it's kosher to be frank about it, to discuss any practical issues or last issues, to say good-bye, to bring a satisfying personal and spiritual closure to the event, whenever and however possible.

Is it kosher to plagiarize?

Most emphatically not. It's never kosher to take the work of another and claim it as your own.

The first time I ever studied Talmud, I remember how impressed I was to read about rabbis who most often would make their statement in the name of one of their teachers. In an age in which we hear about people plagiarizing and taking others ideas' and words without giving proper credit, I was impressed to see that the rabbis' motives were more to impart the truth than to win accolades for some brilliant statement made by some other colleague.

Later I encountered a most unusual sentence in the Ethics of the Fathers 6:6: "whoever reports a saying in the name of its originator brings the world closer to redemption." From Judaism's perspective we see here that a person who chooses to take credit for a statement made by another is a double thief, misappropriating the credit that belongs to the statement's originator, while also deceiving listeners into thinking better of his intelligence than he deserves. Redemption becomes the reward for people that always choose to be motivated in their words by speaking the truth.

If you find a watch and someone calls to claim it, is it kosher to return it to the caller, no questions asked?

According to the Talmud (Baba Metzia 2:7), in order to retrieve a lost object, the owner must be able to clearly identify it. Thus, for example, if one finds a watch and someone calls to claim it, the finder must ask the potential owner to describe it in some way. This is to ensure the owner that the watch is in fact the property of the caller and rightfully belongs to him.

If an object is found and does not possess any marks of distinction, then Judaism says "finders, keepers!"

Is it kosher to take a towel from a hotel as a souvenir?

In a single year, thousands of towels are removed from hotel rooms all around the country. Taking a towel, even though one may think of it as a souvenir, is stealing, plain and simple.

Is it kosher to withhold returning an object that you found that belonged to someone you greatly disliked?

Because Judaism demands that people act honestly, fairly, and justly toward each other, including their own enemies, it would be non-kosher for a person not to return a lost object to someone whom he or she disliked. In fact, a Torah law legislates that "when you encounter your enemy's ox or donkey wandering, you must return it to him" (Exodus 23:4).

❦ What the Experts Say ❧

There is no salvation in falsehood. (Midrash, Ruth Rabbah 5:13)

God hates the person who says one thing with his mouth and another with his mind. (Talmud, Pesachim 113b)

People who tell lies are excluded from the presence of the Shechinah. (Talmud, Sotah 42a)

Everything in the world can be imitated except truth. For truth that is imitated is no longer truth. (Menachem Mendel of Kotsk)

Teach your tongue to say, "I don't know, lest you be led to lie." (Talmud, Berachot 4a)

What is considered lost property? [Something obviously found where it was not supposed to be] If one found a donkey or a cow grazing on the way, this is not lost property. If one, however, finds a donkey and its burden topsy-turvy or a cow running through a vineyard, this is obviously lost property. (Mishnah, Baba Metzia 2:9)

One is forbidden to dye a slave's beard or hair in order to make him appear young. One is not allowed to paint old baskets to make them appear new nor is a person allowed to soak meat in water to make it white and look fat. (Code of Jewish Law, Choshen Mishpat, Laws of Stealing, 358)

One who robs the public must restore to the public. Worse is stealing from the public than stealing from an individual, for one who steals from the individual can appease that individual, and return the theft. The former cannot do this. (Tosefta, Baba Kamma, 10, 14)

The following articles [with no distinguishing marks] belong to the finder: if one finds scattered fruit, small sheaves in a public thoroughfare, round cakes of pressed figs, a baker's loaves, strings of fish, pieces of meat, fleeces of wool which have been brought from the country, bundles of flax and strips of purple, colored wool; all these belong to the finder. (Mishnah, Baba Metzia 2:1)

If you see your neighbor's ox or sheep go astray, do not ignore it. You must take it back to your neighbor. (Deuteronomy 22:1)

Call the attention of a non-Jew to an error he has made in over-
payment to you, for it is better that you live on charity than that
you disgrace the Jewish name. (Sefer Hasidim, Laws of Deception,
chap. 18)

❦ Sources ❧

The seal of the Holy Blessed One is Truth. (Talmud, Shabbat 55a)

Keep far away from falsehood. (Exodus 23:7)

Topic 22

Hospitality

❦ **What's Kosher** ❧

Are there any kosher requirements for being a good host?

Yes, there are rabbinic suggestions for the host and hostess regarding their responsibilities to their guests:

Be cheerful when serving the meal. "It is the duty of the host to be cheerful during meals, and thus make his guests feel at home and comfortable at the table" (Talmud, Derech Eretz Zuta 9).

Provide choices of food when serving. "It was the custom with some in Jerusalem to place all the dishes on the table at once, so that the fastidious guest was not compelled to eat something he did not like, but might choose anything he wished" (Lamentations Rabbah 4:4).

Guests must always eat first. "It is unbecoming for a host to eat before his guest" (Talmud, Derech Eretz Zuta 8).

Include the guest when reciting the Birkat HaMazon (blessing after the meal). The custom is to ask for God's blessings not only on one's family but on the invited guests as well.

Never embarrass a guest. For example, if you have a guest in your house, don't ask him questions about Torah subjects unless you know that he will be able to answer you (Sefer Hasidim, 312).

Hosts (no matter how high in stature) should personally serve their guests. Rabban Gamaliel, the Nasi (head of the Sanhedrin), served the guests at his own son's wedding (Talmud, Kiddushin 32b).

Escort your guests. It is not enough simply to say good-bye to a guest. It's considered Jewish etiquette to walk out of your house with your guest and see him or her to the car. This is a great way of showing guests respect and honor. (Years ago when our congregation invited Rabbi Neil Gillman to be our scholar-in-residence, I drove into New York to pick him up. To this day when I run into him when visiting the seminary where he teaches, invariably the subject of his visit comes up and he remembers my going the extra distance to escort him to New Jersey, giving him door-to-door service.)

Are there any kosher requirements for being a good guest?

The rabbis enumerate a number of responsibilities for being a responsible guest:

What should a good guest say? Ben Zoma used to say, "What does a good guest say? 'How much trouble my host goes through for me. How much meat he has offered. How much wine he has set before me. How many cakes he has brought before me. And all this trouble that he went through for me" (Talmud, Berachot 58a). In other words, a good guest always tries to show appreciation to his host and hostess.

Let guests comply with a host's requests. "A guest should comply with every request that the host makes of him" (Talmud, Derech Eretz Rabbah 6). A modern-day illustration of fulfilling such a request might include a wedding invitation that reads "Black tie requested," indicating a very formal affair. It would only be appropriate, therefore, for a guest to comply with the hosts' wishes and wear a tuxedo.

Guests ought not to bring other guests to the dinner table. "It is unbecoming for a guest to bring another guest. More unbecoming than the two mentioned is the guest who puts his host to great trouble" (Talmud, Derech Eretz Zuta 8). To put this advice into modern-day terminology: if you are invited to someone's house, do not ask your host whether you can bring along with you another couple, unless that couple happens to be staying at your house and is your guest.

Guests should show good table manners. "A person should not bite off a slice, and return the piece into his dish" (Talmud, *Derech Eretz Rabbah* 9:1). In addition, "a person should not drink his goblet in one gulp. This is unmannerly" (Talmud, Betzah 25b).

Follow local practice and custom. "If you are invited to a certain place, conduct yourself in conformity with local usage" (Zohar 1:144a). (That is, when in Rome, do as the Romans do!)

Wait to be served. "A guest should not say to the host, 'Serve me that I may eat,' but must wait until he is invited to eat" (Talmud, Derech Eretz Rabbah 57a).

An observant Jewish professor at a Catholic college was invited to a colleague's Christmas Eve celebration. Is it kosher for her to attend?

If the party were not on a Friday evening, the night of the holy Sabbath, there would be no reason for the Jewish professor not to attend her colleague's party. Part of school life is the friendship and collegiality of both students and teachers, and it is the responsibility and duty of a friend to celebrate with her if and when she can. Of course, there might be a concern on the part of the Jewish professor regarding the food that is being served.

There is certainly nothing wrong with mentioning to her friend that she has certain food restrictions due to the Jewish dietary laws and letting her friend know in advance of the celebration which foods she might be able to eat. Any good friend would surely want to be sure to provide food of which all could partake.

Recently I was invited to a post-Christmas party by my local funeral director (not Jewish). I attended the party, which was held in a local restaurant. The director told me (before I even had to ask) that he would make sure to have kosher food available. Much to my happiness, when I arrived I saw an entire table filled with a variety of kosher Chinese food!

❦ What's Not Kosher ❧

Is it kosher for a visitor to come to your house without any warning?

The rabbis advised that one should not enter a house without warning. In the Talmudic tractate of Derech Eretz Rabbah 5:2 (dealing with common courtesy), it is suggested that a person should not enter a house suddenly, without ringing or knocking. All can learn such good manners from God, who stood at the entrance of the garden of Eden and called to Adam, "Where are you?" (Genesis 3:9).

Is it kosher for a hostess to watch and see whether her guests are eating all of the meal that she prepared for them?

According to the Mishneh Torah (Laws of Blessings 7:6), a hostess is forbidden to watch her guests overattentively. By doing so, she might embarrass them; and causing embarrassment is viewed as a grave transgression.

In fact, a host and hostess are required to go beyond the normal call of duty to see that their guests totally enjoy their experience. The story is told of the eighteenth-century rabbi, Akiva Eiger, who was entertaining some guests on Shabbat. One of his guests spilled a cup of red wine on his white tablecloth. Before the guest could even react, the rabbi bumped the table and knocked over his wine glass. He then proceeded to tell the guest (in order to protect him from embarrassment) that there was likely a problem with one of the table legs and that he would see that it would get fixed.

Is it kosher for a host to serve liquor at a dinner gathering, knowing one of his guests is an alcoholic?

The Torah says that "one should not put a stumbling block in front of a blind person" (Leviticus 19:14). Because alcoholics generally lack the internal strength to drink in moderation, serving alcohol would only work to encourage his addiction, which Torah law forbids.

Is it kosher for a husband to invite a houseguest without first informing his wife?

The Talmud (Baba Metzia 87a) says that "a woman is more apt to be-grudge guests than a man." Although the verse may be interpreted to imply that women have stingier dispositions, others interpret it to mean that women generally bear the major role when it comes to hosting guests. Certainly this is the case in my house. Therefore, it is only proper etiquette for a husband to let his spouse know in advance when he chooses to invite a guest. In this way adequate preparations can be made in advance of the visit.

Is it kosher for a guest to eat everything on his plate?

One would think that it would be entirely proper for a guest to eat everything on his plate, thus signifying to his host his enthusiasm and delight in the good food. However, rabbinic consensus states other-wise and suggests that it is better for a guest not to eat everything on his or her plate, for if he or she does, the host might be embarrassed and think that he had not given the person enough food. Therefore, it's preferable for a guest to leave just a little bit of food on his plate.

❧ What the Experts Say ❧

Rav Huna observed the custom of opening the door of his house when he was about to take his meal, and saying: "Anyone who is hungry may come and eat." (Talmud, Taanit 20b)

In Jerusalem, there was a custom to display a flag in front of the door, thereby indicating that the meal was ready, and that the guests might come in and eat. The removal of the flag was a sign that the meal was finished, and that transient guests should cease from entering. (Talmud, Baba Batra 93b)

Hospitality is greater than a visit to the house of study. It is even greater than welcoming the Shechinah. The hospitable person is rewarded in both worlds. (Talmud, Shabbat 127b)

Hospitality for strangers shows reverence for God's name. (Talmud, Shabbat 127a)

Always be happy when you are sitting at your table and those who are hungry are enjoying your hospitality. (Jerusalem Talmud, Demai 4:3)

Guests should never overstay their welcome. (Talmud, Pesachim 49a)

Don't repeatedly invite someone who doesn't want to come. (Jerusalem Talmud, Demai 4:3)

❦ Sources ❧

Let your house be opened wide, and treat the poor as members of your own family. (Ethics of the Fathers 1:5)

Let anyone who is hungry come and eat. (Talmud, Taanit 20b)

Abraham hastened into the tent to Sarah, and said, "Quick, three seahs of choice flour. Knead and make cakes." Then Abraham ran to the herd, took a tender and choice calf and gave it to the servant boy, who hastened to prepare it. (Genesis 18:6–7)

Topic 23

Kindness to Animals

❧ What's Kosher ❧

When going on vacation, is it kosher to put a dog in a kennel?

There is nothing wrong with putting one's dog in a reputable kennel when one goes on vacation. The important thing to consider is that the kennel has a good reputation and that you are confident that it can care for your pet in a professional manner. Some people choose to have house sitters come and care for their dogs, because they are confident that having their pet stay in an environment with which they are familiar is better for its mental well-being.

If I find a lost or suffering animal, what is the kosher procedure that I need to follow?

The Torah itself legislates that "when you see the donkey of your enemy lying under its burden and would refrain from raising it, you must nevertheless raise it with him" (Exodus 23:5). In this example we clearly see that one is not allowed to let an animal suffer (even if it belongs to your enemy!). Your responsibility when finding a lost or suffering animal is to see whether you can find its owner or at least get it proper medical attention.

Is there a kosher feeding time for one's pet?

A veterinarian or the breeder or store from which you purchased the pet should tell you the best times to feed and the type of pet food that you should buy for your pet. When people are in a rush and need to get a meal prepared for themselves, they may be prone to forgetting to feed their pets.

The Talmud assumes that animals suffer more than people from hunger, presumably because an unfed animal has no idea if it will ever be fed. That is why Judaism reminds us "that a person should feed his animal before eating" (Talmud, Berachot 40a).

Is it kosher for animals to be used for medical research?

Rabbinic opinion varies. One view is that although there is no basis in Jewish law for a legal ban on such experiments, they are morally indefensible. A refuting view asserts that the pain of the animal surely counts less than the pain of sick people who might be helped by such research. This appears to be the prevailing view, provided that all reasonable steps are taken to prevent any unnecessary suffering and to limit the practice strictly to the advancement of human health.

❦ What's Not Kosher ❧

I visited Spain and went to a bullfight. Is bullfighting kosher?

Bullfighting is not kosher, because the law of the Torah forbids inflicting pain on any living creature. Bullfighting causes the animal to die a slow death and therefore would have been outlawed in the Torah, were the activity to have known to have existed. Better to find something else in Spain to entertain you.

Is it kosher to raise a dangerous animal?

The Torah (Exodus 21:35) cites the case of a person's ox that injures his neighbor's ox, which eventually dies. The owner is then required to pay only partial damages for the injury caused to the neighbor's ox, because the ox had no previous history of being aggressive. But if the ox had a previous history of goring, the owner's responsibility is 100 percent. The reason for this is that the owner knows that the animal has violent inclinations, and if he chooses to keep the animal alive, he bears both a moral and legal responsibility for any future injuries the animal inflicts.

Similarly, were a person to raise an animal that could prove dangerous to human beings, rabbinic consensus would say that it was better never to do so, because of its potential threat to other animals and human beings as well.

Maimonides rules as follows in cases of animals prone to cause damage: "Five species of animals are considered prone to cause damage from the beginning of their existence. This applies even if they have been domesticated. Thus, if they cause damage or death by goring, biting, treading, lying down upon, or the like, the owner is liable for the entire amount of the damage. They are a wolf, lion, bear, tiger and leopard. Similarly, a snake that bites, even if it has been domesticated" (Book of Damages to Property, 1:6).

Is it kosher to purchase a pet if you are not sure that you can provide sufficiently for its needs?

Rabbinic advice suggests that one should wait to purchase a pet until one knows for certain that it can be properly cared for. Because of the great concern for compassion toward animals, it makes better sense to be certain that one can properly care for a pet rather than to rush into purchasing one. Young married couples just starting out in life often make the mistake of buying a pet and then realize that they have neither the means nor the quality time to give to it. Better to wait and be sure than rush into becoming a pet owner, only to have to regret it later.

⚡ What the Experts Say ⚡

Humanity was created Friday, before Shabbat and after the creation of animals. Therefore, in the event of human arrogance, one can reply, "A mosquito took precedence over you." (Talmud, Sanhedrin 38)

Jews must avoid plucking feathers from live geese, because it is cruel to do so. (Shulchan Aruch, Even HaEzer 5:14)

When animals lose their young, they suffer great pain. There is no difference between human pain and the pain of other living creatures. (Maimonides, Guide for the Perplexed 3:48)

Do not eat your own meal until you have seen to it that all your animals have been fed. (Talmud, Berachot 40b)

Compassion should be extended to all creatures, neither destroying nor despising any of them. For God's wisdom is extended to all created things: minerals, plants, animals and humans. This is the reason the rabbis warned us against despising food. In this way, a person's pity should be extended to all the works of the Holy Blessed One, just as in God's wisdom, nothing is to be despised. One should not uproot anything which grows, unless it is necessary, nor kill any living thing unless it is necessary. And one should choose a good death for them with a knife that has been carefully examined, to have pity on them as far as it is possible. (Moses Cordovero, *The Palm Tree of Deborah*)

When Moses shepherded the flocks of Jethro, he kept the old sheep back because of the young ones and let those loose first to feed on the tender grass. Then he let the others loose to feed on the grass of average quality. Lastly, he let the strong ones loose to feed on the tough grass. The Holy One said, "Let the one who knows how to shepherd a flock, each according to its strength, come and lead My people." Once a kid ran away, and Moses pursued it until it came to a tree where there chanced to be a pool of water. The kid stood there to drink, and when Moses overtook it he said, "I did not know you ran away because you were thirsty. You must also be tired." So he set it upon his shoulders and carried it back. The Holy One said, "Since you are merciful to the flock of a human being, you shall be the shepherd of My flock, Israel." (Exodus Rabbah 2, 2)

Abraham said to Melchizedek, "How is it you came forth safely from the ark?" "By reason of the charity we practiced there." "But what charity was there for you to practice? Were there any poor in the ark? Only Noah and his sons were there, so to whom could you have been charitable?" "To the animals, beasts, and the birds. We did not sleep but gave each its food throughout the night." (Midrash to Psalms 37)

If an animal falls into a ditch on the Sabbath, place pillows and bedding under it [since it cannot be moved until the end of the Sabbath]. (Talmud, Shabbat 128b)

A human being's animal is his life. (Mechilta)

Fur looks elegant on its original owners. On human beings, it is a sign of callous barbarity. (Rabbi Bradley Artson, *It's a Mitzvah!*, p. 205)

✺ Sources ✺

Do not plow an ox and a donkey together in the same yoke. (Deuteronomy 22:10)

When you see the donkey of your enemy lying under its burden and would refrain from raising it, you must nevertheless raise it with him. (Exodus 23:5)

If you come across a bird's nest in a tree or on the ground, and the nest has young birds and even eggs, and the mother is sitting with her young, do not take the mother together with her children. Let the mother go and take only the young—so that you may fare well and live a long time. (Deuteronomy 22:6)

Topic 24

Marriage

❧ What's Kosher ❧

Are there kosher times to get married?

Jewish tradition places limitations on the choice of a wedding date. For instance, weddings are never held on the Sabbath or on Jewish festivals, so that we do not mix—and consequently dilute—these joyous occasions. In addition, marriage is considered a legal transaction, and business transactions are not permitted on the Sabbath and on festivals. Days that commemorate tragic events in Jewish history are also not appropriate times for a marriage celebration: the period of *sefirah*, when the omer is counted, from the beginning of the second night of Passover and concluding with Shavuot; the period called Three Weeks (seventeenth of Tammuz until the ninth of Av); minor fast days. There is some variation in the observance of these special days, depending on your rabbi's affiliation with a particular branch of Judaism. Better to consult with your rabbi before selecting the date to be sure that your rabbi is available and that the date you chose is a kosher one.

What are the kosher locations for wedding ceremonies?

No Jewish laws restrict the selection of the location of a wedding or its reception. However, there are several kosher guidelines to follow:

There is probably no finer way to highlight the spiritual nature of a wedding than to hold the ceremony in a synagogue. The synagogue provides an aura of sanctity and spirituality, especially if one has a personal attachment to it. The synagogue's social hall is a convenient place to hold the reception. (Hotels and kosher catering establishments are certainly viable alternatives.)

Outdoor weddings are not only acceptable but rooted in Jewish tradition. Customarily, outdoor weddings, especially those held in the evening, were considered to bring good luck because the bride and groom could see the stars, which would remind them of God's promise to Abraham that the Jewish people would be as numerous as the stars in the sky.

Weddings held in the home of the bride and groom are also acceptable. A homespun wedding can add an atmosphere of warmth and intimacy.

Are there kosher guidelines for a wedding reception?

The reception following the marriage ceremony is called a *simcha*, an occasion of ultimate joy. Because a Jewish wedding is considered a religious as well as a social occasion, the meal served at its celebration is an integral part of the ritual, a *seudat mitzvah* (ritually prescribed feast). It is therefore only proper and fitting for the wedding feast to be a kosher meal. The inclusion of a kosher meal adds spirituality to the event and allows all to eat, without having to worry about any restrictions.

The wedding meal ought to begin with the *hamotzi* blessing over the bread and end with blessings after the meal. In the special Grace after the meal, the seven wedding blessings recited under the *huppah* (wedding canopy) are recited once again. This is an opportunity to honor friends of the bride and groom by having them recite selected blessings.

Finally, a kosher practice is to remember the less fortunate at times of celebration. Couples often arrange to share their flowers with hospital patients and leftover foods with the needy by donating them to a local food bank.

What's kosher regarding the bride's choice of wedding dress?

Jewish law does not stipulate what a bride or a groom must wear. Thus, Jews in every country have developed their own style of wedding dress. In some countries the dress is very ornate. For example, Iraqi Jewish brides wear silver bells and golden nose rings.

The most common custom among Jews with an Eastern European tradition, as among the general U.S. population, is for the bride to wear white, a symbol of purity. The custom is for the bride to also wear a veil at the ceremony, reminiscent of the biblical Rebekah, who covered her face when she first saw her future husband, Isaac. Because Judaism believes in the value of modesty, most traditional brides will have their shoulders covered, at least during the ceremony.

For the groom the traditional custom is to wear a *kittel*, a simple white robe that denotes purity, humility, and festivity, over his wedding suit. For the most part only traditional Jewish grooms will wear the *kittel*. Most will wear suits or a tuxedo.

Is it kosher to have a double-ring ceremony?

Orthodox rabbis will not permit double-ring ceremonies, because Jewish law requires only one ring, which the groom gives to his bride. However, double-ring ceremonies, in which the bride and groom exchange rings, can usually take place in Reform, Conservative, and Reconstructionist weddings. Although traditionally the gift of the ring was conceived as a token of acquisition (by which the groom acquired the bride), the double exchange of rings expresses, in a contemporary setting, a partnership, with a mutuality of respect and an equality of status.

What are the elements of a kosher wedding ring?

Jewish law states that for a wedding band to be kosher, it must meet three standards: it must belong to the groom, be of solid metal (customarily gold), and not have gems or stones in it.

Some rabbis permit wedding bands that are etched with a biblical verse as well. Others may have fewer restrictions regarding the qualifications for a suitable wedding band.

Is it kosher for a couple to write their own *ketubah* (marriage contract)?

Yes, a couple may, if they wish and are capable, write their own *ketubah*. (I once had an Israeli couple write the *ketubah* in Hebrew, because they did not particularly identify with the more traditional Aramaic language in which the *ketubah* was originally drafted). It is a good idea to have the rabbi be the final authority as to whether or not it can be used at the ceremony.

What are the requirements for selecting kosher witnesses for the *ketubah* signing?

Jewish law requires two witnesses for the signing in Hebrew of the *ketubah*. A kosher witness must be an adult; religiously observant; and not related by blood to either the bride, the groom, or the other witness. The officiating rabbi and cantor can serve as witnesses unless they are related to the bride or groom. Orthodox rabbis will permit only males to serve as witnesses. Reform, Reconstructionist, and some Conservative rabbis will permit women to participate. Because witnesses will be asked to sign their names in Hebrew, they should prepare for this requirement. To serve as a witness to a Jewish marriage is an honor and an important responsibility, so it is important that the bride and groom choose their witnesses with great care.

Is there such a thing as kosher wedding music for the wedding ceremony?

Music, with its power to elicit strong expressions of joy and tender expressions of love, has always been an integral part of the Jewish wedding ceremony and celebration. Even in Bible times, musicians often accompanied marriage processions. There are no laws regarding wedding music. However, a couple has an opportunity to fashion a unique and meaningful setting. I advise the couples whose marriages I am asked to perform to choose Jewish or Israeli music that echoes the Jewish heritage. The inclusion of Israeli and traditional Jewish wedding dances at the reception also can add a large measure of joy to the celebration.

Avoid using the traditional American piece "Here Comes the Bride," as it was composed by Wagner, a known anti-Semite.

Is it kosher to devise a prenuptial agreement?

In Talmudic times, as soon as a match was made, the parents of the bride and groom negotiated the terms of the dowry. These terms were set forth in a contract called *tenaim* (stipulations). This contract was legally binding, and a fine or penalty was imposed if either party reneged on the arrangement. The *tenaim* were officially sealed by breaking a dinner plate.

Today some still practice the custom of having the traditional *tenaim* that witnesses sign prior to the ceremony. It is also kosher for a couple to formalize a written prenuptial contract relating to the couple's life together. Such a document can include the number of desired children, finances, professional careers, and the role of Judaism in their life.

Is there a kosher procedure for lining up participants for the procession?

Jewish law does not fix the order of the procession and the number of participants in a Jewish wedding ceremony. But some customs that have continued over the years can help serve as guides.

Because Judaism has always emphasized the important role of parents, it is most usual for the bride and groom to be escorted by both their parents. The role of best man and maid or matron of honor has an early precedent. Legend has it that Michael and Gabriel, two angels, attended the wedding of Adam and Eve. They are considered the prototypical friends of the bride and groom.

The groom's friends might be in charge of the ring(s). The bride's friends may be asked to hold the *ketubah* and help lift the veil when the bride sips the wine. Grandparents and siblings may also join the procession.

At the conclusion of the wedding ceremony (after the breaking of the glass), the bride and groom walk up the aisle together, followed, in reverse order, by those who participated in the procession.

How many cups of wine are used in a kosher wedding ceremony?

Jewish law prescribes two cups of wine. The Jewish wedding ceremony began to take its present form about a thousand years ago. Prior to that time, marriage was accomplished in two separate rituals that took place approximately one year apart. In the first ritual, the betrothal ceremony (*erusin*), the couple set the wedding date, after which the bride returned to her family's house for a period of about one year. This allowed the groom additional time to learn a trade so that he could provide financial support for his family.

The second ritual was called *nisuin*, the formal ceremony. Over time the two ceremonies began to take place on the same day. The modern traditional Jewish wedding ceremony still shows the seam that joins the two rituals, in the two cups of wine that the bride and groom share at two points in the ceremony. In more liberal Jewish settings, only one cup of wine is used and is filled twice.

❧ What's Not Kosher ☙

Is it kosher to have a justice of the peace be the officiant?

No, the only kosher officiants are an ordained rabbi or cantor. If one's family is affiliated with a synagogue, one's own rabbi is a wonderful choice. Sometimes two rabbis (of both the bride and groom) co-officiate. A highlight of my career was to co-officiate at a wedding with the rabbi who had been the officiant at my Bar Mitzvah.

Is it kosher to have an interfaith wedding ceremony in which a rabbi officiates with a priest?

All Orthodox and Conservative rabbis, and many Reconstructionist and Reform ones, will officiate only at a marriage between a bride and groom who are Jewish. Jewish law does not permit a rabbi to officiate at an interfaith ceremony. When such a marriage does occur, it is considered valid in civil law but never according to Jewish law.

When an interfaith couple seeks out my advice on what to do in terms of officiant, I counsel them that a civil ceremony (using a judge as officiant) rather than a rabbi and a priest or minister is the better choice. In this way no one is offended, and neither religion needs to be compromised.

I am getting married outdoors. I'd like to use a large oak tree as my *huppah*. Is this kosher?

Jewish law requires that a couple get married under a wedding canopy, which today is available in many sizes, colors, and styles. It can be as simple as a tallit (prayer shawl) held up by four poles or quite elaborate. Regarding the question of using the oak tree as a *huppah*, I checked with several rabbinic scholars, who told me that because the majority of those attending the wedding would not likely think of the oak tree as a *huppah*, it ought not to be used. One couple got married under a small *huppah* held up by four poles, which was situated right under an oak tree.

Is it kosher for a bride and groom after their marriage to immediately go on their honeymoon?

Jewish custom says no, there is no immediate honeymoon! Brides are grooms must spend the first week of married life surrounded by friends and relatives who feed and entertain them. This custom probably originated with the biblical seven-day banquet that Laban prepared for Jacob and Leah (Genesis 19). Although most traditional couples still observe this beautiful custom, the honeymoon trip more often than not displaces it.

Is it kosher for a bride to choose not to wear a veil?

Most brides today in traditional Jewish settings choose to wear a veil, a sign of modesty and humility. In fact, a ceremony called *badeken* occurs before the actual marriage ceremony. During this ceremony the groom, having recognized his bride's face, proceeds to lower the veil.

According to one interpretation, the veiling ceremony developed to prevent a recurrence of what happened to Jacob in biblical times. Laban, Rachel's father, tricked the groom, Jacob, by substituting his older daughter, Leah, who wore an opaque veil, for Jacob's choice, Rachel. In order to avoid Jacob's dilemma, it has been customary for the groom to personally lower the veil over his bride's face. After the bride is veiled, the groom (or sometimes the bride's father) recites the priestly blessing of peace.

❦ What the Experts Say ❧

A man who does not have a wife lives without joy, blessing, and goodness. (Talmud, Yevamot 62b)

When there is no union of male and female, men are not worthy of beholding the Divine Presence. (Zohar 3:59a)

God creates new worlds constantly by causing marriages to take place. (Zohar 1:88a)

When a man weds a wife who is right for him, the prophet Elijah kisses him and the Holy One loves him. (Talmud, Derech Eretz Rabbah 1)

❦ Source ❧

Thus a man leaves his father and mother and clings to his wife, so that they become one flesh. (Genesis 2:24)

Topic 25

Mezuzah

❦ What's Kosher ❧

What are the criteria for a kosher mezuzah?

To be kosher, the mezuzah receptacle (which can be made out of any material—wood, plastic, metal) must contain a piece of kosher parchment, with two passages from the book of Deuteronomy (chaps. 6:4–9 and 11:13–21) inscribed on the parchment by a qualified scribe. Kosher parchment can be purchased in any Judaica store.

Does the mezuzah have to be placed in one particular spot to be kosher, or can it be nailed anywhere?

To be kosher, the mezuzah is positioned on the right doorpost, one-third down from the top. The upper portion of the mezuzah is slanted. Place a mezuzah on the doorpost of every room in a home except for the bathroom.

Is there a kosher ceremony for affixing a mezuzah?

No formal ceremony for affixing a mezuzah exists in Jewish tradition. Generally speaking, the custom is to attach the mezuzah to the doorpost and recite the following blessing: *baruch ata Adonai eloheinu melech ha'olam asher kidshanu be-mitzvotav vetzivanu likboa mezuzah* (praised are You, Adonai our God, Ruler of the Universe, who has made us holy by commandments and commanded us to affix a mezuzah).

If I put up a mezuzah in a strictly kosher way, are there benefits to my family's good health or security?

A mezuzah is not an amulet or good luck charm that will offer you benefits. It is a symbol of one's love for God and a way of identifying your home as a Jewish one.

In recent years an unfortunate superstition has developed around the mezuzah, a belief that Jews who have suffered a tragedy are being punished because their mezuzot are flawed and nonkosher. To avoid having nonkosher mezuzot, Jewish custom is to have a qualified Jewish scribe check them periodically.

Is it kosher to kiss a mezuzah?

Yes, it most certainly is. In Jewish tradition kissing a holy object such as a mezuzah is a gesture of reverence and adoration. Just as many people touch and kiss a Torah scroll as it is carried around the synagogue, many follow the custom of touching the mezuzah with their fingertips and kissing it when entering and leaving their homes or a room.

My philosophy teacher, Rabbi Neil Gillman, quoting one of his students, compared the mezuzah with a speed bump on a road: both are meant to slow us down. When a person enters or leaves one's house and kisses the mezuzah, the person takes just enough time to slow down and be reminded that the home is a sanctified one in which the Divine is present.

When moving away, what's the kosher thing to do with one's mezuzot?

When a Jewish person moves out of a home, he or she is expected to leave the mezuzot for the new occupants if they are Jews. If they are not Jewish, it is best to take them with you and use them for your new dwelling.

Is there a kosher way of rolling the parchment before inserting it in the mezuzah?

The kosher procedure for the parchment is to roll it up so that it will fit into the receptacle. The parchment should be rolled with the Hebrew words on the inside and the Hebrew word *Shaddai* (written on the reverse of the parchment) visible through the aperture.

❦ What's Not Kosher ❧

Some people put up a mezuzah without anything inside it. Is this kosher?

A mezuzah without parchment is like a car without an engine. It simply won't work, and such a mezuzah has no sanctification attached to it. When one purchases a mezuzah from a reputable Judaica store, the seller is always sure to remind the buyer to purchase kosher parchment for the mezuzah. If the seller tells you that the mezuzah comes with parchment inside, in my experience this is usually a sure sign that the parchment inside is a fake (perhaps a photocopied piece of paper).

It is also not kosher for a person to try to write the required biblical verses on paper or parchment and use this in his or her mezuzah. The parchment must be written by a qualified authority in order to be kosher. Unless you are one, you will need to buy the parchment from a reputable Judaica store.

In a Jewish bookstore, I saw a mezuzah to be used for a car. Is this kosher?

Some people view the mezuzah as a charm and good luck amulet. It's not. As with the Star of David and Chai religious symbols, though, wearing a mezuzah (with no parchment inside) that has been crafted as a piece of jewelry can be an expression of pride in one's Jewish heritage.

I have seen mezuzot for cars in stores as well. There is no need or requirement to affix a mezuzah to one's car. So-called car mezuzot do not come with kosher parchment and are often bought by people who feel that somehow they are going to be more "protected" if they put one in their car. If you are looking for God's protection while driving, a better thing to do would be to keep the traditional Jewish prayer for the journey in your wallet or purse and recite it just before taking off in your car.

Is it kosher to put a mezuzah up on my sukkah during the Sukkot festival?

Because the sukkah is a temporary structure, posting a mezuzah on its entrance is not proper.

🦋 What the Experts Say 🦋

Due to the fact that most mezuzot in the homes of hostages, upon examination, were found to be defective, improperly placed, or not on every doorpost, all Jews should check their mezuzot immediately. (Martin Gordon, "Mezuzah: Protective Amulet or Religious Symbol?" p. 8.)

🦋 Source 🦋

Inscribe them on the doorposts of your house and on your gates. (Deuteronomy 6:9)

Topic 26

Mitzvah

✿ What's Kosher ✿

Is there a kosher procedure for fulfilling a mitzvah?

Yes, there is a considerable amount of rabbinic advice regarding the kosher and proper way to perform a mitzvah. For instance, we are told in the Talmud (Kiddushin 31a) that the rabbis valued more the person who performed a commandment when commanded to do so than they did the one who performed a commandment but was not commanded to do so. The rabbis posited that the person who performed the commandment voluntarily would be more consistent.

Next, it was always considered meritorious for a person to hasten and be eager to perform a mitzvah and in a timely fashion. Thus, when a baby is to be circumcised, the custom is to have the ceremony take place in the morning. Or when a person goes up to the Torah for an *aliyah* (ascending to the Torah to recite blessings), the custom is to always take the shortest and quickest route, in order to show enthusiasm for the honor to come.

Ethics of the Fathers 2:1 cautioned that one is to be as attentive to a "light" mitzvah as to a "heavier" one. The rabbis also made a distinction between the lighter and heavier mitzvot. For instance, they considered celebrating a festival lighter (*mitzvah kallah*), whereas the mitzvah to learn Hebrew was a more serious commitment, therefore a heavier one (*mitzvah chamurah*).

One should never think of performing a mitzvah as a burden. Thus, the rabbis coined the phrase *simcha shel mitzvah* to express the joy a person ought to feel when performing a mitzvah. The only way to get the feeling, they suggested, was by doing mitzvot and not seeing them merely as an obligation.

Finally, simply doing mitzvot, even in a joyous manner, was not considered enough. So the rabbis advised that we look for ways to make the mitzvah even more beautiful by doing more than the bare minimum required to fulfill it. They called this idea *hiddur mitzvah* (glorification or adding beauty to the mitzvah). For example, when building a sukkah for the Festival of Sukkot, one should take extra time to decorate it in an especially aesthetic manner, or when buying a tallit to wear, to purchase one that is beautiful and special.

Is it kosher for a woman to perform mitzvot from which women are exempted?

Virtually all rabbinic authorities agree that women may perform the mitzvot from which they have been exempted (that is, time-related positive commandments). Furthermore, most authorities consider performing these voluntarily to be a meritorious act. Therefore, it is not unusual to see women today (including Orthodox ones) donning a tallit and even putting on tefillin, mitzvot from which women were traditionally exempted.

One area of controversy among rabbinic authorities relates to whether women are permitted to recite the appropriate blessing before performing an optional commandment. The phrase "and commanded us" in the blessing presents a problem to some rabbis in the case of optional mitzvot for women. Rabbenu Tam, a twelfth-century rabbinic authority, interpreted the phrase as referring to the collective obligation of the Jewish people and ruled that women, as part of the collective, could recite the blessing. Maimonides, on the other hand, interpreted the phrase as referring to individual obligation in the specific mitzvah and ruled that women could not recite the blessing when performing an optional commandment. Because the custom of Ashkenazic Jewry has been to follow Rabbenu Tam, Ashkenazic women who choose to do so recite blessings on optional mitzvot.

What age is kosher for a person to be able to perform a mitzvah?

For a boy the age is thirteen and a day, according to his Hebrew birthday. For a girl it is twelve and a day, according to the Jewish calendar. The rabbis recommend that parents encourage their children to begin to fulfill some mitzvot even before they reach the age of obligation. Thus, it is not unusual to see a young girl before her twelfth birthday lighting Sabbath candles with her mother.

In an interfaith marriage, is it kosher for the spouse who is not Jewish to perform mitzvot?

Jewish understanding is that the 613 mitzvot were given to the Jews to fulfill, and thus only they have the Jewish obligation to do them. However, the rabbis did say that even before the revelation at Mount Sinai, certain laws were binding on all people. This view held that although the Jewish people were subject to the Torah's extensive provisions, non-Jews were required to observe at least a number of fundamental precepts essential for maintaining a just and decent society. These laws came to be known as the Noahide laws because they were believed to have been incumbent on the sons of Noah and therefore obligatory for all people; from Noah's sons "the whole world branched out" (Genesis 9:19).

The rabbis, in interpreting Genesis 2:16, established six such basic commands:

- People may not worship idols.
- People may not blaspheme God.
- People must establish courts of justice.
- People may not kill.
- People may not commit adultery.
- People may not rob.

A seventh law, that people may not eat flesh cut from a live animal, was added after the flood (Genesis 9:4). Interestingly, this rabbinic tradition is reflected in the apostle Paul's teaching about the Noahides. He required that gentiles abstain from idolatry, from eating blood and the meat of strange animals, and from fornication.

Is it kosher to perform mitzvot without ever having had a Bar/Bat Mitzvah ceremony?

When one comes of age to do mitzvot (thirteen for a boy, twelve for a girl), one may begin to perform mitzvot, whether or not one has had a Bar/Bat Mitzvah ceremony. However, parents are obligated to train their children in the ways of Judaism, and most do. Hand in hand with the Bar/Bat Mitzvah training comes Judaic training. Thus, a person who never had any religious training would be unlikely to really know how to fulfill a mitzvah. I know many adults (especially women) who never had a Bar/Bat Mitzvah. To that end, I, as well as all of my colleagues, now offer courses to help adults rediscover their Judaism. The program is often a one- or two-year course of adult Jewish studies, culminating in a group adult Bar/Bat Mitzvah experience in which class members lead the service and chant a *haftarah* (prophetic portion).

When a person reaches the age of eighty-three, a lovely Jewish custom allows the opportunity of celebrating a second Bar/Bat Mitzvah. It often provides an occasion for family, relatives, and friends to celebrate an important Jewish milestone for a second time. In the 1980s Judith Kaplan Eisenstein, the first declared Bat Mitzvah in the United States, celebrated her eighty-third birthday with her second Bat Mitzvah.

❧ What's Not Kosher ❧

What are nonkosher ways of performing a mitzvah?

It is forbidden to treat a commandment with disrespect (*bizui mitzvah*). There are many ways in which one might show lack of respect for a mitzvah. For example, using a sacred object for a secular purpose is a form of being disrespectful in performing a mitzvah. Thus, counting money using the light of the candles of a *hanukkiah* (Hanukkah candelabrum) is forbidden. One must also guard against the disrespectful treatment of an object with which a mitzvah has once been performed, such as an old pair of tefillin. When these become old and worn, they must not be thrown away but rather buried in order to prevent desecration.

One must also be careful not to perform a mitzvah with the fruits of sin (*mitzvah habaah averah*). For instance, the rabbis said: "if a person has stolen wheat and has ground, kneaded and baked it, and set apart the *hallah*, how can one then recite the blessing over it. It would not be a blessing, but a blasphemy!" (Talmud, Sanhedrin 6b)

Finally, too much stress on performing the commandments could quite naturally result in pure, mechanical behavior in which acts are performed without proper feeling and devotion. To avoid that, the rabbis instituted the concept of *kavanah*, meaning direction or concentration. *Kavanah* refers to the need for correct thoughts and application of the mind before one performs a commandment. Undoubtedly, this is why the rabbis created blessings to recite before performing a mitzvah. The blessing is intended to offer praise to God and remind us of the importance of the sanctified act.

Is it kosher to think that one should have to perform all 613 mitzvot?

No, this is impossible and not a kosher thought. First of all, several hundred of the mitzvot (dealing with animal sacrifices and the like) are no longer applicable and therefore no longer required. And second, performing mitzvot is not intended to be a competition. The idea is to continue to climb the ladder of observance each year by adding new mitzvot to your repertoire.

My teacher taught me that men and women do not have the same obligation to perform commandments. Is this kosher?

There is virtually no distinction between men and women in the area of moral responsibility covered by the so-called negative commandments ("You shall not"). However, there is a distinction between men and women with regard to positive commands ("You shall"). Women are obligated according to Jewish law in virtually all of the positive commandments that are independent of time, but they are exempt from most, though not all, time-bound positive commandments. The rabbis give quite a number of reasons for this rabbinic dispensation, including the fact that women are excused from the time-related mitzvot because of their familial duties and responsibilities. Others believed that women have greater potential for spiritual growth than men because of their less aggressive nature. Thus, they need to have fewer commandments in order to achieve spiritual perfection.

Is it kosher to translate the word *mitzvah* as good deed?

The word *mitzvah* means a commandment, specifically a divine one. That is its primary meaning, and the rabbis emphasized to their students that a mitzvah was a religious obligation. That being said, the word *mitzvah* has also come to mean a good or pious deed (even though not all mitzvot are related to goodness), as in "it's a mitzvah to help a blind person cross the street."

Is it kosher to think that God will reward you for doing a mitzvah?

The rabbinic sages advise that one should do a mitzvah for its own sake and not in expectation of receiving a reward (Ethics of the Fathers 1:3). The fear of God was always to be the determining factor in one's actions. That being said, both the Bible and Talmud refer to performing mitzvot. For instance, the Bible promises long life for honoring parents and chasing away a mother bird before taking her eggs (Exodus 20:12; Deuteronomy 22:6–7).

The belief that God will somehow reward and protect a person trying to fulfill a commandment certainly has a number of adherents. For example, friends and relatives of some Jews setting out on a journey (such as a trip to Israel) will give the travelers *tzedakah* (charity) money to distribute on arrival at their destination. The underlying belief here is that God will protect a person en route who is going to perform an act of *tzedakah*.

Is it kosher for a person to know the reason for performing a mitzvah before doing it?

Most rabbinic authorities believe that the yoke of the commandments is to be cherished without the necessity to probe the reasons behind them. Therefore, it is perfectly kosher to perform a mitzvah without knowing the precise reason why God or the rabbis gave it to us. Many people I know who keep kosher really don't have a rationale that satisfies them, and yet they continue to keep kosher because they feel that Jewish tradition obligates them to do so. When my father-in-law, of blessed memory, a university professor, was asked by one of his colleagues why he kept kosher and ate only salad in the university cafeteria, he simply responded: "It reminds me that I am a Jew."

❦ What the Experts Say ❧

Live by the commandments; do not die by them. (Talmud, Sanhedrin 74a)

A commandment is to the Torah what a lamp is to the sun. (Midrash, Psalms 17:7)

One who loves mitzvot is not sated with mitzvot. (Midrash, Deuteronomy Rabbah 2:23)

Rabbi Eleazer ben Shammua said: "The man who fears God delights greatly in God's commandments" (Psalms 112:1). "In His commandments, not in the reward of His commandments." (Talmud, Avodah Zarah 192)

He who sits and does not sin is rewarded as if he had performed a mitzvah. (Talmud, Kiddushin 39)

The commandments of the Torah should be performed in a two-fold manner: by the body and by the mind. (Zohar 1:72a)

What difference does it make to God whether one kills the animal at the throat or at its back? But the commandments were given to purify the people. (Tanchuma Shemini 5)

It is well to spend an extra third to perform a mitzvah in a more satisfactory way. (Talmud, Baba Kamma 9)

Ranking the commandments in importance (Talmud, Makkot 23b–24a):
Rabbi Simlai said: "Moses gave to Israel 613 commandments. David came and comprehended them in 11 (Psalm 15).
"Isaiah came and comprehended them in 6: 'He that walks righteously, and speaks uprightly, he that despises the gain acquired by oppression, that shakes out his hands from holding of bribes, that stops his ears from hearing of blood, and shuts his eyes from looking upon the evil, he shall dwell on high' (Isaiah 33:15).
"Micah came and comprehended them in 3: 'He has told you, O man, what is good, and what God requires of you—do justly, love mercy and walk humbly with your God' (Micah 6:8).
Amos came and comprehended them in 1: 'Seek me and live'" (Amos 5:4).

Rabbi Joshiah said: Just as you must not allow the *matzah* to get sour, so you must not let the commandment get sour by delay. If a mitzvah comes your way, do it at once. (Mechilta Pischa, Bo, 9)

Rabbi Elazar said: People on a mission to perform commandments will not be harmed, neither on the way nor on the way back. (Talmud, Pesachim 8b)

If a person causes another to do a commandment, the Scripture regards him as if he had done it himself. (Avot de Rabbi Natan, 5:1)

A stolen *lulav* is unfit for mitzvah use. (Mishnah, Sukkah 3:1)

Unlike other distinguished rabbis, Rabbi Israel Salanter would often pour only a small amount of water over his hands for the ritual washing before the meal, even though the law recommends that as much water as possible ought to be used. Those who witnessed his conduct were amazed that he was content with the minimum requirements of the law. "Yes," the rabbi said. "I know that it is a mitzvah to use a good deal of water, but have you noticed that the poor girl has to bring in the water from the well outside in the bitter cold? I am not anxious to perform special acts of piety at the expense of the poor girl's toil." (Hasidic folktale)

❧ Sources ❧

Greater is one who is commanded to do something and does it, than one who is not commanded to do something and does it. (Talmud, Kiddushin 31a)

Run to perform a light commandment as you would to perform the most important. (Ethics of the Fathers 4:2)

Topic 27

❦ ❧

Office Work

❦ What's Kosher ❧

Is it kosher for an office worker to quit her job at any time?

Although Jewish law recognizes the right of employees to quit a job at any time, in practice it does restrict this right. If a worker quits and the employer is forced to pay those who replace that worker with a high wage, it is kosher for the employer to deduct the additional amount from the wages owed the worker who quit. If, however, the employer is able to hire a new worker at the same rate of pay, then the worker who quit is not penalized.

Is it kosher for an office worker who sees a fellow worker stealing to tell his or her employer?

Jewish law says that one should not stand idly by when one sees wrong-doing. Therefore, it would be perfectly kosher to let one's employer know. However, because Judaism allows for repentance and second chances, it might be more appropriate to first confront the fellow worker, allowing for an explanation and a second chance. This would be a more *menschlich* (considerate) thing to do, and perhaps the warning would serve as a wake-up call to improved behavior.

❧ What's Not Kosher ❧

Is being a workaholic kosher?

Although to work in Judaism is a mitzvah, being a workaholic is not kosher. Americans work very hard. So hard in fact, that they often put work at the emotional and spiritual center of their lives. To restore balance in our lives, God commanded us to set aside one day a week as the day of rest, relaxation, and rejuvenation. But alas, many people continue to choose to work, even on weekends. Eventually work becomes all that there is in life, sometimes leading to emotional breakdowns and broken marriages.

It is not kosher for workers to try to take on more work than they are capable of doing. For the compulsive worker, work often becomes an end in itself. Workaholism can bring with it all kinds of health problems, not to mention neglecting one's family and avoiding other personal responsibilities as a spouse or parent. There is nothing wrong with working hard, but overdoing it is un-Jewish and not kosher.

Is it kosher to play video games or shop online while on the job?

No, it's not kosher to spend time playing games or taking care of personal business when you are being paid to work, except during lunch or other breaks. It is strictly kosher for a worker to give a full day's work during work hours. Many employees violate this norm by engaging in personal phone conversations, playing games on their computers, and taking longer breaks than are permissible. Productivity of workers was of great importance to the rabbis who formulated the laws. It is not surprising, therefore, that the Jerusalem Talmud (Peah 8:8) states that "fifty productive workers are better than two hundred who are not."

Is it kosher to take paper clips home from the office?

If the paper clips belong to the business for which one is working, then it is kosher to use them only for business matters and not for personal use. Taking them home is for personal use; doing so is not only not kosher, but it might well be violating the biblical law "you shall not steal"!

Is it kosher to work shorter hours if unsupervised?

No, working shorter hours just because one thinks he or she can get away with doing less is not permissible. Although there is a general tendency for a worker to begin a job and to labor faithfully only to eventually become lazier (especially in light of lack of supervision), a worker has a duty to honor his or her agreement and to work the agreed-upon hours.

Is it kosher to engage in office gossip?

Office gossip is strictly forbidden, anywhere, anytime. One is forbidden to say anything negative about another person, even if it is true, unless the person to whom one is speaking or writing has a legitimate need for this information. Even the relatively innocuous form of gossip, involving talking about the minutiae of another person's life, is nonkosher. Although the damage done by this form of gossip may be minor, it almost always leads to the more damaging kind. So instead of talking about the juicy tales of peoples' lives, try spending more time saying nice things about them.

If a fellow worker steals something belonging to you and you learn the thief's identity, is stealing it back kosher?

Stealing is stealing, strictly forbidden by Jewish law. Therefore, it is not kosher to steal, even if one does it merely in a playful manner meant to confuse or perhaps annoy.

One of my favorite stories related to this question tells of a Jew who once observed the commandments scrupulously but was also known to be a pickpocket. One day he visited his rabbi's office to return a watch he had found in the fulfillment of the mitzvah of returning a lost article. After he left, the rabbi realized that the man who returned the watch had picked his pocket. He inquired, and the man had to tell him the truth—it was indeed he. The rabbi then asked how he could reconcile these two acts—returning the watch and picking his pocket. "Well," said the man, "the Torah says you must return a lost article. That's a mitzvah. But business is business."

Honesty in business dealings is paramount in Jewish law. Even the thought of appearing like a thief to others was of concern to the rabbis. Many centuries ago Ben Bag is quoted as saying: "You must not steal your own property back from a thief, lest you appear to be stealing" (Sifra 38b).

✻ What the Experts Say ✺

A worker is not permitted to labor at night and to hire himself out during the day, to plow with his cow in the evenings and hire her out in the mornings, nor should he go hungry and afflict himself in order to feed his children—for this is tantamount to stealing from the labor of the employer. (Tosefta to Baba Metzia 8:2)

A worker is enjoined not to deprive the employer of the benefit of his work by idling away his time, a little here and a little there, thus wasting the whole day deceitfully. The worker must also be very punctual in the matter of time. (Maimonides, Mishneh Torah, Laws of Hiring, chap. 13, sec. 7)

✻ Source ✺

Fifty productive workers are better than two hundred who are not. (Jerusalem Talmud, Peah 8:8)

❦ ❧

Organ Transplants

❦ What's Kosher ❧

Is it kosher to mark on my driver's license that I am willing to donate my organs?

In 1990 the Rabbinical Assembly of America (the union of Conservative rabbis in which I bear membership) approved a resolution to "encourage all Jews to become enrolled as organ and tissue donors by signing and carrying cards or driver's licenses attesting to their commitment of such organs and tissues upon their deaths to those in need." Today most rabbinic authorities in all branches of Judaism would permit the donation of one's organs to benefit another. Two main issues work in tandem with the issue of organ transplantation. Saving a person's life and acting kindly to others are values so sacred in Judaism that if a person's organ can be used to preserve someone else's life, using the organ in that way is actually an honor to the deceased. Enabling a person to live through a donation of an organ is an act of *hesed* (kindness), and the fact that the organ is a gift freely given is an important part of how both the donor and the recipient perceive it.

Although it is forbidden to mutilate a corpse for the purpose of harvesting organs, most rabbinic authorities agree that this prohibition can be set aside in order to save a life. It is in the rabbinic interpretation of saving a life that we get differing opinions.

There is the greatest consensus of rabbinic opinion that eye or corneal transplants are permissible. Transplantation of a healthy kidney to replace a patient's nonfunctioning kidney is also permissible. The general rule is that the rabbis permit organ transplants when they can be accomplished without major risk to the donor's life or health.

The most restrictive rabbinic opinion would permit donations only when there is a specific patient who stands to lose his or her life or an entire physical faculty. According to this opinion, for example, if the person can see out of one eye, a cornea may not be removed from a dead person to restore vision in the other eye. Only if both eyes are failing, such that the potential recipient would lose all vision and therefore incur serious danger to life and limb, may a transplant be performed. Moreover, according to this more restrictive view, the patient for whom the organ is intended must be known and present. Donation to organ banks is not permitted according to this view.

A new organization that has come to my attention is the Halachic Organ Donor Society, located in New York City. Its mission is to disseminate information regarding Jewish legal issues and rabbinic opinions concerning organ donation. It also offers card-carrying membership in a society that allows people to donate organs in accordance with their particular halachic belief.

Each year in November there is also a National Donor Sabbath. Clergy in all religious denominations speak to their members to try to raise awareness about the critical need for organ and tissue donors and discuss their religious beliefs and traditions related to this topic.

Is it kosher to use artificial organs or animal organs (including a pig's) for transplants?

The use of animal or artificial organs is permissible and serves to help solve two of the major ethical problems regarding transplants. The first is the moral problem of assuring that a vital organ is not removed from a legally living person (so that the transplantation is not an act of murder). The other is the practical problem of providing enough organs for those who need them.

Although some have raised questions about the use of animal parts for direct transplant or for making artificial organs, no Jewish source considers this to be a moral issue. Judaism, after all, does not demand vegetarianism; and if we may eat the flesh of animals under the kosher dietary laws, then we may certainly use animal parts for saving a life. Judaism, in fact, posits that if the use of animal parts can save a human life, we have a moral and religious obligation to use them, and they do not even have to be from a kosher animal.

Is it kosher to donate one's body to science for a medical student to dissect as part of his or her education?

The majority of my rabbinic colleagues would argue that to allow use of one's body parts for medical science is both an honor to the deceased and a real mitzvah in that it helps the living. Of course, one must have the express written permission of the deceased's family.

Objections to the donation of one's body for science center around the desecration of the body and the delay in its burial after death. Many Orthodox rabbis take a very hard line on this issue, claiming that any invasion of the corpse for purposes of a transplant is warranted only if a patient will immediately benefit thereby. Many others do not object to the use of bodies of persons who gave their consent in writing, provided that the dissected parts are carefully preserved so as to be eventually buried with due respect according to Jewish law.

When is it kosher to declare someone officially dead?

Waiting even a short time is generally too long today, if doctors are able to use a dying person's heart to save the life of an awaiting transplant patient. Consequently, many rabbis, including my professor, the late Rabbi Seymour Siegel, suggested that a flat electroencephalogram, indicating cessation of spontaneous brain activity, be sufficient to determine death. In 1988 the Chief Rabbinate of Israel approved heart transplantation, effectively accepting that a flat electroencephalogram guarantees the patient can no longer independently breathe or produce a heartbeat. This has become the accepted opinion of virtually all modern Jewish authorities, with the exception of some Orthodox rabbis.

What's Not Kosher

Is it kosher for people to sell their organs and body parts for profit?

Judaism would not permit people to sell their body parts for a profit. For Judaism God owns everything, including our bodies. We consider them as being on loan to us for the duration of our lives and to be returned at the time of death. One immediate implication of this principle is that we do not have the right to sell that which does not belong to us.

At present many countries have laws that flatly prohibit the purchase or sale of body parts. U.S. law has tended to divide body parts into categories. Payment for nonregenerative or nonrenewable tissues used in transplantation, such as hearts and kidneys, has been prohibited. On the other hand, payment for renewable tissues, such as blood, hair, and semen, has been permitted.

Another concern with regard to selling body parts is the fear that vulnerable populations will be exploited (that is, that the poor and others whose social circumstances give them few choices and little medical sophistication will become "tissue factories" for the well-to-do). Given repeated advances in our ability to partition and manipulate the human body, the debate over the status and treatment of the body's components is likely to continue for many years to come.

What the Experts Say

We may cure and save ourselves with all things, even those that are forbidden, except those things that are connected with idolatry, incest and murder. (Rabbi Elliot Dorff)

The authorized removal of the eyes of a deceased person in order to restore sight to the blind is not an act of mutilation, which is forbidden, but an act of healing and restoration, which in Jewish law takes precedence over almost all other religious injunctions. (*CCAR Yearbook,* vol. 53, 1953, p. 153)

One who is sick and in danger of death, and the physician tells him that he can be cured by a certain object or material that is forbidden by the Torah, he must obey the physician and be cured. (Maimonides)

❧ Sources ❧

You shall live by them, but you shall not die because of them. (Talmud, Yoma 85b)

Whoever saves one life, it is as if he saved the entire world. (Mishnah, Sanhedrin 4:5)

Parents' Obligations to Children

What's Kosher

Is it kosher for a father of a child who is an alcoholic to ask him to leave the house?

As the book of Deuteronomy (6:7) says, a parent is required to diligently instruct his child. Using the approach of instruction, it would be kosher for the father to make his child aware of his illness and tell him that unless he involves himself in a program that will help to break his addiction, he is not allowed to stay at home. This approach is generally known as the tough-love approach, which instructs parents to desist from providing financial and emotional support to a badly behaving child, specifically because they do very much love their child. By permitting such a child to stay at home, a parent discourages improvement. In addition, this child might well have a negative influence on any siblings who still are living at home.

Note that this kosher approach does not mean cutting off all communication with one's child if he or she has an addiction. Rather, what it means is that a parent must avoid expending excess emotion and money for a self-destructive child at the expense of the other children.

Is it kosher for a father to coach his son's baseball team?

Although no Jewish law prohibits a child from playing on a team that his father coaches, this situation could lead to a conflict of interest between the father as coach and as parent of his son. Centuries ago Rabbi Pappa of Talmudic fame (Ketubot 105b) cautioned judges not to adjudicate cases of someone they either loved or hated, for fear of judging unjustly.

A coach must offer equal treatment to all of his players, whereas a father has an obligation to show special attention to his own child. Sometimes these two roles are mutually exclusive, making it difficult for a father to have to coach his own son.

I always cringed at summer camp when I was umpiring a baseball game in which my son played. My fear was the possibility of calling him safe at the plate in a close call, where other players might judge me as being unfair, simply because he was my son.

So if you want to coach a team and have a son who wants to play, it's advisable (if possible) to find your son a different team.

Is it kosher for a father to teach his son karate to protect him from bullies?

Yes, there is nothing wrong if a father chooses to teach his son karate or send him to a karate class. In fact, the Talmud itself mandates it. Years ago the rabbis obligated a father to teach his son how to swim (Talmud, Kiddushin 29a). In Talmudic times, when travel often required traversing water in small boats, the ability to swim was critical to survival.

Fathers (and mothers too) are thus obligated to teach their child any skill on which the child's life may depend. Such skills might include driving carefully, being mindful of proper hygiene, and yes, swimming and boating too!

What's the kosher thing for a mother to say when her child accidentally spills tomato soup on a white tablecloth?

When such things happen, many parents are apt to explode and yell and scream at their child. The kosher thing to say would be "Don't worry, it was an accident. Let's clean it up together." The child feels badly enough as it is, so to be angry and accuse him of clumsiness will serve only to embarrass him more. The important thing for a parent to remember here is to be cognizant of the child's feelings.

Is it kosher for a child to correct a parent?

According to the Talmud (Sanhedrin 81a), if a parent unwittingly transgresses a law in the Torah, his child shall not reprimand him by saying, "Father, you have transgressed a law." Rather, a child should "gently" explain to his father, "Does not the Torah say such and such?" Thus, it is kosher to correct a parent; however, one must make the correction without causing a parent embarrassment.

❦ What's Not Kosher ❧

Is it kosher for a parent to be his child's only Hebrew school teacher?

Although Jewish law obligates a parent to teach his child Torah (Talmud, Kiddushin 29a), there is still great value in sending one's child to a religious school where he or she has the benefit of interacting with other children. A school setting also provides a connection with a community of learners that simply is impossible when one's parent is the only purveyor of Jewish education.

Is it kosher for a parent to threaten a child with physical punishment?

It is not in keeping with Jewish tradition for a parent to threaten a child with physical punishment. Parents need to show compassion to their children, especially when they misbehave and do the wrong thing.

In one of the famous episodes on the *Leave It to Beaver* television sitcom, Beaver's father makes a remark that both frightens the boy and causes him to believe that he is no longer wanted as a family member. As a result, the Beaver proceeds to find an adoption agency in an attempt to get himself adopted by new parents. Although this is only a humorous episode in a sitcom, there are scores of real-life stories of children who, when physically threatened, either run away or try to inflict injury on themselves.

It would be wise to remember the words of the rabbis, who advise that "if you must strike a child, strike him only with a shoelace" (Talmud, Baba Batra 21a). Clearly, the intention here is to warn a parent never to cause physical harm to one's child.

Is it kosher for a parent to favor one child over another?

From the stories in the Torah we learn that it is best not to play favorites. All parents have a moral obligation to make sure to treat their children with equal respect, fairness, and love. Furthermore, it is a parent's obligation to ascertain their child's emotional way and to treat him or her in manner that recognizes and values that way.

The hatred of Joseph's brothers due to his father's special affinity for him and their jealousy over the gift of the colored cloak caused the brothers to sell Joseph into slavery to travelers who were heading toward Egypt. When the rabbis of bygone years studied this episode, the ethical implications became clear: "A man should never single out one of his children for favored treatment, for because of the two extra coins' worth of silk [that Jacob had woven into Joseph's special coat], Joseph's brothers became jealous, and one thing led to another until our ancestors became slaves in Egypt" (Talmud, Shabbat 10b).

Is it kosher for a parent to snoop?

It's absolutely forbidden for a parent to snoop and pry into someone's private affairs. As a youngster my family shared a phone line (called a party line) with another family. I remember how tempted I was to listen in on numerous occasions when I picked up the phone, only to find two other people with whom I had no relationship whatsoever already speaking.

So the next time you're tempted to read a private letter or e-mail addressed to your spouse or child, to read that person's diary, or to listen to phone messages intended for someone else, don't do so unless that person has given you permission. When my son and I are in a room together and he receives a call on his cell phone, I always leave the room. It's important to allow him space and freedom to speak openly, without his father standing and hovering close by.

If a mother tells a child to do something and the father then rebukes the child for it, what is a kosher response for a child?

According to rabbinic consensus, a child ought always to avoid causing a quarrel between his parents. Thus, Sefer Hasidim (Parents and Children, par. 531) suggests in this case that the child ought not to implicate the mother by saying, "It was Mother who asked me to do it." For then the child would be to blame if his father became enraged with his wife and shouted at her.

❧ What the Experts Say ❧

The Rabbis say that the best skill that parents can teach their children is the study of Torah, for it will provide them in this world and sustain them in the World to Come. (Talmud, Kiddushin 82a)

A parent who does not rebuke his child leads him into delinquency. (Exodus Rabbah 1:1)

A parent should never show favoritism among his or her children. (Talmud, Shabbat 10b)

Rabbi Judah once said that "anyone who does not teach his child a craft may be regarded as if he is teaching his child to steal." (Talmud, Kiddushin 29a)

A father must teach his child to swim. (Talmud, Kiddushin 29a)

A father is responsible to marry off his sons and daughters, to clothe his daughter as befits her, and to provide her with a dowry. (Otzar Dinim U'minhagim)

If you must strike a child, strike him only with a shoelace. (Talmud, Baba Batra 21a)

A father should never excessively terrorize his children. (Talmud, Gittin 6b)

If a parent does not teach his son Torah, it is as if he had merely created an image. (Zohar 2:93a)

A person should not threaten a child even with as small a thing as boxing his ears. Rather, he should punish him immediately, or say nothing. (Semachot 2:5–6)

If a father has a son who is a glutton and a drunkard, he should not destroy his entire family and his other children for the benefit of that one. Therefore, the father should act as if this son never existed and expel him from his house, rather than ruin himself and his family on account of one son. (Sefer Hasidim)

If a small child is capable of shaking the *lulav* [palm branch] correctly, his parents should buy him his own *lulav*. (Talmud, Sukkah 28a)

A parent should not promise to give a child something and then not give it, because in that way the child learns to lie. (Talmud, Sukkah 46b)

The parent who teaches his son, it is as if he had taught his son, his son's son, and so on to the end of the generations. (Talmud, Kiddushin 36)

A father once came to the Baal Shem Tov with a problem concerning his son. He complained that his son was forsaking Judaism and morality and asked the rabbi what he could do. The Baal Shem Tov answered: "Love him more." (Hasidic tale)

Judaism invented family education by obligating parents to create an ambiance for their children permeated by Jewish conversation and ritual, Jewish artifacts and values. (Dr. Ismar Schorsch, chancellor of the Jewish Theological Seminary of America)

I think parents should forget the genius bit—what you want is a human being, a *mensch*—not a genius. (Dr. Jerome Bruner, noted Jewish psychologist)

❧ Sources ❧

Teach them [God's words] diligently to your children. (Deuteronomy 6:7)

Anger in a home is like a worm in a fruit. (Talmud, Sotah 3b)

Educate a child according to his own way. (Proverbs 22:6)

Topic 30

Prayer

❧ What's Kosher ☙

Must I pray only in Hebrew for it to be kosher?

Not at all! Although Hebrew is the preferred language, Jewish law de-
crees that one may pray in any language that one understands. And
even if one knows Hebrew (but does not understand it), it is always
kosher to look at and ponder the English, usually found on the opposite page of the prayer book, so that one will know what he or she
is saying or praying for.

What are some kosher guidelines for helping a worshipper find more meaning in Jewish prayer?

Here is some kosher advice, based on rabbinic suggestions from various sources, that will help make your prayer experience come alive
and be more meaningful:

Before entering the synagogue, briefly pause to arouse your awe
and love for God and the respect for the sanctuary. If you can
do this a few minutes before services begin, all the better.

When finding a seat, sit closer to where the cantor and rabbi are
situated so that you can hear well and participate more fully.

And it is a good idea once you get comfortable with a certain location to continue to maintain that location (Code of Jewish Law, Orach Chayim 90:19).

If you wear a tallit, try wrapping it fully around your head as you put it on, briefly meditating on being close to God. Then sit down, close your eyes, calm yourself, and put yourself in a peaceful mood. (The Kotzker Rebbe once said that the time spent in sharpening the ax is as important as the time spent in chopping the tree.)

Bring a book of Bible commentary or a prayer book with commentary that you can read and peruse during services.

Don't be afraid to close your eyes during services. It can help you to block out distractions and concentrate.

Follow the prayers in English translation, and it will help you better to sense the meaning of what you are saying.

During every prayer service, it's kosher to add some of your own private and personal prayers and thoughts.

Try chanting and swaying during prayer services. This will help you enter into the prayers themselves.

Like anything else in life that is done well, kosher praying requires adequate preparation and practice. The more you attend and familiarize yourself with the prayer service, the better you will become.

Is it kosher to pray alone, or do I always have to go to synagogue to be with other Jews?

According to the rabbis, communal prayer is of greater significance than private prayer. Our sages have taught that God listens more readily to congregational prayer than to an individual's prayer. Though an individual is permitted to pray alone if unable to participate with a group (many people who have to be at work early in the day will pray at home by necessity), the preferred situation has always been group prayer. There is clearly an extra dimension to community prayer. Having other people around us when we pray reminds us that we must never be selfish when saying our prayers but include others as well in our thoughts. It is not by chance that the most important formal prayers are all written in the first person plural. We pray to *our* God, and we ask that God's blessing be upon *us*.

Is it kosher to count women as part of the minyan of ten?

A minyan is a quorum of ten adults.

Rabbi Nachman of Bratslav said, "Nine righteous people do not make a minyan, but one common person, joining them, completes the minyan."

Today the Reform, Conservative, and Reconstructionist branches of Judaism include adult women in their count of the minyan. The Orthodox still do not.

If I can't keep up with the service, is it kosher to skip parts of it?

One should take his or her time and not race through the prayer book. When a service is moving too quickly for a worshipper, it is better to skip parts of the service and say the rest with full concentration than to try to pray all of the prayers in a rushed fashion. Prayer is called service of the heart, and heartfelt prayers that are said with feeling are the most kosher kinds of prayers and most likely to find their way to God.

I remember my seminary professor, the late Abraham Joshua Heschel, telling our class that to pray is to take hold of a world. That's another way of saying "don't rush."

If I have time in the morning to recite only a few prayers, what would be some kosher guidelines?

I would single out three prayers to say in the morning as a minimum when one is pressed for time. The first is the Shema: "Hear O Israel, Adonai is our God, Adonai is One." This prayer comes closest to Judaism's credo and is a confession of the Jewish faith, proclaiming that God is one and reminding us of our obligation to love God with all our heart and soul.

The second core prayer is the Amidah. The longest prayer, its nineteen morning blessings consist of three main thoughts: the glory of God, hope for personal and group well-being, and thankfulness for God's blessings.

Finally, concluding every worship service is the Aleynu prayer, which includes the universal prayer for the day when all people will be under the dominion of One God.

Is it kosher to meditate?

Absolutely. In fact, meditation is a traditional activity in Judaism. Genesis 24:63 says that Isaac went out into a field to meditate, which the rabbis interpreted to mean that he prayed. And in the Talmud we learn that the early Hasidim would spend an hour before prayer in meditation, to direct the mind to God.

The Hebrew high school students in my synagogue meditate at most of their evening services, and several of the students have led the entire student body in guided meditation.

Is there a kosher direction to face while praying?

Yes, when in the West, praying is always done facing east, toward the holy city of Jerusalem. For this reason the ark in U.S. synagogues is designed to face eastward. (Those in other parts of the world face Jerusalem in relation to their location.) If you are praying at home and forget which way is east, it is a good idea to put a *mizrach* (east) plaque or picture on a wall that faces east as a constant reminder.

My friend invited me to Christmas midnight Mass. Is it kosher for me to go and join in the prayer service?

Rabbi Moses Isserles (b. 1525), in his Notes to the Code of Jewish Law, writes that for the sake of retaining goodwill and avoiding bad feelings, Jews who find themselves in the midst of a non-Jewish holiday celebration should join in the festivities. He suggests that they should not seek out such celebrations but if invited should certainly be allowed to go.

Many Jews have attended church with Christian friends and neighbors, both for the regular Sunday services and for special ceremonies for a friend or funeral. When they do go to church however, they ought to go as visitors, not participants. Nor should they feel required to kneel during services (even for the sake of conformity) or for that matter answer *amen* to prayers offered in the name of Jesus. These actions would contradict the tenets of Judaism, and some Christians might even interpret them as disrespectful or even as subtle mockery. Generally, I would recommend a benign and compassionate attitude toward our Christian friends' religious services.

❧ What's Not Kosher ❧

You see an accident ahead with ambulances and fire trucks. Is it kosher to pray that the people involved are not anyone you know?

When most people see an accident ahead while driving, many thoughts go through their minds. Many wish that nobody they know is involved. To turn this wish into a prayer and subsequently pray to God that no one you know is involved in the accident is not kosher. First of all, the prayer is in vain, because a person in this case would be praying to have undone what has already occurred.

A better prayer and a kosher one would be that you hope that all the survivors recover in a timely fashion and that God be with them.

Every night before going to sleep, I pray for my family's health and welfare. Is this kosher?

It is meritorious to say prayers at nighttime, especially the Shema, which is the most traditional. However, a prayer petitioning for the welfare of only your family is a selfish prayer. A better prayer would include not only those in your family but all of those in need of healing. And to add a prayer for peace in the world would not be a bad idea either.

Is it kosher to expect that God will answer my prayers?

It's kosher to believe that God will hear your prayers. However, to expect your every prayer to be answered in the way you want it to be answered is not reasonable and not kosher. For God does not always grant a person that for which one prays. Sometimes God says no.

People are often disappointed when praying to God for something specific and not getting an answer to their satisfaction. However, people who have faith and pray regularly have told me that their prayers have helped them physically, psychologically, and spiritually. For instance, I had a student who took her driving test and failed on successive tries. She asked for my advice, and I told her to pray to God for the courage and determination to relax when taking the test and for renewed confidence as well. The next time she took the test, she passed with flying colors!

Which kind of prayers are not kosher?

Not all prayers are considered proper ones, according to the rabbis:

We may not pray that an overabundance of good be removed from us (Talmud, Taanit 22).

Rabbi said: "It is not permitted to pray that God send death to the wicked" (Zohar Chadash 105).

To pray for the impossible is a disgrace. It is as if a person brought into a shed a hundred measures of corn and prayed, "May it be Your will that they become two hundred" (Tosefta, Berachot 7).

To pray for something that has already happened is considered a prayer in vain. For example, if a man's wife is pregnant and he says, "May it be God's will that my wife give birth to a boy," that is a prayer in vain (Talmud, Berachot 54a).

❦ What the Experts Say ❧

When ten or more people pray together, the Divine Presence is with them. (Talmud, Berachot 8a)

One who is standing outside Israel when praying should direct his or her heart toward the Land of Israel. (Talmud, Berachot 30a)

When you pray, always know before Whom you stand. (Talmud, Berachot 28b)

Rabbi Iddi said in the name of Rabbi Yochanan: "People should not pray if they have to use the bathroom." (Jerusalem Talmud, Berachot 2:3)

One whose mind is not at ease should not pray. (Talmud, Eruvin 65a)

Prayer without intention is like a body without a soul. (Yeshuot Meschicho)

A person should purify his or her heart before praying. (Exodus Rabbah, Beshallach 22:3)

The person who stands in prayer will keep his eyes down and his heart upward. (Talmud, Yevamot 105)

Rabbi Eliezer said: "If a person prays only according to the exact text and adds nothing from his own mind, that prayer is not proper imploration." (Talmud, Berachot 28)

Prayer of the congregation is always heard by God. (Maimonides, Mishneh Torah, Laws of Prayer 8:1)

Rabbi Jonah would recite the Amidah in the synagogue in an undertone, lest he disturb others. But, if he prayed at home, he would recite it aloud so that his sons might learn it by hearing it from him. (Jerusalem Talmud, Berachot 4)

Never has a tearful prayer been uttered in vain. (Zohar 1:132b)

Rav said: "Whoever has in his power to pray on behalf of his neighbor and fails to do so, that person is a sinner." (Talmud, Berachot 12b)

❧ Sources ❧

You shall fear the Lord your God. . . . Him shall you serve.
(Deuteronomy 10:20)

How many times ought a person to pray? Our rabbis taught: One
should not pray more than three times a day, for the three Patri-
archs instituted the three statutory prayers: Abraham, the morning
service [Genesis 19:27]; Isaac, the afternoon service [Genesis 24:63);
and Jacob the evening service [Genesis 27:11].

Topic 31

❦❧

Repentance

❦ What's Kosher ❧

Are there kosher guidelines for repenting?

There are four basic stages to doing repentance. The transgressor must recognize his or her sin, feel sincere and honest remorse, undo any damage he or she has done, and resolve never to commit the sin again.

What is the kosher number of times that one is obliged to ask another's forgiveness?

Jewish law requires a person who has wronged another to seek forgiveness a maximum of three times. After three requests have been made and refused, one is not required to seek forgiveness again.

❦ What's Not Kosher ❧

Is it kosher for a person who has been wronged and offered an apology not to accept it?

Withholding forgiveness is cruel and in and of itself a sin. The person who is wronged ought to accept an apology that is offered with sincerity and honesty. The Torah (Leviticus 19:18) reminds us not to bear and hold a grudge against another. A grudge one bears against another only festers and creates more anger and is not healthy. Therefore, when you have wronged another and have been offered an apology, it is only proper to accept it.

Are the High Holy Days the only time to repent?

Although one of the basic themes of Rosh Hashanah and Yom Kippur is repentance, and there are a myriad of confessional statements throughout the High Holy Day prayer book, one may and is encouraged to repent at all times. The Talmud says that one should repent every day, because one never knows when one's last day will be. For in this manner one's whole life will be spent in repentance.

One who repents daily is safeguarding oneself against becoming involved in more serious sins. Rabbi Levi Yitzchak of Berditchev offers some especially kosher advice. Each night he would sit down with pen and paper and review his actions of the day. When he completed this, he would review his list and say to himself: "Today I did some things that were wrong, but tomorrow I won't repeat them."

Is it kosher to forgive a murderer?

According to Jewish law, one can never completely forgive one who has committed the ultimate crime—the taking of another's life. Saadia Gaon defined several other sins as so heinous that they entail irretrievable harm and cannot be atoned for by repentance: corrupting, misleading and misinforming a multitude, ruining the reputation of an innocent person, and keeping misappropriated articles.

People have been faxing requests for God's intervention to the Western Wall; some ask forgiveness by e-mail. Is this kosher?

It is best to ask for forgiveness face-to-face rather than by fax, e-mail, or telephone. There is no substitute for the personal touch, and although apologizing in person may be a bit more uncomfortable, it is the kosher way to do it!

A person who had been a thief served his time in jail and never stole again. Ten years later someone reminded him of his days as a thief. Is this kosher?

According to the Talmud (Baba Metzia 56b), one must never say to a person who has repented (and changed his or her way of life), "remember your former transgressions." Saying this only causes embarrassment. When there is no real purpose in saying something to someone else, better to be silent!

What kind of repentance is not kosher?

If a person repents and returns to sinning, that is no repentance (Pesikta Rabbati, 44). True repentance requires that such a person will not return to his evil ways and repeat the crime. It is not kosher to repeatedly sin and repent.

Rabbi Simcha Bunam once asked his students how we can tell when a sin we have committed has been pardoned. None of the students knew the answer, so the rabbi answered his own question by saying: "We can tell by the fact that we no longer commit that sin."

☙ What the Experts Say ☙

Because piety is a difficult way of life to adopt, it is good to start when you are young. The most admirable kind of repentance is when a person still possesses his strength and vigor, and his passion threatens to overwhelm him, but he subdues it. By controlling his intensely strong desire, he really is performing a powerful feat. (Sefer Hasidim, Laws of Repentance, chap. 6, par. 61)

A twinge of conscience in a person's heart is better than all the floggings that such a person may receive. (Talmud, Berachot 7)

In the place where penitents stand, even the wholly righteous cannot stand. (Talmud, Berachot 34b)

As long as the candle is burning, it is still possible to make repairs. (Rabbi Israel Salanter)

If a man has beheld evil, he may know that it was shown to him in order that he learn his own guilt and repent; for what is shown to him is also within him. (Baal Shem Tov)

One who confesses has a share in the world to come. (Mishnah, Sanhedrin 43)

Twenty-four things hinder repentance: four of these are grievous offenses. If one commits any of them, God gives him no opportunity to repent because of the gravity of the offense. Offenders of this type are: He who leads the people to sin; this includes someone who prevents them from doing a good deed; he who diverts another from the good to the evil, such as a seducer or enticer; he who sees that his son is falling into bad ways and does not stop him; being under his control, the son would desist if checked by the father; hence, it is as if he actually led him to sin; he who says: "I will sin and then repent." This includes one who says: "I will sin and on Yom Kippur I will atone."

Five of the twenty-four misdeeds shut the ways of repentance to those who commit them. They are: he who stands aloof from the community; since he is not among them when they repent, he does not share the merit they attain; he who opposes the rulings of the sages; since his opposition induces him to stand away from them, he remains ignorant of the ways of repentance; he who makes a mockery of the divine precepts; since they are held in contempt by him, he does not eagerly obey them, and if he does not obey, how can he attain merit? he who insults his teachers; and he who hates rebuke, because he leaves himself no way of repentance; for it is reproof that induces repentance.

Five of the twenty-four misdeeds are of such a nature that anyone who commits them cannot attain complete repentance, because they are sins against a fellow human, without knowing it is in order to compensate him and ask his pardon. Offenders of this category are: he who curses the people and not an individual, of whom he might ask forgiveness; he who shares with a thief; he who finds lost property and does not announce it, that he may restore it to its owner; when he repents after some time, he does not know to whom he should restore it; he who despoils the poor, orphans, and widows; these people are wretched and not well known, they migrate from town to town, and have no acquaintance whereby to ascertain how to refund what he has robbed; he who takes bribes to tamper with justice, thus encouraging the bribing litigant and leading him to sin.

Five of the twenty-four offenses are such that the person who commits them is not likely to repent, because they are regarded by most people as trivial, with the result that the sinner imagines that it is no sin. Offenders of this class are: he who shares a meal that is insufficient for its owner; since this is a tinge of robbery, he imagines that he has not done any wrong, saying, "I did not eat without his consent"; he who makes use of a poor person's pledge; since a poor person's pledge happens to be only an ox or a plow, and the user says to himself: "The articles have not depreciated, and I have not robbed him"; he who gazes at women lustfully, supposes that there is nothing wrong in it, and does not realize that the lustful look is a grave sin, as it is written: "You shall not follow the desires of your heart and your eyes" (Numbers 15:39); he who elevates himself at the expense of another's degradation, and thinks to himself that this is no sin, since the other person is absent and has not endured shame; nor has he actually shamed him by comparing his own good deeds and wisdom with the other person's deeds or wisdom, implying that he is honorable while the other is contemptible; he who suspects honest men, saying to himself that it is no sin. "What have I done to him?" he says: "Is there anything more to it than a mere suspicion that maybe he has done it and maybe not?" He does not realize that it is sinful to regard a worthy person as a transgressor.

Finally, five of the twenty-four misdeeds are such that anyone who commits them will always be attracted to them, and they are hard to give up. One should therefore be careful lest one become addicted to them, for they are all extreme obnoxious traits.

They are: gossip, slander, wrath, evil thought, keeping bad company. (Maimonides, Mishneh Torah, Laws of Repentance 4:1–5)

Rabbi Meir said that when one truly repents, the entire world is pardoned. (Talmud, Yoma 86b)

❦ Sources ❧

Then they shall confess their sin which they have committed. (Numbers 5:7)

Repent on the day before you die. (Ethics of the Fathers 2:10)

Topic 32

Sabbath

❧ What's Kosher ❧

Is it kosher to visit someone who is sick on Shabbat?

Yes, it is. However, visiting on Shabbat is only permissible if one can walk to the sick person's house or the hospital. Driving in an automobile on the Sabbath for such a purpose is not permissible.

Is it kosher to play in a baseball game on Shabbat?

Individual sports and amusements in themselves, where no other violation of the Sabbath is involved, are permissible. Thus, ball-playing in a private domain, or anywhere that carrying an object is allowed, is permissible.

Is it kosher to violate the Sabbath if an emergency arises?

In Jewish law saving a life and safeguarding a person's health takes precedence over the laws of the Sabbath. Consequently, when an emergency arises, one may engage in activities normally prohibited on the Sabbath.

Is it kosher for a man to light Shabbat candles?

The primary but not exclusive obligation for lighting Sabbath candles belongs to women. The traditional explanation is found in the Talmud (Shabbat 31b), where Rashi comments that because a woman was the cause of man's downfall (Eve when tempted by the serpent), causing the light of the world to be dimmed, it is a Jewish woman's obligation to light the candles and bring back light. But if for some reason the woman of the house cannot carry out the candlelighting duty (if she is ill, giving birth, or away), the obligation rests with the man; and it is kosher for him to light the candles on the family's behalf.

Single men and women who run their own households are obligated to light Sabbath candles.

My grandmother always served gefilte fish at her Sabbath dinners, but my mother did not. Did my mother do anything that was not kosher?

Although I grew up eating gefilte fish as an appetizer at our Sabbath dinner, there is no requirement to serve it. The serving of gefilte fish in many traditional Jewish households likely relates to the custom of families serving fish at least once during the Sabbath. (Fish, the rabbinic sages say, was created on the fifth day, followed by man, who was created on the sixth day [Friday]; and both were created to glorify the seventh day—the Sabbath). Because the cost was often beyond many families' reach, Eastern European household communities created the much less expensive gefilte fish.

Gefilte fish means filled or stuffed fish. It got its name because after two or three types of boned fish (carp, pike, and whitefish) used in its preparation were ground up and seasoned with onions, salt, and pepper, the mixture was stuffed into the skin of the fish and cooked for an hour or more.

Is it kosher to take a cruise that travels on the Sabbath?

The Talmud (Shabbat 19a) stipulates that one may not set out on a journey by ship unless he or she boards the ship at least three days before the Sabbath begins. This applies only to trips made for business or social purposes. If the purpose of the trip is charitable, the rabbis permit one to board the ship immediately before the onset of the Sabbath.

The rabbis granted permission to travel on the Sabbath in such circumstances if the owner of the ship is a non-Jew, if the trip is not made specifically for the sake of Jews onboard, and if on the Sabbath the sailors on the ship perform no work specifically for the Jews onboard. To do so would be nonkosher and in violation of Sabbath law.

From very early Talmudic times, the rabbis recognized that if Jews were to maintain contact with the outside world, it would be necessary for them to travel on the Sabbath. Because of the distances between large cities and the length of time required to cross large bodies of water, it would have been impossible for Jews to carry on normal business dealings or to engage in social or charitable activities if they had not been able to travel on the Sabbath.

Is it ever kosher to carry money on the Sabbath?

Although all rabbinic authorities strictly forbid the carrying of money on the Sabbath, Moses Isserles (1525–1572), an Ashkenazic rabbinic authority, remarks that a person may carry money on the Sabbath if he finds himself in a situation where he must spend the Sabbath at an inn and is afraid that the money might be stolen if he leaves it unattended in his room. Contemporary authorities have applied Isserles's position to the problem of muggings. Some modern authorities permit the elderly, being prime targets of muggers, to carry money on the Sabbath because it was established that muggers often become violent when they discover that their victims are not carrying money.

What are some kosher guidelines for preparing for the Sabbath?

Psychologically, it is necessary to prepare for a moment of heightened experience if it is to be fully appreciated. Thus, the approach of the Sabbath should be anticipated with special acts of preparation. We are told in the Talmud (Betzah 16a) how many of the sages personally prepared themselves and their homes for the Sabbath. The sage Shammai actually began his preparations on Sunday. If he saw a choice article of food, he immediately set it aside for the Sabbath.

Today taking a bath or shower, tidying one's home, cooking a festive meal, and putting money in a *tzedakah* (charity) box before lighting Sabbath candles are traditional activities for preparing oneself and one's home for the Sabbath. Before the approach of the Sabbath, one should make sure to empty one's pockets so as not to carry things that one should not carry on the Sabbath.

What kosher activities can I do on Shabbat afternoon?

Taking a walk, napping, playing a board game, reading for pleasure, and studying Torah are all appropriate activities for the afternoon of the Sabbath. In the summer months beginning with the Sabbath after Passover, the custom is to read and study Pirke Avot (Ethics of the Fathers), a Talmudic tractate that teaches one how to be a better person.

❦ What's Not Kosher ❧

Is it kosher to hire a non-Jew to do the work of a Jew on Shabbat?

Jewish law (Maimonides, Mishneh Torah, Laws of Shabbat 24:4) states explicitly as a general rule that we may not ask a non-Jew to do anything on the Sabbath that we may not do ourselves. Because of the exceptions to this rule, the institution of the so-called Shabbes-goy (a non-Jew working for a Jew on the Sabbath) came into being. The exceptions are in the following cases:

- Illness or other emergencies
- Lighting a fire in cold weather
- To relieve an animal in pain
- Where the act is done by a non-Jew for his own purpose, even though a Jew may benefit (Talmud, Shabbat 122b)

These exceptions have been stretched to the point that some Sabbath observers have non-Jews do every manner of work around the house that is usually forbidden. The idea of using a person in this way to me is repugnant and ought not to be encouraged.

The rabbis laid down the general principle that if the non-Jew is independent, is paid for the job as a whole, and is not told specifically to work on the Sabbath, it is kosher for him to do his work (Code of Jewish Law, Orach Chayim 244:5, 252:2). For instance, one may give his clothes to the laundry, ask a non-Jewish tailor to fix his garments, or ask a non-Jew to do any other similar type of work, even if he knows that it will be done on the Sabbath, as long as the non-Jew is free to decide when the work should be done. We have a custodian in our synagogue who is not Jewish who does work on the Sabbath. Because he is assigned specific duties on the Sabbath as part of his total responsibilities, it is entirely kosher to have him do this work on the Sabbath.

In the winter it's already dark by the time I get home (five o'clock). Is it still kosher to light Shabbat candles?

Candles must be lit at sundown, usually eighteen minutes before sunset and approximately forty minutes before nightfall. They may be lit earlier in the day, and if they are, the person lighting the candles must begin observing the Sabbath at that time. Lighting them when it is already dark is not kosher, because with darkness the Sabbath has arrived, and lighting candles on the Sabbath is not kosher.

Is it kosher to use electricity on Shabbat?

Many traditional Jews consider electricity to be a form of fire, and Jewish law prohibits making a fire on the Sabbath. Those who do not use electricity do not turn on a radio or television or use any electrical appliances on the Sabbath. Some authorities who doubt whether electricity can truly be labeled fire explain the ban on electricity as a protective measure, to safeguard against other violations that might stem from permitting the use of electrical appliances. More liberal Jews generally will use electricity on the Sabbath.

Is it kosher to use one candle for candlelighting on the Sabbath?

Jewish law requires a minimum of two candles for Shabbat candle-lighting. Some commentators have noted that the two candles represent the two important references to the Sabbath in the Bible: "Remember the Sabbath" (Exodus 20:8) and "Observe the Sabbath" (Deuteronomy 5:12).

A variety of customs has emerged over the centuries, differing from community to community and from family to family. Some people have been known to light seven candles, or a seven-branched candelabrum, to correspond to the seven days of the week or the seven-branched menorah that was a centerpiece in the Temple in Jerusalem. The Talmud (Shabbat 23b) encouraged this custom: "The multiplication of candlelight is a Sabbath blessing." My maternal grandmother had the custom of lighting thirty-two candles, one for each of her grandchildren and great-grandchildren!

Is it kosher to think that Jewish law requires that all work be prohibited on the Sabbath?

Anyone who takes the Bible literally may conclude that no kind of work is permitted on the Sabbath. For the Torah explicitly says: "But the seventh day is the Sabbath unto the Lord your God, in it you shall do no manner of work" (Exodus 20:1).

However, the biblical command does not specify all the kinds of work that are forbidden other than kindling a flame, plowing, harvesting, reaping, gathering wood, and the like. The Talmud further refines the definition of work prohibited on the Sabbath, enumerating thirty-nine major classifications of work that are not permissible. Additionally, other categories of work should be avoided because they are not in the spirit of Sabbath rest. These categories incorporate all the types of work that were involved in the construction of the tabernacle.

The common belief that any manner of work is prohibited on the Sabbath is incorrect. Jewish law does not prohibit physical exertion on the Sabbath. An observant Jew may walk up a steep hill not only to attend synagogue but even without a destination. Serving the

Sabbath meal to family, friends, or strangers is permitted even though serving and clearing the table entail considerable physical activity. Lifting furniture within one's home (called one's private domain) is permitted on the Sabbath.

By the same token, some minor activities that do not require strenuous activity are nevertheless avoided because they violate the spirit of the Sabbath. For example, discussing business matters or reading business correspondence is not kosher.

Is it kosher to use a timer to turn on lights on the Sabbath?

Almost all rabbinic authorities agree that it is kosher to use a timer to switch lights on and off on the Sabbath. Not all agree, however, that a timer may be used for other purposes. Rabbi Moshe Feinstein, a leading Orthodox authority, permits using a timer to switch electric lights on and off on the Sabbath only because it is now a widely accepted practice among Orthodox Jews. But he opposes a timer's use for preprogramming an electric stove or food warmer to heat precooked food on the Sabbath. Feinstein is clearly apprehensive that the use of the timer in connection with warming food might ultimately lead to use of the timer to set some sort of work process into motion on the Sabbath.

Is it kosher to use a timer and have it turn on your television for Shabbat viewing?

Many rabbinic authorities have deemed turning on a television as synonymous with using fire and therefore prohibited. There are other reasons for opting not to watch television on the Sabbath. Dennis Prager and Joseph Telushkin, co-authors of *Nine Questions People Ask about Judaism,* have suggested that Shabbat and television have antithetical purposes. Whereas the purpose of television is to entertain and enable people to kill time, the Sabbath's purpose is to teach people how to sanctify time. Even though people are known to watch television for more than five hours each day, keeping the television off one day of the week liberates a person from dependence on it. Telushkin and Prager say it best when they write that "Shabbat is a natural day, no artificial additives are permitted. Therefore, no television!" (p. 167).

Is it kosher to drive on Shabbat?

Conservative Jews are permitted to drive to and from synagogue, but that is all. Although Reform and Reconstructionist Jews are permitted to drive on Shabbat, the Orthodox rabbis do not permit it. The basis of the prohibition is the verse in Exodus 16:29: "Let everyone remain where he is: let no one leave his place on the seventh day." This law was originally directed at the gatherers of manna, the heavenly food that fell in the desert. Travel on the Sabbath in Bible times, by riding on an animal, was also forbidden.

I do not use a car on Shabbat. I think that the biblical idea of asking people to stay home or near their home on the Sabbath is an attempt to mold the Sabbath day into one of spirituality and serenity.

❦ What the Experts Say ❧

Call the Sabbath a delight. (Isaiah 58:13)

The most important ingredient in creating a Jewish home is the celebration of the Sabbath. (Abraham Joshua Heschel)

More than Israel has kept the Sabbath, it has been the Sabbath that has kept the people of Israel. (Achad Ha'Am)

The messiah will come when the entire Jewish people keep two Sabbaths in a row. (Talmud, Shabbat 118b)

The world is like the Sabbath eve, and the world to come is like one long Sabbath. (Midrash, Ruth Rabbah 3:3)

On the Sabbath an additional soul is given to us, an increased capacity for lofty thoughts and holy desires. (Talmud, Betzah 16a)

Sabbath clothing should not be the same as weekday clothing. (Talmud, Shabbat 113)

The Sabbath is the Queen of the week. (Talmud, Shabbat 119a)

Break the Sabbath so that this sick person may live. Thus you will keep many Sabbaths. (Talmud, Yoma 85b)

Rabbi Hanina said: "A joyous spirit should be the rule on the Sabbath." (Talmud, Shabbat 12a)

ꙮ Sources ꙮ

Remember the Sabbath day to keep it holy. (Exodus 20:8)

Observe the Sabbath day to keep it holy. (Deuteronomy 6:12)

Topic 33

❧ ❧

Sex

❧ **What's Kosher** ❧

Is it kosher to masturbate?

The answer to this question is, like many others, "it all depends who you ask." Traditional Judaism forbids masturbation by males and has little to say about masturbation by females.

Modern rabbinic views vary on the subject of permissibility. For instance, the esteemed Orthodox rabbi and author of *Judaism on Pleasure*, Reuven P. Bulka, considers masturbation an instrument for focusing only on the self and strongly condemns it. Rabbi Elliot Dorff (a Conservative rabbi), in his book *Matters of Life and Death*, writes that masturbation in and of itself should no longer carry the shame it had for our ancestors: the original grounds for opposing it (that a man has a finite amount of seed and spilling saps a man's strength) are no longer tenable, and it is a way of dealing with one's sexual energy before marriage. Others agree with him, positing that learning about one's body is permissible. Therefore, they have declared masturbation as a form of permissible release, because it can work to discourage young people from sexual experimentation with others.

Rabbi Shmuley Boteach, the rabbi of Oxford University and author of the book *Kosher Sex*, writes that every act of masturbation serves as a powerful release that in turn lessens our vital need for sex with another person. In the context of marriage, the lessening of need for sex can be disastrous.

Is oral sex kosher?

Although other more traditional rabbis are likely to say no, many others say it is. Their thinking posits that Judaism opposes the willful destruction of seed but not sexual practices (like oral sex) that sometimes involve the spilling of seed but that husband and wife pursue for purposes of pleasuring one another. For a Jew sex is holy so long as it is always designed to increase the mutual dependency and intimacy of husband and wife.

The great medieval codifier, Maimonides, while advising husbands and wives to abstain from an overindulgence in nonmissionary sex, still writes that the actual law is this: "A man's wife is permitted to him and therefore, whatever he and his wife wish to pursue sexually, they may do. They may have intercourse whenever it pleases them and he may kiss any organ he wishes, and he may have intercourse in a natural or unnatural manner" (Mishneh Torah, Laws of Marital Sex 21:9).

Must the lights be off to have kosher sex?

The ancient rabbis strongly advocated that lovemaking take place in the dark. The dark requires a couple to see with the eye of their minds. Fantasy and mystery is more easily integrated into the experience.

Rabbinic consensus also held that sex should take place well into the evening, at a time when husband and wife are more relaxed and released from the cares of the world. But the Talmud also offers that one might have intercourse during the day, because otherwise the husband, overcome by sleep, might perform perfunctorily and end up despising his wife.

The Talmud also adds that it is a particular mitzvah for scholars to have intercourse on Friday night, thus joining the holiness of the Sabbath with the holiness of marital sex—a double mitzvah!

Is it kosher for a man to fantasize about another woman while making love?

The rabbis differ as to whether it is kosher for a man to fantasize about another woman when he has sex with his wife: "'so that you do not follow your heart and eyes in your lustful urge' [Numbers 15:39]. Deducing from this Rabbi taught: One may not drink out of one goblet and think of another. Rabina said: This is necessary only when both are his wives" (Talmud, Nedarim 20b). Rabina's opinion permits sexual fantasies about another woman not available in the household. Such fantasies would not threaten a woman's status in her own household as would a fantasy about a co-wife.

In our own times, some Jewish sources would permit a man to fantasize about a beautiful but unavailable movie star if it helps intensify lovemaking with his own wife. However, a fantasy that might lead to infidelity (that is, one about a neighbor's wife) would be inappropriate and nonkosher.

Is birth control kosher, and if so, which are the most appropriate methods?

Judaism is relatively permissive with regard to artificial contraception on the woman's part. This is because she is technically not commanded to procreate (although when she marries she joins with her husband in the fulfillment of this mitzvah). Secondly, her use of birth control does not involve the serious transgression of destroying seed.

As in so many other cases, religious authorities vary on which purposes and methods of contraception they will permit. The most lenient authorities would say that birth control is permissible as long as normal intercourse can take place and one's body derives natural gratification from the other. From the point of view of Jewish law, the diaphragm and the contraceptive patch are two of the most favored forms of birth control, for they prevent conception and have little if any impact on the woman's health. If the contraceptive pill or implant is not contraindicated by a woman's age or body chemistry, it is usually the form of contraception that rabbinic authorities next most favor. Couples like these methods of birth control because they are easy to use and very reliable. Jewish authorities recommend them because their success rate minimizes the possibility of the couple later considering an abortion as a form of retroactive birth control.

Because rabbinic law enjoins that only a man is commanded "to be fruitful and multiply" (Genesis 1:28), Judaism is far more restrictive about condoms, whose use violates the strict prohibition against the wasting of seed. The severe rabbinic stricture on the wasting of seed was related to the belief that the male seed was really a person in miniature waiting to be planted in female soil and that the number of such seeds was limited. Because we now know that this is not true, many rabbinic authorities permit the use of condoms. In addition, because condoms are known to protect not only against pregnancy but against sexually transmitted diseases, particularly AIDS, there is a stronger push for their use.

In terms of frequency of having sex, what's kosher?

Because the rabbis in bygone years considered women to be more inhibited than men in expressing their sexual needs, they prescribed a minimum schedule of sexual relations based on their husband's professions (which in turn affected the men's availability): "For men of independent means, every day. For laborers, twice weekly. For donkey drivers, once a week. For camel drivers, once very thirty days. For sailors, once every six months" (Mishnah, Ketubot 5:6).

The Talmud (Ketubot 62b) also forbade a man who wished to change to a trade that would require him to travel further from home to do so, on the grounds that his doing so would make lovemaking with his wife less frequent.

The woman's right to sexual intercourse is referred to as *onah*, and it is one of the wife's three basic rights (the others are food and clothing) that the *ketubah* (Jewish marriage contract) stipulates. Today most rabbinic authorities would agree on several principles regarding sex and its frequency. First, a husband has a duty to give his wife sex regularly and to ensure that sex is pleasurable for her. Simply performing his marital duty pro forma is not in keeping with the Jewish ideal. The Torah requires joy, frivolity, even spontaneity in the sexual relations between husband and wife.

A husband is also obligated to watch for signs that his wife wants to make love and to offer it to her without her asking for it.

Although it is a man's duty to engage in regular sexual relations, a woman must also make herself available to her husband for those relations. Even though a man cannot force himself on his wife, neither can a wife continue to refuse her husband's sexual advances. It is even considered desirable according to rabbinic consensus for the wife to solicit her husband to the sexual act. Nevertheless, the laws of modesty suggest that she be a bit less brazen and more subtle than her husband.

❧ What's Not Kosher ❧

Are there times when it is not kosher to have sex?

Even within marriage there are times when it is not permissible to have sex. For example, the Torah forbids a man to have relations with his wife during her menstrual cycle and for a specific time afterward. These laws are euphemistically known as *taharat ha-mishpacha* (family purity). Jewish law also forbids sexual intercourse between husband and wife by force, when one of them is drunk, when the husband has decided to divorce his wife, when there is strife, or when the wife fears her husband (Talmud, Nedarim 20b). Conjugal relations are also forbidden on Yom Kippur, the Day of Atonement, and other minor fast days.

Is it kosher to engage in nonmarital sex?

Although it is probable that only a small minority of Jews maintain the ideal of chastity before marriage, sex within marriage continues definitely to be the ideal. Although the Torah never explicitly outlaws nonmarital sex (except of course in the case of adultery and incest), the rabbis forbade it. Sex outside marriage simply did not fit their ideal of holiness and could lead to continued promiscuity after marriage.

The only Mishnaic rabbi explicitly to outlaw nonmarital sex was Rabbi Eliezer, who wrote: "He sleeps with many women and does not know who they all are. She receives many men and does not know whom she received. It will turn out that a man will err and marry his sister, and a woman will err and marry her brother, and the world will be filled with *mamzerim* [children born of forbidden marriages]" (Sifra, Kiddushin 7:5).

Rabbi Michael Gold, who wrote *Does God Belong in the Bedroom?*, relates how his own synagogue continues to promote the Jewish ideal of sex within marriage. An unmarried couple who were living together applied to become members. After much discussion the synagogue decided that they could join as two singles but not as one family. In this way the synagogue would reflect the ideals of Judaism.

Is it kosher to be gay?

According to Jewish tradition, the marital state of a man and a woman is considered the kosher ideal. And the primary reasons for marriage are to have companionship and children. That being said, there are a variety of views on homosexuality. To begin, homosexual conduct between males is mentioned more frequently and more heavily condemned in the traditional Jewish sources than such conduct between females. The emphasis is on the sexual act between males rather than mental homosexual tendencies.

New medical knowledge about the origin of homosexuality has led the more liberal branches of Judaism to rethink their stance against homosexuality, in some cases to the point of equating monogamous and loving homosexual relations with the same type of heterosexual relations. For some denominations of Judaism, no change is called for; yet for others, that matter has become the source of deep controversy.

The Conservative movement, in a 1990 Rabbinical Assembly resolution, came out in support of affording full civil equality for gays and lesbians and welcoming them as members in our congregations. A number of modern rabbis from various movements have attempted to interpret the traditional sources on homosexuality as they apply to gay Jews today. Three basic approaches have emerged: (1) a reaffirmation of the traditional prohibition, tempered by a call for compassion for homosexuals; (2) a rejection of the traditional prohibition in favor of fully embracing the sexual needs of gays; (3) an attempt to rework Jewish law in light of a modern scientific understanding of homosexuality.

Is pornography kosher?

Pornography, in which sex is photographed, filmed, or put into magazines for sale, is not kosher. In many ways pornography resembles prostitution. Both involve the exchange of money for sex. Because of its dehumanizing nature and use of obscenities, it violates the law and spirit of Judaism. The issue for Judaism is that pornography does not enhance the passion and romance between a couple but rather replaces them with something alien. Because the purpose of sex is to foster and sustain emotional intimacy between husband and wife, whatever a couple does is permitted if it leaves their passion for each other intact. Here lies the problem, for in most cases pornography will serve as an end in itself rather than a tool for the excitement of passion.

Pornography recognizes only our animal bodies, not our holy spirit. It may be ethical in that it does not hurt anyone, but it does violence against the divine soul. That is why pornography, in all of its modern manifestations, destroys the holiness ideal of Judaism and is not kosher.

❦ What the Experts Say ❧

There is a small organ in a man. If he starves it, it is satisfied. If he feeds it, it whets his appetite for more. (Talmud, Sukkah 52b)

Everyone knows why the bride enters the bridal chamber, but if anyone speaks obscenely about it, even if seventy years of happiness have been decreed and sealed for him on High, the decree is changed for him into evil. (Talmud, Ketubot 8b)

When there is no union of male and female, men are not worthy of beholding the Divine Presence. (Zohar 3; Acharei Mot 59a)

He can do as he wishes with his wife. He can have intercourse any time he wishes. He can kiss any part of her body, and he can have intercourse both in the usual way and in an unusual way or on her limbs, provided that he does not spill his seed. Some are more lenient and rule that unnatural intercourse is permitted even if it involves a spilling of the seed, provided it is only done occasionally and he does not make a habit of it. All of these are permitted. Whoever sanctifies himself in that which is permitted is called holy. (Moses Isserles in his notes to the Shulchan Aruch, Even HaEzer 25:2)

If a man sees that his evil impulse is conquering him, let him go to a place where he is unknown, put on black clothes, wrap himself in a black cloak, and do what his heart desires, but let him not publicly profane God's name. (Talmud, Kiddushin 40a)

If a man forbids himself by vow from having intercourse with his wife, the School of Shammai says she must go along with the vow for up to two weeks. If it lasts longer, the court can compel him to divorce her, but the school of Hillel says for only one week. (Mishnah, Ketubot 5:6)

If someone was originally employed in a trade near his home and wished to change to a trade in which he would have to travel far from home, his wife may prevent him from changing, on the grounds that their sexual relations would become less frequent. (Rabbi Obadiah of Bartenura)

A man should never force himself upon his wife and never over-power her, for the Divine spirit never rests upon one whose sexual relations occur in the absence of desire, love and free will. The Talmud (Pesachim 49b) tells us that just as a lion tears at his prey and eats it shamelessly, so does an ignorant man shamelessly strike and sleep with his wife. Rather, act so that you will warm her heart by speaking to her charming and seductive words. (Iggeret Ha-kodesh, Moses Nachmonides)

Although intercourse was reserved for the night, if because of one's nature one finds himself forced to sleep at night and ought not to be aroused or excited, or if the woman's nature is such that she is overtaken by sleep at night and is not sexually receptive at that time, one is permitted to have intercourse during the day, with due sexual modesty, in order that intercourse be performed with acceptance and love and not by force. (Meiri to Talmud, Niddah 17a)

He sleeps with many women and he does not know who they all are. She receives many men and does not know who she receives. It will turn out that a man will err and marry his sister, a woman will err and marry her brother and the world will be filled with *mamzerim* [children born of a forbidden marriage]. (Talmud, Sanhedrin 4:1)

Ben Azzai said: He who does not engage in propagation of the race acts as though he sheds blood and diminishes the divine image in the world. (Talmud, Yevamot 63b)

Our rabbis taught: There are three partners in the creation of man. The Holy Blessed One, his father and his mother. (Talmud, Niddah 31a)

❦ Sources ❧

Be fruitful and multiply. (Genesis 1:28)

You shall not commit adultery. (Exodus 20:13)

Thus shall man leave his father and mother and cleave to his wife, and they shall be one flesh. (Genesis 2:24)

Topic 34

Shopping

✺ **What's Kosher** ✺

Is it kosher to sample a fruit at the supermarket before purchasing it?

Unless the produce manager is offering free samples of fruit to taste, it is not kosher to pick and taste without asking permission. To do so would be tantamount to stealing, because you didn't pay for it.

If a woman accidentally breaks one of the glasses while shopping for glassware, is it kosher for her not to pay for it?

Many stores today have a sign that says Break It, You Pay for It. Such a sign legally binds a shopper who breaks an item to pay for that item. Even without a sign, the storeowner would have the right to insist on repayment for the value of the broken glass.

I once accidentally broke a bottle of ketchup in a supermarket. The store manager came over to me and told me not to worry. He didn't want me to pay, realizing that I did not act maliciously and that it was totally unintentional.

Jewish law calls the store manager's decision *lifnim meshurat hadin*, going beyond the letter of the law. Jewish law often holds to a moral standard rather than a purely legal one, allowing a person the possibility of going beyond the letter of the law. That's what kindness and mercy are all about.

Is it kosher to shop daily for yourself, beyond what the family needs (like food)?

Shopping for oneself every day would appear to be excessive yet would be permissible if one could afford to do so and not deny the family its basic needs. However, rabbinic advice would always caution against overindulgence when it comes to material things. One must always put one's family's basic needs before one's own needs.

Is it kosher to purchase a product and then return it because of dissatisfaction?

When one makes a purchase and has a change of heart (for any reason), one is surely permitted to return it. However, before purchasing any product, one should always check the store's return policy to be certain that a purchase is returnable for full cash refund or store credit. If the store's policy is that all purchased items are final sales and non-returnable, then the store has no obligation to the customer, regardless of the customer's dissatisfaction with the item.

❦ What's Not Kosher ❧

Is it kosher to buy a handbag from a street vendor when you know it might be stolen goods?

There is no way to know for certain whether the items that this vendor was selling were counterfeit or even stolen. However, common sense would suggest that if the vendor is selling incredibly underpriced items, either the vendor has acquired them illegally or they are counterfeit. Jewish law would forbid a person from purchasing them. This is based on the Mishnah Baba Kama 10:9: "one may not buy wool, milk or kids from shepherds. Nor may one buy wood or fruit from the watchmen of orchards." You cannot know for certain that the shepherds or watchmen have stolen the items from their employers, but common sense suggests that if they are selling precisely those items they are paid to guard, they have probably acquired them illegally.

With no intention ever to buy, a shopper went to several stores and asked salespeople to show him watches. Is this kosher?

I can remember numerous times when my wife and I went comparison shopping for various items, often taking up a considerable amount of the salesperson's time. However, when the salesperson asked, "Can I help you?" my wife answered with honesty, "Just looking, thank you." According to rabbinic thinkers, all consumers have an obligation to merchants to act fairly: "Just as there is wrongdoing in buying and selling, so there is wrongdoing in words: One may not say to a storekeeper 'How much does this item cost?' if one has no intention of buying it" (Talmud, Baba Metzia 4:10).

   This ruling is not made to discourage a person from doing comparison shopping. If you are truly considering buying an item, you have every right to compare prices in various stores. What you are forbidden from doing is raising the salesperson's hopes, stealing his or her time just to satisfy your curiosity or to acquire information about the product in order to later buy from a cheaper online vendor.

Is it kosher to buy products produced by exploited workers?

Hundreds of thousands of very poorly paid and even slave laborers (many of whom are children) around the world are exploited by their bosses. They work in unsanitary conditions for unimaginably long hours. If you do business with people who take advantage of their workers by exploiting them, you help ensure that these businesses will continue to take unfair advantage of their workers. It would therefore be nonkosher to buy such products.

The cashier returned more change than I was entitled to. Is it kosher for me to keep it?

Many people in a similar situation would likely choose to keep the change, often saying or at least thinking that the store makes enough money already. However, because Judaism values truth and honesty, the kosher thing to do would be to tell the cashier that he or she has made a mistake and return the additional change. Another reason for doing this is that when accounting is done at the end of each day, a cashier who has made an error in favor of the customer will often be penalized and have that amount of money deducted from his wages. Ethics of the Fathers (2:7) has this simple reminder when it comes to money: "Let your fellow's money be as precious to you as your own."

Is it kosher while in a checkout line to push ahead in front of another customer?

It is not proper to push ahead in line. The person who does this is asserting that somehow his or her time is more valuable than that of others in line. All are equal in God's eyes, and rabbinic consensus would say to wait your turn in line even when you are impatient and in a rush.

After shopping I found several items in my grocery bag that I had neither purchased nor paid for. Is it kosher to keep them?

Because you had not paid for the items, they belong to the store and not to you. It would therefore only be proper that you return them to the store where you did your shopping. Even though you might be tempted to keep them (reasoning that they were accidentally placed in your bag and no one would ever know the difference), it is your responsibility to return them to the store, imagining that they were simply lost property.

I had a friend to whom this happened. When he called the store to let the cashier know what had happened, the store manager told him to give the items to a local food pantry.

❦ What the Experts Say ❧

It is forbidden for vendors to buy from any thief any property they have stolen, since it encourages criminals and causes the thief to steal other property. For if a thief finds no buyer, he will not steal. (Maimonides, Mishneh Torah, Laws of Theft 5:1)

A person should not pretend to be interested in making a purchase when he or she has no money. (Talmud, Baba Metzia 55b)

It is the same for the buyer as it is for the seller. They are both subject to the law of wrongdoing in price. (Mishnah, Baba Metzia, chap. 4)

Just as there is wrongdoing in buying and selling, so there is wrongdoing in words: One may not say to a storekeeper "How much does this item cost?" if one has no intention of buying it. (Talmud, Baba Metzia 4:10)

An overcharge or an undercharge of more than one sixth of the value of a commodity invalidates the sale. (Talmud, Baba Metzia 30b)

If a poor man is examining a cake [with the intention of buying it] and another [knowing that the poor man is about to make the purchase] comes and buys it, the latter is called a wicked man. (Talmud, Kiddushin 59a)

Rabbi Judah ben Ilai declared that a shopkeeper should not give to child-customers sweetmeats to attract their patronage. The other rabbis permitted this [because the merchant does not prevent his competitor from doing likewise]. (Mishnah, Baba Metzia 4:12)

If one person seeks to buy or rent either land or movables and another person comes and buys it, the second person is called wicked. (Code of Jewish Law, Choshen Mishpat, chap. 237, sec. 1)

Don't return evil for evil. Don't say, He cheated me on weights and measures. I'll repay him in kind. (Sefer Hasidim, par. 1080)

❦ Source ❧

You shall not falsify measures of length, weight or capacity. You shall have an honest balance, and honest weights. (Leviticus 19:35)

Suicide

❦ What's Kosher ❧

Is it kosher to commit suicide?

The Talmud (Baba Kamma 8:6) makes it clear that Jews may not injure themselves, let alone kill themselves. Either of these actions is viewed as harming or destroying what belongs to God and thus a violation of our conditional use permit, as it were. Therefore, suicide is morally wrong.

Is it kosher for a person who commits suicide to be afforded all the normal Jewish rites of a funeral and burial?

Because suicide is traditionally considered an act of blasphemy and a transgression of Jewish law, the bereaved are generally required to follow a different pattern of mourning. According to this perspective, only those aspects of the mourning ritual that affirm life are to be observed. In addition, the location of the grave may be affected. Some cemeteries include a special separate section for suicides on their outskirts. *Keriah* (the traditional cutting of the clothing) is performed, but a eulogy is not always offered. Interestingly, even traditional Judaism holds that the customary mourning practices should be observed in every detail (even in a case of a suicide), if not doing so would lead to the family's honor being questioned.

All of this being said, the Jewish people have always been sensitive to the state of mind that would lead a person to commit suicide. Thus, only rarely are self-inflicted deaths labeled as suicides within the context of Jewish law. Rather, Jewish law labels the individuals as having suffered from temporary insanity, exempting them from falling into the category of a willful suicide and allowing them a normal Jewish funeral.

Having participated in the funerals of persons who committed suicide, I feel (as do many of my colleagues) that the traditional laws regarding suicides are insensitive to the mental anguish suffered by the person who commits suicide, as well as by the survivors. A reexamination of them would entirely be in order.

Is martyrdom a kosher kind of suicide?

The rabbis decreed that only with regard to three cardinal sins—idolatry, incest, and murder—should a person prefer to make the supreme sacrifice rather than be forced to commit any of these transgressions. If one were coerced to violate any other commandment, rabbinic consensus says that one should spare oneself from death and violate the law.

After announcing this principle, though, the Talmud (Avodah Zarah 18a) goes on to introduce two other factors that can either broaden or narrow the occasions on which one must give up one's life. If the action demanded of Jews is in private and only for the heathen's own pleasure, then they may even bow down to idols to save their lives. On the other hand, if the demand is specifically to cause Jews to violate Jewish law, or if the heathen's demand requires Jews to transgress Jewish law (even if only for the heathen's pleasure), then one may not even "change one's shoe strap from white to black" (that is, violate even a Jewish custom) but rather choose to die in defense of Judaism.

❧ What's Not Kosher ❧

Is assisted suicide kosher?

Jewish law forbids both suicide and aiding a suicide. Assisted suicide combines active euthanasia (acting with the intention of taking another's life for a benign purpose, such as relieving agonizing and incurable pain) with suicide. In assisted suicide both the person who wants to die and his or her assistant contribute to executing the death. Assisted suicide has been practiced quietly in North American hospitals for many decades, although it is only since Dr. Jack Kevorkian's highly publicized and controversial efforts to help people die that the practice has become a matter of public knowledge and concern.

I sympathize enormously with people going through an agonizing process of dying. Some Jewish ethicists take a more liberal stance on withholding or withdrawing life support systems, including artificial nutrition and hydration, to enable nature to take its course. However, the bottom line is that Jewish law permits neither suicide nor assisted suicide.

Jewish law has always demanded that we take a much more active role in ensuring that the dying are not abandoned to physical pain or social ostracism. When a person says, "I want to end this," we need to respond to his or her mental distress; but our response must be a kosher one. This would include supplying sufficient pain medication, treating clinical depression if that is present, and most important, providing the personal and social support that people in these circumstances need. We must also make the mitzvah of *bikkur cholim* (visiting the ill) a critical part of our mission as Jews. Hospice care is an important system in which a whole team of people, including family and friends, support the patient physically, psychologically, and socially.

❧ What the Experts Say ❧

If a minor has committed suicide, it is considered as if he had done the deed unwittingly. If an adult killed himself and it is evident that the act was prompted by madness or through fear of terrible torture, as was the case of Saul who feared the Philistines, he should likewise be treated as an ordinary deceased person. (Code of Jewish Law, Condensed Version, Laws of Suicide, chap. 201:3)

The Law Committee has generally regarded the suicide as an emotionally overwrought person, and therefore not responsible for his action. It would be almost impossible to ascertain a person's motives and lucidity at the time of such an act. (Rabbinical Assembly of America, "Statement on Suicide")

It is the general custom among Liberal congregations to bury a suicide victim in their family plots. (Solomon Freehof, *Reform Jewish Practice,* p. 145)

A suicide is a sentinel who has deserted his post. (Bachya ibn Pakuda, *Duties of the Heart,* chap. 4)

Who is to be ruled a willful suicide? Not one who climbs to the top of a tree or to the top of a roof and falls to his death, as these may have been accidents. Rather, a willful suicide is one who says, "I am climbing the roof, or the tree, and I am going to throw myself to my death," and others see him climb to the top of the tree or to the top of the roof and fall to his death. Such a person is presumed to be a suicide and no mourning rites whatsoever should be observed. A man found strangling or hanging from a tree or lying dead on a sword is presumed to have committed suicide willfully, and none of the mourning rites are withheld from him. (Talmud, Semachot 2:2–3)

The essential principle is that when dealing with a case of suicide, we ascribe his actions to any extrinsic motive we can find, as for example, to terror, despondency, insanity. (Rabbi Yechiel Epstein, Aruch Ha-Shulchan, Yoreh Deah 345:5)

King Saul said to his arms-bearer, "Draw your sword and run it through me, so that the uncircumcised [Philistines] may not run it through and make sport of me." But his arms-bearer, in his great awe, refused; whereupon Saul grasped the sword and fell on it. (1 Samuel 31:4)

✤ Sources ✤

You shall not murder. (Exodus 20:13)

I have put before you life and death, blessing and curse. Choose life. (Deuteronomy 30:19)

Synagogue Behavior

❧ What's Kosher ☙

What is considered kosher dress when in a synagogue?

Most synagogues require males to always wear *kippot* (yarmulkes) when in the synagogue building, even if it is not the sanctuary. When in the sanctuary the custom in Orthodox synagogues would have married women cover their heads and all males wear *kippot*. Conservative synagogues require males to wear *kippot* and females to have the option of covering their heads as they choose. Reform and Reconstructionist Jews have personal autonomy.

On the Sabbath or a Jewish holiday, festive clothing is entirely in order.

Are there any kosher guidelines for conduct during prayer services?

Sefer Hasidim (4:26) has some wonderful advice for kosher prayer conduct. You should not begin to pray in the middle of laughter, giddiness, joking, and banter nor in the middle of an argument.

While praying, you should place your feet close together, cast your eyes downward, and direct your heart upward. You should not pray merely by thinking the words but articulate the words with your lips, so that you can hear what you are saying. And don't raise your voice in public prayer; this can disturb other worshippers.

What's the kosher thing to do when you drop a prayer book?

It's proper to kiss either a prayer book or a Bible after it has fallen to the floor. Kissing is a sign of respect and reverence, and both of these books have God's name in them.

Is it kosher to chew gum in the sanctuary?

Chewing gum is rather disrespectful to the words of the siddur (prayer book), and chomping on gum just doesn't look nice in the sanctuary. Many of my colleagues would agree with me and say that it would be better not to chew gum while praying. Eating food in a sanctuary is strictly forbidden.

Is it kosher to arrive late to services?

Many people do, some because they choose to and others because they live a substantial distance from the synagogue. Coming to services on time is meritorious. However, latecomers are permitted to make up the prayers that have already been said by standing next to their seat and saying the missed prayers. This is perfectly kosher and done even in the most traditional synagogues.

What's kosher to do when your baby cries or your three-year-old begins to get cranky during services?

When a baby begins to cry and interrupts services, or a young child gets rowdy or cranky, the kosher thing to do would be to take the child out of the sanctuary until he or she is relaxed and ready to return. Some newer synagogues today have built a crying room in the sanctuary. People seated in this soundproof room can see and hear the rabbi and cantor, but congregants cannot hear them. I am not in favor of such rooms and see no need for them. A crying room isolates a family from the rest of the congregation and does not create the kind of warmth I like to see in a congregation. A parent who simply uses common sense when it comes to dealing with a child's unruly behavior will likely be doing the kosher thing.

❦ What's Not Kosher ❧

Is it kosher to talk while praying?

The Code of Jewish Law (Sanctity of the Synagogue, chap. 13:1) says that one must always act with reverence and refrain from conversing in the synagogue. In addition, "People should not act irreverently in a synagogue, as for example: senseless laughter, frivolous behavior, and meaningless chatter" (Code of Jewish Law, Orach Chayim 151:1).

Is it kosher to sleep in a synagogue?

Although it would be permissible to sleep in one of the synagogue rooms (Sabbath observers who are visiting a synagogue may do this because they do not use a car on the Sabbath), sleeping in the sanctuary is not kosher.

Is it kosher to save seats on the High Holy Days?

It is kosher to find oneself a regular seat when in the synagogue. Regular worshippers often tell me how good they feel knowing that they have found a comfortable place in the sanctuary that they return to each week in order to pray.

But saving a seat for someone is not really the proper thing to do. Many people get annoyed when people try to save seats on Rosh Hashanah or Yom Kippur. Some will leave a tallit (prayer shawl) on a seat the night before the holiday, to return to it only the next day.

My advice is that if you are interested in a certain seat (and your synagogue does not have reserved seating), you should arrive at the synagogue early enough to get the seat of your choice.

When is it not kosher to enter a synagogue sanctuary?

When the ark is open and people are standing, when people are reciting one of the standing prayers (such as the Amidah), or when the rabbi is speaking, entering the sanctuary is not kosher. Many synagogues will have ushers standing at the door who will tell people when they can and cannot enter.

❧ What the Experts Say ❦

Woe to the person who converses in the synagogue. Such a person demonstrates that he does not belong there. The person who comes to the synagogue early and leaves late merits a goodly portion. (Zohar 1:256a)

The person who does not enter a synagogue in this world will not enter a synagogue in the World to Come. (Jerusalem Talmud, Berachot 5:1)

A person carrying a Torah scroll should not vent his anger by pounding his fist on it or by striking someone with the scroll. (Sefer Hasidim, chap. 8:90)

It is considered entirely proper to clean the mud off of one's feet before entering a synagogue to pray. (Code of Jewish Law, Orach Chayim 151:8)

❧ Sources ❦

And my sanctuary you shall revere. (Leviticus 19:3)

It is forbidden to eat, drink, or sleep in places of worship, even if it is only a short nap. (Code of Jewish Law, Condensed Version, Laws of Sanctity and House of Study, chap. 13:4)

Topic 37

Tallit

❦ **What's Kosher** ❧

Is it ever kosher to wear a tallit at night?

The only permissible time to wear a tallit (prayer shawl) in the evening is at the Kol Nidre service of Yom Kippur. The reason is for added sanctity. At other times the tallit is permitted to be worn during the day only. It is customary for rabbis and cantors and those leading the services to wear a tallit, even at night.

At an Orthodox synagogue, I saw many teenage boys without a tallit. Is this kosher?

In Talmudic times only married men wore tallitot, and this was an indication of their marital status (Talmud, Kiddushin 29b). Today the practice of unmarried men wearing tallitot varies with the community. In many Orthodox synagogues, especially those that follow the Polish or Polish-Sephardic rites, an unmarried man does not wear a tallit. However, when leading the congregation in prayer and when being honored with an *aliyah* (ascending to the Torah to recite blessings), all men wear a tallit.

Is it kosher for a woman to wear a tallit?

Wearing a tallit is one of those religious obligations from which Jewish law exempts women. The exemption was made because the woman's obligation is considered to be to the home and family. Because the tallit must be worn during daylight hours at a specific time, the wearing of a tallit is not incumbent on women.

This being said, we do know of women who wore them in Talmudic times. Today almost all Conservative, Reform, and Reconstructionist synagogues permit women to wear a tallit. Some modern Orthodox ones do as well.

Is it kosher to bury a person in his tallit?

Jewish law requires a man to be buried in his tallit. However, one of the fringes is torn off so as to render the tallit invalid. The law was enacted to make the symbolic point that the obligations of Jewish law are no longer required of a person who is deceased. In more liberal settings, women who had customarily worn a tallit are also buried in theirs.

I've seen people praying with their tallit over their head. Is this kosher?

Yes, it is perfectly kosher to drape a tallit over one's head. Supposedly this helps with concentration and blocks out distractions.

My Orthodox cousin wears some sort of undergarment with fringes sticking out over his pants. Is this kosher?

Yes, it's called a small tallit or *tallit katan* and is perfectly permissible. Originally, fringes were attached to the four corners of the overgarment, as prescribed in Deuteronomy 22:12: "You shall place twisted cords on the four corners of your garment." When wearing such an overgarment all day became too cumbersome and inconvenient, and when styles changed and overgarments no longer always had four distinct corners, a lightweight undergarment that could be draped over the neck was used in its place, the *tallit katan*.

Is it ever kosher to kiss my tallit?

Yes, after reciting the prayer shawl blessing, it is customary to kiss the neckband (called the *atara*) as a sign of reverence. In addition, there are several times during services when the custom is to kiss the ritual fringes. The most well-known time is during the third paragraph of the Shema (Numbers 15), where the word *tzitzit* (fringe) appears three times. Each time the word is recited, it is kosher to kiss the tzitzit.

What makes for a kosher tallit?

A tallit must have a neckband and four kosher tzitzit on its corners to be fit to wear. It may be made of linen, wool, or silk but may not contain both linen and wool, because of the prohibition of mixing fabrics in the same garment (Leviticus 19:18). The tzitzit must be of the same material as the tallit. The strand of blue (*techelet*) that was part of the tzitzit in ancient times is no longer required because the exact shade of the blue is no longer known, although some tzitzit being sold today have the blue thread, whose color the sellers claim is authentic.

What does one do with one's tallit if one has to go to the bathroom?

When going to the lavatory during morning prayer services, one is required to remove one's tallit, because taking it into the bathroom is disrespectful. One can simply leave the tallit at one's seat and put it back on when returning. Repeating the blessing again is not necessary.

❦ What's Not Kosher ❧

Does a tallit have to have stripes to be kosher?

A tallit does not have to have stripes at all to be kosher. Years ago most of the store-bought ones had stripes, usually black or blue in color. Today tallitot come in all colors and a variety of designs. Neckbands that traditionally used to have the blessing for wearing a tallit now commonly have a biblical verse or even a view of ancient Jerusalem sewn onto them. I have seen cantors wearing a tallit with a neckband whose words were *Shiru l'Adonai shir chadash*, sing to God a new song. As Jewish communities continue to encourage artisans to handcraft all kinds of ritual items and garments, the array of prayer shawl designs expands too.

Is it kosher to use a tallit with a defective or missing fringe? What does one do with the torn fringe?

To be kosher a tallit must have four kosher fringes (with the proper numbers of double knots and coils). If one of the fringes is missing, it is no longer kosher to be worn. One may replace the missing or defective fringe with another kosher one.

According to the Code of Jewish Law (Laws of Fringes 9:19), even a fringe that has fallen off or has been removed ought not to be thrown into the rubbish heap, because one slights thereby a divine commandment. Some people are strict about discarded fringes and place them in a book to serve as a bookmark, because, having used them to perform a precept, performing another with them is only proper.

A man in my synagogue put on tefillin before his tallit. Is this kosher?

According to the rabbis, a tallit is always put on before tefillin because it is worn every day of the year, whereas tefillin are not worn on the Sabbath and festivals.

❧ What the Experts Say ❧

I wrap myself in a tallit with fringes to fulfill the mitzvah of my Creator, as written in the Torah: "They shall put fringes on the corners of their garments in every generation." (Meditation before donning a tallit)

How does the mere act of looking upon tzitzit serve to remind one of God's commandments? I suggest that it's like a uniform worn by soldiers in the army. When wearing a uniform, one is especially mindful to whom one owes one's allegiance. (Rabbi Hayim Donin, *To Pray as a Jew*, p. 155)

Have mercy on us and rebuild Your city speedily in our days, and return us to peace in our holy land, and let us merit the return and revelation of the *hilazon* [mollusk], that we may be privileged to fulfill the commandment of *techelet* [blue] in the fringes. (Prayer book of Rabbi Nachman of Bratslav)

❦ Source ❧

God said to Moses: Instruct the people of Israel that in every generation they shall put fringes on the corners of their garments and bind a thread of blue to the fringe of each corner. Looking upon it, you will always be reminded of all the mitzvot of God and fulfill them and not be led astray by your eyes. Then you will remember and observe all of my mitzvot and be holy before your God. (Numbers 15:37–40)

Topic 38

Teacher-Student Relationships

❧ **What's Kosher** ❧

Is it kosher for a student to speak up when the teacher appears to be showing favoritism?

Because Jewish tradition emphasizes the respect that a student must show his or her teacher, the rabbis were concerned that students would hold their tongues when they saw their teacher judge a case and favor one side. Thus, the Talmud felt compelled to warn students that when such a matter occurs, the Torah mandates that they speak up. If a student were to remain silent and not speak up, he or she might be committing an offense greater than the teacher's, because the teacher's error is probably innocent, whereas the student's silence is not.

When I was in rabbinical school, a teacher asked a classmate of mine to answer a question during a Bible lesson. The student was unable to do so. Obviously upset and angry, the teacher asked him to leave the room and come back next time better prepared. After class several students (who felt that the teacher wrongly embarrassed the student) approached the teacher, asking to have a meeting concerning what had happened to the student he had expelled from class. The professor eventually apologized.

Is there a kosher way to study?

The Ethics of the Fathers (1:6) suggests that a person get himself a study partner with whom to learn and study. Called *hevruta* learning (from the Hebrew word *haver*, "friend"), the idea was that studying with a friend is a way to build a friendship while at the same time gaining deeper insights into the texts.

"As one piece of iron sharpens another, so do two students sharpen each other when they study together" (Talmud, Taanit 7a).

Is it ever kosher for a teacher to give one student a test that differs from all the other students'?

If there is a valid reason for doing so, Judaism would not only commend but require a teacher to give a particular student a test that was different from the one given to the others in the class. "Educate a child according to his way," the book of Proverbs (22:6) teaches. In other words, each child is unique and ought to be taught in a manner that best recognizes and values that way.

Centuries ago Maimonides recognized the individual differences among students, which led him to employ different methods of motivation for different students. By the same token, because some students express themselves well in written work and others orally, a student whose oral skills are better than his written skills would be at a disadvantage when taking a written exam.

A few years ago I had a student with several learning disabilities. In a class requiring a final project with lots of choices and possibilities, I spoke to his parents to get their advice on the best choice of project for this particular student. In the end the student presented his final project—a musical masterpiece.

Is it kosher to socialize with one's teacher?

"To eat a meal where a great teacher is present is to feast upon the radiance of the Divine Presence" (Talmud, Berachot 64a). The answer to this question depends on the situation. In bygone years it was customary for teachers to invite older students to their homes to share meals and camaraderie. When I was an undergraduate student at the seminary, it was common to get an invitation to a Shabbat meal by a different professor each week. It was wonderful to get to know a teacher on a more personal basis and to ask him questions that one would not normally be able to do in class.

However, teachers who choose to invite high school or elementary students to their homes need to be careful of potential suspicion of impropriety. There have been all too many cases in recent years of teachers having inappropriate sexual relations with their students.

Are there any special teaching techniques that are considered to be kosher?

Rabbinic consensus considered a teacher the most exalted person in a student's life, worthy of even greater honor than that given to a parent. Not surprisingly, they had many ideas about teaching methodologies, some of which sound progressive even today. Here is a brief summary of the techniques that were intended to make for kosher learning. I still try to use all of them when I teach my students.

Take into account a student's mood. Rabbah would begin his lesson by first putting his students into a joyous, cheerful mood (Talmud, Pesachim 117a).

Teach interesting material. Rabbi said: One should always study that part of the Torah to which a student's interest draws him. (Talmud, Avodah Zarah 19a)

Seat students together. If a student is inattentive, it's best to put that student next to a diligent one. (Talmud, Baba Batra 21a)

Repeat the teaching. A teacher must not become angry with his students if they do not understand him, but must repeat his explanation as many times as necessary until they do understand. (Code of Jewish Law, Yoreh Deah 246:10)

Be dramatic. Rabbi was once lecturing when he noticed that his audience was falling asleep. Searching for ways to arouse them, he suddenly called out, "A woman in Egypt gave birth to six hundred thousand children all at once."

One student, Rabbi Ishmael ben Yose, stirred out of his boredom, asked, "Who could that be?"

Rabbi said loudly: "It was Yocheved, when she gave birth to Moses, because he is equal to six hundred thousand people." (Song of Songs Rabbah 1:65)

ℱ What's Not Kosher ℜ

Is it kosher for a student to call his teacher by his first name?

Maimonides, the great medieval philosopher and educator, did not permit a student to call his teacher by his first name. Doing so was considered disrespectful. To show a teacher proper respect, the custom in those days was for the student to bow to his teacher and say, "Peace be unto you, my master and teacher." A student was also never permitted to sit down nor stand up in his teacher's presence unless so instructed and permitted. And when leaving the presence of the teacher, the student was never to turn his back but step backward while facing his master. The student was also required to rise at the sight of his teacher. In some rabbinical schools today, rising when a teacher walks into the classroom is still the custom.

Nowadays it is still the norm for students to call their teachers by their last names. My own students who feel particularly close to me have chosen to call me Rabbi Ron. I'm happy that they do!

Is it kosher to be bashful in class?

Jewish tradition generally regards shyness as a positive trait but not when it comes to classroom learning and study. Ethics of the Fathers (2:6) teaches: "A bashful student, one too unassertive to ask questions, will always remain ignorant."

For Jews, asking questions is a national pastime, with the great sages asking every conceivable question about every conceivable topic. Students whose nature is generally passive must try to learn to ask more questions, even challenging their teacher on occasion. So when you have a question, don't be afraid to ask it.

Is it kosher for an angry teacher to teach?

A kosher teacher is one who displays patience, self-control, and respect in his or her classroom. Being angry and having a bad temper would disqualify one from being a Jewish educator.

Often, if students do not understand a concept and have a bad-tempered teacher, they will be afraid to ask a question, fearing that they will be mocked or yelled at.

Maimonides recommends that a teacher never shout or scream when speaking. Instead, the teacher should talk gently, give a friendly greeting, and always dwell on the merits of his students, without ever disparaging them (Mishneh Torah, Laws of Study 5:7).

The following Talmudic statement underscores the unpleasant consequences of studying with an ill-tempered teacher: "If you find a student who has difficulty with his studies, attribute it to his teacher's failure to show a pleasant countenance" (Taanit 8a).

✶ What the Experts Say ✶

The Teacher

The easily angered person cannot teach. (Ethics of the Fathers 2:5)

Rabbi Perida had a student with whom he found it necessary to rehearse a lesson many times before the latter comprehended it. One day the rabbi was hurriedly called away to perform a charitable act. Before he departed, however, he repeated the lesson at hand the usual number of times, but, on this occasion, his student failed to learn it.

"Why is it, my son," asked Rabbi Perida, "that the repetitions this time have been thrown away?"

The student answered: "Because, Master, my mind was so pre-occupied with the summons you received to discharge another duty."

"Well, then," said the Rabbi, "let us begin again."

And he repeated the lesson again the usual number of times. [Rabbi Perida was rewarded with a long life.] (Talmud, Eruvin 54b)

A teacher must be conscientious in his work. A teacher who leaves his students and goes out of the room or engages in other work while in their presence or shows carelessness in teaching comes under the ban of the Prophet Jeremiah: "Cursed be the one who does the work of God deceitfully" [48:10]. (Maimonides, Mishneh Torah, Laws of Torah Study 2:3)

The Ark was overlaid with gold from within and from without, so too the teacher's inner and outer self should be consistent. (Talmud, Yoma 72b)

If a teacher is incompetent, his words seem to the students as harsh as falling rain. If the teacher is competent, his teaching is distilled gently like dew. (Talmud, Taanit 7a)

If the teacher taught and his students did not understand, he should not be angry with them or fall into a rage, but should repeat the lesson again and again until they have grasped the full meaning of the rule he is expounding. (Maimonides, Mishneh Torah, Book of Knowledge, Laws of Study 4:4)

The Student

One who teaches a child, it is as if he had created it. (Talmud, Sanhedrin 19b)

No teacher should be appointed for the young unless that teacher is a God-fearing person and possesses the qualities to teach accurately. (Code of Jewish Law, Yoreh Deah 245:17)

❦ Sources ❧

A person should always live in the same town as his or her teacher. (Talmud, Berachot 8a)

All kinds of service that a servant must render to his master, a student must render to his teacher, except that of taking off his shoes. (Talmud, Ketubot 96a)

Whoever contends against the ruling of a teacher, it is as though that person contended with the Divine Presence. Whoever expresses resentment against one's teacher, it is as though one expressed it against the Divine Presence. (Talmud, Sanhedrin 110a)

A student is required to pay his respects to his teacher on festival days. (Talmud, Sukkah 27b)

The Bible says: "And you shall honor." This means, one shall not stand in one's teacher's regular place, nor sit in his regular place, nor contradict his statements. When one asks one's teacher a law, one must do so with reverence. One must not be quick in replying to one's teacher, nor interrupt his words. For whoever does not observe the marks of respect toward one's teacher is deemed a wicked person before God. (Numbers Rabbah 15:17)

Topic 39

✿ ✿

Tefillin

✿ What's Kosher ✿

I once saw a person don tefillin and wear them on his right arm rather than his left. Is this kosher?

According to rabbinic consensus, right-handed people wear the hand *tefila* on the left hand, and left-handed people wear it on the right hand. According to one interpretation, the practice is based on a reading of the Hebrew word *yadcha*, meaning "your hand," which appears in the verse "you shall bind them for a sign on your hand" (Deuteronomy 6:8). If the Hebrew letter *hey* is added to the end of the word *yadcha*, the word can then be pronounced *yad kayheh*, meaning "the weaker hand." According to this interpretation, the hand part of the tefillin is to be wrapped around the weaker hand—the left hand of a right-handed person, the right hand of a left-handed person.

Is it kosher to wear tefillin on the intermediate days of a Jewish festival?

Some Jews, particularly Hasidim and Sephardim, believe that the intermediate days of a festival are holy and hence must be observed fully. Accordingly, as on other holidays, they do not put on tefillin on these days. Other Jews choose to wear tefillin on these days, because there are no work restrictions.

Is it kosher for women to wear tefillin?

As with the tallit, Jewish law exempts women from performing rituals that must be carried out at a specific time of the day. Because tefillin are worn during the morning service, women are free from this obligation. We do know, however, that some women in Talmudic times, such as Michal, daughter of King Saul, wore tefillin. Today many observant women in the Conservative branch have chosen to wear tefillin. I have also seen modern Orthodox women wearing them, and surely some Reform and Reconstructionist women do so as well.

When is the kosher time for a boy to begin to wear tefillin?

Usually, boys are trained to start wearing tefillin one to two months before their thirteenth Hebrew birthday. During the training period, boys don tefillin but do not recite the blessing.

A pair of tefillin were for sale in a Judaica shop for $750 and another for $200. Is this kosher?

Tefillin are made of leather by hand and are expensive to make. The difference between a $200 pair and one selling for much more has to do with the quality and size of the parchment; the beauty of the scribe's Hebrew calligraphy; and the quality, thickness, and durability of the leather. With a more expensive pair of tefillin, each of the boxes is made of one single piece of leather; less expensive ones have the box cojoined to its base. Both, however, are kosher for use.

⚡ What's Not Kosher ⚡

Is it kosher to wear tefillin without ever having them checked?

Every few years a person is required to have a qualified scribe check his tefillin, to be certain that the parchment in the tefillin boxes bears no defects. People often choose the weeks before the new year, Rosh Hashanah, as a time to do the checking.

A man came to our synagogue on Shabbat and donned tefillin. Is this kosher?

Tefillin are never to be worn on the Sabbath or on a Jewish festival. According to the rabbis, tefillin are worn as a sign of one's willingness to affirm God's presence and power. Because the Sabbath and holidays in themselves are observed to indicate one's devotion to God, it is unnecessary and improper to wear tefillin on those days. Furthermore, if tefillin had to be worn on the Sabbath, a person might be tempted to carry them to synagogue; and carrying on the Sabbath is forbidden.

Is it kosher to translate the word *tefillin* as phylacteries?

I have never known a Jewish person who puts on tefillin to call them phylacteries. In the New Testament (Matthew 23:5), *phylacteries* is the word used for tefillin. The word, derived from the Greek *phylakterion*, means a "safeguard," and implies that tefillin are amulets. Although in early societies jewelry and other objects were worn on the head, hands, and arms to protect against evil spirits, there is no evidence that this ever applied to the wearing of tefillin. Therefore, better to translate tefillin as tefillin.

Is it kosher to sit while putting on tefillin? And what is the kosher order for putting them on?

No, the Code of Jewish Law requires a person to stand when donning tefillin. One must not shake the tefillin out of the bag, because that is considered an act of contempt toward a mitzvah. Rather, one must gently take them out by hand. First, the hand tefillin (*tefillin shel yad*) is placed on the arm, wrapped seven times, and the benediction recited. Next, the head tefillin (*tefillin shel rosh*) is placed on the head and the blessing recited. Then, in the final stage, one makes three coils on the middle finger, one around the middle finger joint and two around the lower finger joint. The remainder is then wound around the palm. When this is properly done, the three Hebrew letters (*shin, dalet, yud*) spelling the word *Shaddai* will be seen on the hand. When the tefillin are taken off, the order is reversed.

❧ What the Experts Say ☙

I put on tefillin to fulfill the mitzvah of my Creator, as written in the Torah: "Bind them as a sign on your hand, and set them as a symbol above your eyes." The tefillin contain four passages from the Torah. They teach us the unity and uniqueness of God, recall the miracle of the Exodus, declare God's dominion over all that is in the heavens and on earth and affirm our duty to serve God with all our being. We place one tefillah on the arm, pointed toward the heart, that we may recall God's outstretched arm and be reminded to direct our impulses and desires to His service. We place the other tefillah on the head to remind us of the duty to devote all the power of our mind to the service of God, Blessed be the One. (Meditation before putting on tefillin)

Rabbi Nachman bar Yitzchak asked Rabbi Chiyya bar Avin: "What is written in the tefillin of the Master of the World?" Rabbi Chiyya answered that God's tefillin contains the verse "Who is like Your people, a nation singular on earth?'" (Talmud, Berachot 6a)

❧ Source ☙

And it shall serve as a sign on your hand and as a reminder on your forehead—in order that the teachings of Adonai may be in your mouth—that with a mighty hand Adonai freed you from Egypt. (Exodus 13:9)

Topic 40

❧ ❦

Torah Reading

❧ What's Kosher ❦

Is there a kosher way of approaching the Torah when going up for an *aliyah*?

Judaism says, "hasten to perform a mitzvah" (Ethics of the Fathers 4:2). Therefore, one should always approach the Torah by the shorter way and leave by the longer one to indicate one's eagerness for the Torah and one's reluctance to leave it. If the approach and the descent are of equal distance, one should ascend on the right and descend on the left (Code of Jewish Law, Orach Chayim 141:7). This is reminiscent of practice in the Jerusalem Temple, where the ascent to the altar was from the right side and the descent from the left (Talmud, Zevachim 63a). Also, the entrance to the Temple was on the right side.

In more traditional synagogues there is a custom of people descending the pulpit backward so as not to turn their back on the ark — like exiting from an audience with a king.

Is there a kosher procedure for reciting the Torah blessings for an *aliyah*?

Yes. Before the first Torah blessing is recited, the *gabbai* (ritual assistant) removes the mantle from the Torah scroll. The person having an *aliyah* then grasps the two handles of the scroll and opens it, and the reader, using the pointer, indicates the place to be read. *Aliyah* honorees who are wearing a tallit (that is, all male honorees and females who have adopted the practice) now touch the fringes to the place indicated and kiss them. Females who do not wear a tallit may use a prayer book or the Torah belt to touch the scroll for the same purpose.

The honoree should grasp the scroll handles while reciting the blessing. During the Torah reading, the honoree steps aside to make room for the reader but continues to hold one handle of the scroll. After the honoree recites the second Torah blessing, it is customary for him or her to move to the side of the reading table and remain there until the completion of the next *aliyah*. Staying near the Torah is considered an act of respect.

If the cantor finds an error in one of the words while reading the Torah, what is the kosher thing for him to do?

If an error is discovered during the Torah reading, another scroll should immediately be taken from the ark and used for completing the prescribed reading. If no other Torah scroll is available, the reading is completed in the first scroll and the required number of people are still called up. Authorities differ as to whether Torah blessings should be recited in such a case. Each congregational rabbi generally is entrusted to make this important decision.

The Torah reader never showed up at a morning service in a synagogue. A layperson read the Torah portion using a *Humash* (Bible). Is this kosher?

Because no Torah reading was present, it was perfectly correct to have someone read from a printed Bible while someone followed in the Torah scroll itself. In such a case, though, the usual custom is not to have the Torah blessings recited.

What are the kosher occasions on which the Torah is read?

The Torah is read on all Sabbaths, the three pilgrimage festivals (Sukkot, Passover, and Shavuot), the High Holy Days (Rosh Hashanah and Yom Kippur), Rosh Chodesh (new Jewish month), Hanukkah, and Purim. It is also read on fast days, including the ninth of Av, the seventeenth of Tammuz, and the Fast of Gedaliah. Finally, the Torah is also read on Mondays and Thursdays, which were traditional market days in bygone years.

Is there a kosher order of preference for persons entitled to an *aliyah*?

Generally speaking, when there is a Bar/Bat Mitzvah, congregations will afford most if not all of their Torah honors to the family of the Bar/Bat Mitzvah. Here is the kosher order of preference for persons entitled to an *aliyah*:

1. Bridegroom and bride
2. Bar/Bat Mitzvah
3. Parents naming a baby
4. Bridegroom on the Sabbath after his wedding
5. Father of a baby girl to be named
6. Person commemorating a *yahrzeit* (anniversary of a person's death)
7. Father of a baby to be circumcised on that day or during the coming week
8. One observing a *yahrzeit* for one's parents during the coming week
9. One who has to recite the blessing of *gomel* (blessing of gratitude traditionally recited after recovering from a serious illness or safe return after a long trip)
10. One who is about to leave on a journey or has just returned from one
11. A distinguished guest in the community
12. Person rising from a shivah (seven days of mourning)

Traditionally, it is kosher to reserve the third and sixth *aliyot* for persons of great learning and piety, as is the *aliyah* that concludes each of the Five Books of the Torah. These aliyot were considered lucky and more prestigious.

Is there a kosher phrase to say to someone who has returned to his seat after having an *aliyah*?

Shaking one's hand is the civil custom, whereas the Jewish custom would be to say to the person *"yasher koach,"* which essentially means "well done!"

Is it kosher to add additional *aliyot* to the traditional number that are given on any Torah reading day?

The number of *aliyot* is fixed on all occasions, except the Sabbath, when the number may be increased. Today this is discouraged in many synagogues lest we prolong the service.

Must a *kohen* be given the first *aliyah*? If one is not in attendance, is it kosher to give the honor to someone else?

Jewish law mandates that a *kohen* (Jewish priest) be called for the first *aliyah*, a Levite for the second, and an Israelite for the third and succeeding prescribed *aliyot*. The Talmud (Gittin 59a) comments that this order is "for the sake of peace." If no Levite is present, the *kohen* often takes the second *aliyah* as well, especially in more traditional synagogues. If no *kohen* is present, a person who is not a *kohen* may be called. A Levite would be the first choice to substitute for a *kohen*.

In more liberal Jewish settings, the stringent rules related to *aliyah* preference are often waived, and there is little concern over who gets which *aliyah*.

Is it kosher for a person to recite the Torah blessings using a phonetic card with English translation?

Most congregations have such a card on the lectern, next to the Torah. There is no problem with reciting the blessings in Hebrew using this card. The card with phonetics allows a non-Hebrew reader to participate in this very important honor.

If a person is called to the Torah in one synagogue and offered an *aliyah* at another synagogue the same day, is it kosher for him to accept?

Yes, it is perfectly kosher for a person to receive two *aliyot* on the same day. This happened to a member of my congregation who went "*shule* hopping" in Jerusalem on Shabbat, visiting four different synagogues for morning Sabbath services. Two congregations took notice that he was a tourist, and each gave him an *aliyah*.

❧ What's Not Kosher ❧

During the Torah reading an entire family went up for an *aliyah* and recited the blessings. Is this kosher?

Jewish law mandates that one individual is entitled to one *aliyah*. Some Conservative rabbis will permit two persons to take an *aliyah* but seldom more. The custom of a two-person *aliyah* is quite common at a service to celebrate a Bar/Bat Mitzvah. Here Torah honors are limited, and a family will surely wish to include more of its relatives. In Reform settings, where the rabbi has a great deal of personal autonomy, it is entirely possible that more than two persons may be seen reciting the Torah blessings for an *aliyah*.

The only time that Jewish custom encourages a so-called group *aliyah* would be on the holiday of Simchat Torah, when even in traditional settings all children would be called to the Torah as a group, often standing under a large tallit draped over their heads.

Is it kosher for a non-Jew to go up to the Torah for an *aliyah*?

Only Jewish adults (age thirteen and over) have the obligation and privilege of ascending the *bimah* (raised platform) to recite Torah blessings. Because a non-Jew is not obligated, it would be nonkosher to offer an *aliyah* to him or her.

In liberal Jewish settings with a great deal of personal autonomy, some rabbis do permit an interfaith couple to have a joint *aliyah*.

An Israeli visiting the United States is offered a Torah honor on the second day of Shavuot. Is it kosher for him to accept?

Because the Israeli is attending synagogue on a day when he would not be normally observing a festival in his own country (Israel observes only one festival day for Shavuot), the Code of Jewish Law says that he should not be called up to the Torah (Kitzur Shulchan Aruch, Laws of Reading the Torah, chap. 23).

⌇ What the Experts Say ⌇

It is a tree of life [that is, the Torah] to those who hold fast to it, and all of its supporters are happy. (Proverbs 3:18)

Torah is illumination. (Proverbs 6:23)

The person called for an *aliyah* should wear a tallit. (Orach Chayim 14:3)

The Torah should be publicly read on Mondays, Thursdays and Saturdays. (Talmud, Baba Kamma 82a)

Both the one called up and the Reader must stand while the Torah is read. A feeble person is permitted to lean slightly, if necessary. (Kitzur Shulchan Aruch, Laws of Reading the Torah, chap. 23)

⌇ Source ⌇

The scroll is opened and one who is called up for an *aliyah* looks at the passage to be read, and taking hold of two handles, he closes his eyes and says *Barechu et Adonai ha-mevorach* [Praised is God who is to be praised]. (Kitzur Shulchan Aruch, Laws of Reading the Torah, chap. 23)

Topic 41

❧ ❧

Torah Study

❧ **What's Kosher** ❧

What is the kosher time to study Torah?

Although there is not one proper time for Torah study, it is proper according to the Code of Jewish Law (Laws of Torah Study 27:1) to set a fixed time to study Torah and keep to that schedule. One is also advised that if he has a very important business transaction, he should first study at least one verse of Torah or one law and then attend to his business affairs.

Many traditional synagogues have a Torah study session immediately following daily worship services. Shabbat and festivals are also especially good times to engage in Torah study. Many synagogues and Jewish communities have formed weekly Torah study groups in which people come together and learn Jewish texts. In the professional world, it is not uncommon to find Jewish men and women engaged in Torah study during their lunch hours—often called Lunch and Learns.

What is the kosher age to begin studies?

Jewish law says the younger the better. There are more Judaic preschools in the United States and Canada than ever before in the history of these two countries.

And it is never too late to begin Torah studies if one did not begin as a child. The great Rabbi Akiva did not begin his studies until age forty! According to him (Mishneh Torah, Laws of Study 1:10), one is obligated to study until his or her death.

One student in my Hebrew school class did almost nothing but ask questions during the whole class. Is this kosher?

Although it is not kosher to manipulate the class such that no one else gets a chance to be heard, it is entirely kosher for students to ask questions. In fact, Ethics of the Fathers (2:5) cautioned that "one who is bashful will never learn." The rabbis had no desire to belittle shy people. They were noting, however, that being overly passive and not asking questions will limit one in terms of the depth of one's knowledge.

Is it kosher for children and their parents to study together?

Very much so. Jewish law instructs parents to be the purveyors of Jewish information and knowledge for their children. In recent years more and more opportunities are being provided for parents and children to learn and study together. Rabbi Menachem Mendel of Kotzk once advised parents who want their children to study: "If you truly want your children to study Torah, study it yourself in their presence. They will then follow your example." Parents who do choose to study with their children will provide them with outstanding role modeling.

What are some kosher guidelines for studying Torah?

Among the many are these ten pieces of advice, culled from a variety of Jewish sources:

- Fix a set time for Torah study, and do not wait for free time in order to study.
- Do not use your study for purposes of deriving a profit from it.
- Study for the sake of putting your study into action.
- Always study with a study partner.
- Study with a desire to transmit your knowledge to others.

- Never think you have mastered it all.
- Be an active class participant and ask questions.
- Never retire from studying.
- Do not boast of your learning.
- Never misquote things that you have learned.

Is it ever kosher to study alone, without a partner?

Even though studying with a partner is always preferred, Sefer Hasidim 3:18 advises that a student should study alone if any of the following apply: a student has a teacher or study partner who is arrogant and will not concede his errors; the teacher is short-tempered, and the student is afraid of being punished if he does not know the answer to a question; or the teacher is unqualified.

Two brothers must complete a project that either can carry out while the other can devote his time to Torah study. What's the kosher way to decide who will do what?

According to Sefer Hasidim 3:19, if one has a poor memory and cannot retain information and the other has a good memory, then the forgetful one should stay on the job. But if the one with the good memory is a loafer and the forgetful one a dynamic fellow, then the man of action should study Torah.

❦ What's Not Kosher ❧

Is it kosher after studying a book of the Bible and mastering it never to return to studying it again?

One should never think that one has mastered any Jewish text, and therefore constant review and reexamination is in order. So committed is the Talmud to the significance of review that the rabbis say: "He who repeats what he has learned one hundred times cannot be compared to he who repeats what he has learned one hundred and one times" (Talmud, Hagigah 9b).

If one is interested in more esoteric Talmudic material, is it kosher to study the more esoteric before laws that have more practical application?

Most rabbis would advise that one should begin one's study with a tractate that deals with laws that have practical application in daily life rather than one that is less relevant and has less application to everyday things. The idea here is that one is required to put one's study into action, something one is more likely to be able to accomplish by studying the more relevant tractate.

❧ What the Experts Say ☙

Turn it [the Torah] over and over, for one can find everything in it. (Ethics of the Fathers 5:22)

Without sustenance, there can be no Torah. And if there is no Torah, there can be no sustenance. (Ethics of the Fathers 3:21)

The world stands on three things: on Torah, worship and deeds of kindness. (Ethics of the Fathers 1:2)

Make your home a regular meeting place for scholars. (Ethics of the Fathers 1:4)

One who has acquired Torah has acquired eternal life. (Ethics of the Fathers 2:8)

A person who uses Torah for personal gain perishes. (Ethics of the Fathers 4:7)

When you rise from study, ponder carefully what you have learned. See what there is in that which you learned which you can put into practice. (Letter of Nachmanides)

A foolish student will say, "Who can possibly learn the whole Torah?" A wise student will say, "I will learn two laws today, and two tomorrow, until I have mastered the whole Torah." (Song of Songs Rabbah 5:11)

Words of Torah are forgotten only through inattention. (Talmud, Taanit 7b)

Do not say when I have leisure, I will study. You may never have the leisure. (Ethics of the Fathers 2:4)

Torah is acquired through forty-eight virtues: by study, by attentiveness, by orderly speech, by an understanding heart, by a perceptive heart, by awe, by fear, by humility, by joy, by ministering to sages, by cleaving to colleagues, by acute discussion with students, by calmness in study, by study of Scripture and Mishnah, by a minimum of business, by a minimum of sleep, by a minimum of small talk, by a minimum of worldly pleasure, by a minimum of frivolity, by patience, by a generous heart, by trust in sages, by acceptance of suffering, by knowing one's place, by contentment with one's lot, by guarding one's speech, by taking on personal credit, by being loved, by loving God, by loving all creatures, by loving charitable deeds, by loving rectitude, by loving reproof, by shunning honor, by not boasting of one's learning, by not delighting in rendering decisions, by sharing the burden with one's fellow, by influencing him to virtue, by setting him on the path of truth, by setting him on the path of peace, by concentrating on one's studies, by asking and answering questions, by absorbing knowledge and contributing to it, by studying in order to teach and perform mitzvot, by sharpening the wisdom of his teacher, by being precise in transmitting what he has learned, and by quoting his source. (Ethics of the Fathers 6:6)

If you truly wish your children to study Torah, study it yourself in their presence. They will follow your example. Otherwise, they will not themselves study Torah but will simply instruct their children to do so. (Rabbi Menachem Mendel of Kotzk)

At first the Torah is called "God's Torah." But after a student studies it, the Torah is called "one's own Torah." (Rashi on Kiddushin 32b)

✾ Sources ✾

These are the deeds that yield immediate fruit and continue to yield fruit in time to come: honoring parents; doing deeds of kindness; attending the house of study punctually, morning and evening; providing hospitality; visiting the sick; helping the needy bride; attending the dead; probing the meaning of prayer; making peace between one person and another, and between man and wife. And the study of Torah is the most basic of them all. (Mishnah, Peah 1)

Every Jewish person is required to study Torah, whether poor or rich, healthy or ailing, young or old and feeble. Even a beggar is under the obligation to study. . . . Until what period in life is one obligated to study? Until the day of one's death. (Maimonides, Mishneh Torah, Laws of Torah Study 1:10)

Topic 42

❦ ❦

Visiting the Sick

❦ What's Kosher ❦

Are there kosher preferred times for visiting the sick?

Regarding the appropriate time of day to visit, the Code of Jewish Law (335:4) specifies that "One must not visit the sick during the first three hours of the day—for every invalid's illness is alleviated in the morning, and consequently one will not be troubled to pray for him or her; and not during the last three hours of the day—for then the illness grows worse and one will give up hope to pray."

For therapeutic reasons hospital visiting hours are generally during the middle of the day and in the early evening. In the early morning the patient is likely to be sore and disheveled and might be confronting the prospect of emotionally or physically distressing treatment. In the evening pain tends to be worse. Therefore, the visitor is well advised to respect standard visiting hours, even after the patient is back home.

I like to make my hospital rounds in the early morning, when patients are not likely to have any other visitors. It gives me a chance to spend some quality time with the person in private; and because we are alone, it allows for deeper conversation and sometimes even prayer.

Is there a kosher amount of frequency and length of a visit?

Jewish tradition suggests frequent visits. Raba says, "One must visit even a hundred times a day, so long as the visitor does not trouble the sick person" (Talmud, Nedarim 39b). The rabbis were cognizant of both a patient's desire for visitors' attention and his or her right to privacy.

Whether in the hospital or at home, visits should be brief. It is better to visit several times or even frequently for brief periods than to spend one long period with a patient. If you are not sure about how long to stay, it's better to leave early. Often the patient will say, "It's nice that you've taken the time to come and visit." This is a good clue that it's time to leave.

Finally, if you visit in a hospital and find the patient asleep, leave a note to wish the patient well.

Is it kosher to pray in the patient's presence?

Jewish tradition says that prayer is an essential component of the mitzvah of *bikkur cholim* (visiting the sick). The Code of Jewish Law (335:4) teaches that one should pray either in the presence of the patient or elsewhere. By offering a prayer, we may stimulate hope and strength for the patient and help him or her release tension and worry.

Prayer is not necessarily what a patient may want. Therefore, my custom is to ask a patient whether he or she would like me to offer a prayer (or perhaps pray together) and only pray if the patient accepts the offer. I have also used *niggunim* (melodies without words) in my pastoring, which I have found to bring comfort to a patient.

When taking leave of a patient, the kosher thing to do is to wish that patient a *refuah shelayma*, a whole recovery. This short prayer asks God to bring healing and in my estimation conveys far more meaning than the usual "take care."

Is it kosher to touch the sick person?

Physical interaction is a critical component of healing. The wisdom of Rabbi Yochanan, who said to his friend Rabbi Elazar who was seriously ill "give me your hand," resulted in Rabbi Elezar being raised by him (that is, his spirits were lifted) (Talmud, Berachot 5b).

Modern therapeutics have confirmed the wisdom of giving a person one's hand. The touch of a friendly hand, the caress, the kiss of friendship can be a strong stimulus in well-being.

It is important to be judicious in touching a sick individual. Extending the palm of your hand, for example, rather than your fingers, affords a more secure grasp and tells the patient you are confident. Generally, a visitor will know when a patient is receptive to being touched. If in doubt, you can ask: "Would you like me to hold your hand?"

Should I sit or stand when visiting a person in the hospital? What's kosher?

Jewish tradition teaches that the Divine Presence hovers above the head of the sickbed (Zohar). The Code of Jewish Law (335:7) teaches its version of bedside manners. It instructs the visitor to sit reverently in front of the sick person, rather than on the bed, because sitting might obstruct the Divine Presence and create the impression that the visitor, not God, is the ultimate health provider. This advice implies that by sitting on the same plane, both visitor and patient are under God's protection.

When I visit a patient in the hospital, I always try to position myself so that the patient can easily see and hear me without strain. And I never sit on the bed.

Is it kosher to visit a person afflicted with Alzheimer's who doesn't even know who you are?

Yes, it certainly is right to take time to visit a person who has Alzheimer's disease. Though cut off from society, he or she is still a member of society, deserving of care and attention. The Talmud is very explicit in recognizing the dignity of persons with dementia: "Rabbi Joseph learned: This teaches us that both the tablets and the fragments of the tablets were deposited in the ark. Hence, we learn that a scholar who has forgotten his learning through no fault of his own must not be treated with disrespect" (Talmud, Menachot 99a).

When visiting an Alzheimer's patient, proceed in a calm and orderly manner. Be aware that there may be mood swings. so speak slowly and in simple language that is easy to comprehend. I have also been told that there are few patients for whom touch is more meaningful. Therefore, you may wish to brush the patient's hair or stroke the arm.

Is it kosher to visit a terminally ill person who is near death?

According to Jewish law, even a corpse must be attended to until it is buried, so it stands to reason that one must attend to a dying person alone and not abandon him or her in the last minutes of life. A number of times I have been in the hospital room when a person takes his last breath. Family members in the room have shared with me how comforting it was to have me there. If the family is present, ask whether they would prefer you to stay or go.

Is it kosher to visit persons in the hospital you do not know?

Bikkur cholim, visiting the ill, is a mitzvah for all Jews; and thus it is entirely proper to visit hospitalized people, even if you do not know them very well at all. Most synagogues and Jewish communities have *bikkur cholim* groups, where persons can sign up to make hospital visits on a rotating basis. I can honestly say, having asked members of my own synagogue's *bikkur cholim* group whether their visits to persons whom they don't know are appreciated, in almost all cases the answer is an unequivocal yes. The key is to be sensitive to the patient's desire for company or solitude.

❧ What's Not Kosher ❧

Is it kosher to visit someone in the hospital with no forewarning?

If you are planning to visit one who is sick, it's better to call him or her first, so that the person, who might be feeling lonely and a bit depressed, will have the added pleasure of anticipating the visit. It is also possible that the person might not be feeling up to any visitors; by calling in advance, you can get a heads-up on the situation.

One more reminder: the Talmud (Derech Eretz 5, 2) says: a person should not enter a house suddenly, without ringing or knocking. This is sound advice. Whenever I visit people in the hospital and see a door closed, I either knock or go to the nurses' station, asking them to check with a patient to request permission to visit. Asking permission shows respect and provides the patient a measure of control over his or her environment.

Is it kosher for you to visit someone you dislike who is ill?

Scholars differ about whether one should visit an enemy who falls sick. One argument against it is that one could create an impression of gloating over another's misfortune, thereby causing depression in the person being visited. In other words, if it is impossible to convey empathy and concern to a sick person, it might be best to stay away.

Is it kosher to offer theological explanations to a sick person you are visiting?

In general, Jewish tradition views negatively any attempt to speculate about whether God might have reasons for bringing suffering on a particular individual. The reason for this is that speculation is not directed toward healing. Thus, to suggest any reason for a patient's suffering is not helpful.

Although Judaism does have a goodly number of theological views concerning illness, the visit is not the appropriate time to discuss them. A kosher visit is one in which the visitor reaches out to the sick person, expressing concern and offering words of encouragement that urge striving for recovery.

Is it ever kosher not to visit a sick person?

Because Jewish law prohibits behavior that endangers one's own life, we are not encouraged to visit where direct contact would cause the visitor or the patient to become seriously ill. This is not to be construed as an excuse to avoid visiting but rather as a prevention against putting one's own life in danger.

Tradition also forbids a person to visit a person with a severe headache, because visiting might cause an intense strain (Code of Jewish Law, 335:8).

Finally, the Code of Jewish Law (Laws of Visiting the Sick 193: 10) forbids visits to persons with eye and bowel diseases. These were considered diseases that cause embarrassment to the afflicted person. A good rule of thumb to follow would be that if you think a patient would be embarrassed on account of his or her illness, it's better not to visit!

❧ What the Experts Say ❧

Visit the sick and lighten their suffering. Pray for them and leave. Do not stay long, for you may inflict upon them additional discomfort. And when you visit the sick, always enter the room cheerfully. (Rabbi Eliezer ben Yitzchak, *Orchot Chayim*)

It was once taught: There is no measure for visiting the sick. What does "no measure" mean? Rabbi Joseph explained: "It means that the rewards for doing so are unlimited." (Talmud, Nedarim 39b)

Even the great should visit the humble. If a poor man and a rich man fell ill at the same time, and many go to the rich man to pay him honor, they should also go to the poor man, even if the rich man is a scholar. (Sefer Hasidim chap. 35, par. 587)

A person should not visit his enemy during his illness, for the sick person might think that his enemy rejoices in his misfortune. (Code of Jewish Law, Condensed Version, chap. 193, sec. 1)

When Rabbi Judah visited the sick, he would say, "May the Almighty have compassion upon you and the sick of Israel." Rabbi Yose said, "May the Almighty have compassion upon you in the midst of the sick of Israel." (Talmud, Shabbat 12b)

Whoever visits a sick person helps the person to recover. (Talmud, Nedarim 40a)

Rav Shisha son of Rav Idi said: "One should not visit the sick during the first three or the last three hours of the day, lest he thereby omit to pray for him." During the first three hours of the day his [the invalid's] illness is alleviated; in the last three hours his sickness is strongest. (Talmud, Nedarim 40a)

Relatives and close friends should visit as soon as a person becomes ill. Others should visit after the first three days of illness. (Jerusalem Talmud, Peah 3:7)

❧ Source ❧

Visiting the sick is an act of kindness. (Talmud, Baba Metzia 30a)

Topic 43

❦ ❧

War

❦ What's Kosher ❧

Is it kosher for a Jew to be a conscientious objector?

Judaism does allow for conscientious objection to war. It finds warrant in the Bible (Deuteronomy 20), which lists exemptions for those who are too weak for military duty, interpreting weakness to include those who have no stomach for bloodshed. Those who are faint of heart and afraid of battle may return home, because they may cause general weakness to the morale of the other soldiers. Later in rabbinic literature, these rules seem to apply more to a nonobligatory war—that is, a war that is not for self-defense but for territorial expansion.

Are there any kosher guidelines relating to how to conduct a war?

Although warfare evidently was accepted as a Jewish fact of life, Jewish law placed significant restrictions on how a war was to be conducted. Often ambassadors were called to negotiate disputes in an attempt to avoid war (Judges 11:12–28; 1 Samuel 11:1–10). Israelites were always forbidden to attack unless they first issued a demand that the enemy surrender (Deuteronomy 20:10ff.). When the Israelites besieged a city, they were forbidden to cut down fruit trees (Deuteronomy 20:19–20). The Vietnam War was an example of deliberate wartime ecological destruction, with more than a half million acres of land in South Vietnam sprayed in order to deprive enemy troops of food. Maimonides said that when Jews go to war and lay siege to a city for the purpose of capture, the city may be surrounded only on three sides (not four), in order to give the enemy an opportunity to flee for their lives.

Though it was customary in the ancient Near East for triumphant armies to take prisoners, the Torah always insisted that Jewish soldiers show proper respect for the human feelings of women who became their captives (Deuteronomy 21:10–14). The rabbis even limited war by deeming it a violation to bear arms on the Sabbath, though later laws amended this law in special circumstances.

Were all Jews in bygone years obliged to participate in a war, or were there any kosher exemptions?

Not all Jews were obligated to participate in battle. The book of Deuteronomy (chap. 20) clearly exempts significant categories of men from the battlefield: one who has built a house but not moved into it (a newlywed); one who has planted a vineyard and not consumed its fruit; one who is betrothed but not yet married; or even one who is fearful and faint-hearted.

What is the kosher procedure regarding redemption of captives in war? Who has priority over whom?

Redeeming captives within Jewish tradition is an important responsibility. The Talmud tells us that community funds intended for other purposes could be used to pay ransoms. The rabbis also debated situations in which there was more than one captive and a choice had to be made as to whom to save first.

According to the Mishnah of Horayot 13a, when a man and a woman are exposed to moral degradation in their captivity, the man's ransom takes precedence over the woman's. If a man, his father, his mother, and his teacher were in captivity, the man takes precedence over his teacher; his teacher takes precedence over his father; and his mother takes precedence over all of them.

According to the rabbis, a scholar takes precedence over a king, for if a scholar dies, there is none to replace him, whereas if a king of Israel dies, all are eligible for kingship. A king takes precedence over a high priest, and a high priest takes precedence over a prophet.

Is the current war in Iraq a kosher war?

The ancient rabbis distinguished between two types of wars: *milchemet mitzvah*, a commanded or required war, and *milchemet reshut*, a permitted war. For example, Israel's strike to begin the Six Days' War really was a defensive effort against an aggressor, and therefore most authorities agree that it was required. Operation Iraqi Freedom does not clearly fit in this category.

Other wars, including those intended to stop another nation from unjustly expanding its boundaries, are merely permitted. Waging an optional war requires additional consultation, and the power to make such wars is limited.

An analysis of rabbinic opinion suggests that the strongest reason for waging an optional war is to weaken the power of a potential enemy that would otherwise be likely to attack. Some may even require such a war as close to a required war.

The modern rabbinic community must do its best to analyze what our national leaders tell us. And yet they emphasize that if the evidence truly does equal the arguments for making war in Iraq, if Hussein's regime was indeed building and stockpiling weapons of mass destruction, then there is also good reason to believe that this regime, which has compiled a record of aggression against other countries and its own citizens, continues to harbor aggressive intentions. It would therefore be kosher to judge Iraq to be a threat to peace and security, if not today or tomorrow then surely at some point in the realistically near future. Under these circumstances it would be kosher to view the U.S. attack on Iraq as a preemptive required war (which would be kosher) rather than as a permitted one.

❧ What's Not Kosher ❧

Is it ever kosher to humiliate an enemy?

Recently we witnessed incredible photographs of U.S. soldiers capturing and humiliating Iraqi fighters. For a soldier to humiliate the enemy is absolutely a violation of Jewish ethics. One of the Talmud's most famous stories (Gittin 55b-56a) concerns a man named Kamtza who had an enemy named Bar Kamtza; Kamtza was unexpectedly offered the opportunity either to reconcile or avenge himself on this man. Kamtza (humiliated by his host) ultimately chose revenge, and as a result the whole Jewish people suffered.

Is it kosher to go to war with an enemy before trying to make peace with it?

The Torah admonishes that "the people of Israel must first offer peace to their enemies, and attack only if these efforts are rebuffed" (Deuteronomy 20:10).

❧ What the Experts Say ❧

When siege is laid to a city for the purpose of capture, it may not be surrounded on all four sides, but only on three in order to give an opportunity for escape to those who would flee to save their lives. (Maimonides, Mishneh Torah 7:7)

When in your war against a city . . . you must not destroy its trees. You may eat of them, but must not cut them down. (Deuteronomy 20:19–20)

Conscientious objection to military service is in accordance with the highest interpretation of Judaism. (Resolution of the Central Conference of American Rabbis, 1936)

We recognize the right of the conscientious objector to claim exemption from military service in any war in which he cannot give his moral assent, and we pledge ourselves to support him in his determination to refrain from any participation in it. (Resolution of the Rabbinical Assembly of America, 1948)

The following do not move from their place to join the army: He who built a new house and dedicated it, planted a new vineyard and used its fruit, married his betrothed, or took home his brother's childless widow. (Mishnah, Sotah 8:4)

If someone comes to kill you, kill him first. (Talmud, Sanhedrin 72a)

Do not rejoice when your enemy falls in battle, and do not be glad when he is brought down. (Proverbs 24:17)

If your enemy is hungry, give him bread to eat, and water to drink when thirsty. (Proverbs 25:21)

Common soldiers advance and start the battle, but it is the experienced veterans who go down into the fray and are victorious. (Talmud, Berachot 53b)

A leader who does not stutter before he goes into battle is not a leader. (Golda Meir, commenting on Levi Eshkol's ineffectual speech shortly before the Six Days' War of 1967)

❧ Sources ❧

Nation shall not lift up sword against nation, neither shall they learn war anymore. (Isaiah 2:4)

Seek peace and pursue it. (Psalms 34:15)

One does not wage war, whether profane or holy, before one offers peace, as it is written: When you come near to a city to fight against it, then proclaim peace unto it. (Midrash, Leviticus Rabbah 9)

In a war of defense, everyone comes out to fight, even the groom from his chamber and the bride from her bed. (Talmud, Sotah 8:7)

Topic 44

❦ ❧

Witnesses

❦ What's Kosher ❧

Is it kosher to allow use of a polygraph in a Jewish court?

In recent years various rabbinic authorities have discussed and debated the role and acceptability of a polygraph (lie detector machine). Many have concluded that the court could rely on the polygraph under certain conditions, although never as a single piece of evidence on which to base a court decision.

I looked at my *ketubah* and noticed that only one witness signed, though the contract requires two witnesses' signatures. Is my marriage still kosher?

Although there are varying opinions as to whether a marriage is valid, many authorities would say, "yes, it is kosher," even though only one witness signed the *ketubah* (Jewish marriage contract). There are many examples in the Code of Jewish law when the testimony of one witness (instead of the required two) is valid, such as in cases when a monetary transaction is involved. Likewise, if a person is about to commit an illegal act, one witness may testify in order to prevent him from committing it.

Is it kosher for a person to witness a conversion by listening to the blessings recited on the phone?

According to some rabbis, the answer is yes. I once went to the *mikvah* (building for ritual bathing) for purposes of the conversion of two children. Three witnesses are required to serve as the Bet Din (the Jewish court of law) that is charged with witnessing the converts' immersion and signing the conversion documents. The cantor and I were two of the Bet Din members. The third, an Orthodox rabbi, was ill and called in to the *mikvah* to let us know he was not available to come in person. However, he said that he would sign the conversion documents if we brought a telephone into the *mikvah* area and allowed him to listen to the children recite the blessings.

For purposes of conversion (and divorce too), Jewish law requires three witnesses to sign their names to the document. However, the rabbis have always stated that in the case of an emergency, two will suffice.

✾ What's Not Kosher ✾

Is it kosher for women to serve as witnesses?

Traditional Jewish law disqualifies a woman from serving as a witness in a Jewish court. The rabbis give many reasons for this, but credibility was not one of them. Some felt that to require all women to testify at all times might very possibly contradict their private role in Jewish life, and they were excused from having to perform this duty. Others believed that Jewish law forbade women from testimony because in Talmudic times women owned no property and were supported totally by their husbands. Therefore, if a woman had been allowed to testify and her testimony proved accurate, damages could not be collected from her, as would be done in the case of a man who gave incorrect testimony. Moses Maimonides, in the Mishneh Torah, comments that when the Bible refers to witnesses (Deuteronomy 17:6), it uses the masculine form *edim* (witnesses), implying that only men can serve as witnesses.

Note that in Talmudic and later times women were called as witnesses in matters in which they were particularly knowledgeable, such as women's purity, and in cases in which a husband was missing and only a woman was available to offer testimony. In the thirteenth century Rabbi Meir of Rothenberg stated that if a man is murdered and his wife is the sole witness who can identify the body, and she testifies that a mole on the body of the corpse is identical to the mole of her husband's body, her testimony is accepted, and on that basis she can remarry.

In Reform, Reconstructionist, and Conservative Judaism, women have full equality. They may sign as witnesses on all religious documents.

What makes a witness nonkosher?

Biblical law disqualifies ten types of witnesses:

- Women, because they tend to allow their emotions to rule their judgment.
- Slaves, because they have not acquired the habit of thinking independently.
- Minors, because of their mental immaturity.
- Imbeciles, because they cannot think at all.
- Deaf-mutes, because they can neither hear the questions nor answer them clearly.
- The blind, because they could not have been "eyewitnesses" to any act or event.
- Relatives of the parties involved in the case, because their testimony would be biased.
- Those personally involved in the case, because their testimony would naturally be slanted in their own favor.
- A shameless person (for example, one who eats and drinks in the streets because of an uncontrollable lust for food). Such an insensitive individual cannot be expected to grasp the importance of telling the truth before a court of justice.
- A wicked person (one who is defiant, undisciplined, and not committed to religious observance). Thus, a compulsive gambler, a thief, or a usurer is not fit to testify in court. Some would even dis-

qualify a Jew who is not conversant in Torah and Talmud, for in the eyes of the sages, there was no excuse for ignorance.

A good rule of thumb today for choosing kosher witnesses is that they be pious, reliable, and of good repute.

Is it kosher to witness a crime and refuse to testify?

Because justice is the foundation of society, anyone who deliberately impedes justice according to Jewish law is guilty of perpetrating an act of injustice. This is based on the Bible verse "if a person sins and hears the voice of adjuration, he being a witness, whether he has seen or known of it, if he does not utter it, then he shall bear his iniquity" (Leviticus 5:1). Thus, if one who could give testimony that would help a court of justice come to a decision fails to do so, he or she has committed a sin.

As a rule, courts of justice under Jewish law require the testimony of two witnesses to establish a fact.

Can my best friend, who is not Jewish, serve as witness to the *ketubah* signing at my wedding?

A Jewish marriage requires two Jewish people to serve as witnesses. Therefore, it is not permissible to have a non-Jew be a witness at the *ketubah* signing.

❦ What the Experts Say ❧

One who has an ill feeling towards another will make every effort to bring his enemy down. He will even distort his testimony in order to hurt the other. But it is unlikely that two righteous witnesses will collude to perjure themselves. For this reason, the law requires two witnesses for conviction. (Hinnuch)

The testimony of a witness who accepts a reward for testifying is null and void. (Abridged Code of Jewish Law, Litigation and Testimony 181:4)

We have learned that Rabbi Shimon ben Shetach said: "I once saw a man running after his friend into a deserted area and I ran after him and found a sword in his hand and blood dripping and a man killed, and I said: 'Evil man, who killed this man, either you or I, but what can I do, for your life is not given into my hands, for behold the Torah said: "According to the statement of two or three witnesses shall the convicted one die" [Deuteronomy 17:6], but the Almighty will extract payment from you.'"

Before Rabbi Shimon left, a snake came and bit the man and he died. (Talmud, Shevuot 34a)

Be not a witness against your neighbor without cause. (Proverbs 24:28)

Examine the witnesses diligently, and be careful in your speech, lest from it they learn to die. (Ethics of the Fathers 1:9)

Whoever lends money without witnesses will weep in the end and none will heed him. (Talmud, Baba Metzia 75)

Since a witness has given his evidence, he cannot change it. (Talmud, Ketubot 18)

You cannot give evidence in your own favor. (Talmud, Ketubot 27)

❧ Sources ❧

A single witness may not validate against a person any guilt or blame for any offense that may be committed; a case can be valid only on the testimony of two or more witnesses. (Deuteronomy 19:15)

If a person sins and hears the voice of adjuration, he being a witness, whether he has seen or known of it, if he does not utter it, then he shall bear his iniquity. (Leviticus 5:1)

You shall not bear false witness against your neighbor. (Exodus 20:13)

Sources
of Jewish Law

Jewish law must be preserved but it is subject to interpreta-
tion by those who have mastered it and the interpretation
placed upon it by duly authorized masters in every genera-
tion must be accepted with as much reverence as those
which were given in previous generations.

Louis Finkelstein

I have chosen to conclude the book with a chapter that presents a
concise summary of the sources of Jewish law. I hope that you will
find that a better understanding of the source books of Jewish practice and their history will help you place the laws, customs, and traditions in their proper perspective.

May you always appreciate both the beauty and importance of
living a kosher life.

What is the earliest source of Jewish law?

The Torah, sometimes called the *Humash*, Pentateuch, or the Five
Books of Moses, is the earliest source of Jewish law. The Torah consists
of the books of Genesis, Exodus, Leviticus, Numbers, and Deuteronomy. Reverence for and acceptance of the Torah are the foundation of
Jewish law and its interpretation. Although the Torah does contain
guiding principles from which Jewish law and its interpretation spring,

it does not contain all of Jewish law. A parallel can be found by comparing the Torah to the United States Constitution. Although the Constitution is a relatively brief document, library shelves are filled with many thousands of volumes based on it. These books contain additional laws interpreted by the courts. Similarly, Jews look to the Torah as authoritative on many basic traditions but constantly seek the rabbinic interpretation of the law that followed in order to definitely learn how to live as authentic Jews.

What is the Talmud?

The Talmud is the major source for the rabbinic interpretation of the law. The Mishnah, which is part of the Talmud (sometimes called the Oral Law), sought to explain the laws as set forth in the Torah. For example, the Torah did not go into detail concerning the observance of the Sabbath. What did it mean that one should not work on the Sabbath? What is the definition of *work*? The Mishnah, consisting of the teachings of the *tanaaim*, scholars and sages who lived prior to 220 C.E., answered these and many other questions.

Judah HaNasi and his associates sifted through, evaluated, and edited a large number of legal opinions that had been expressed over the centuries in the learning academies. The product of their work was the Mishnah, a six-volume collection of legal opinions. It deals with topics from Jewish holidays and observing them to issues of what one does when one's ox wounds another's animal.

The Mishnah is divided into six sections or Orders, called *Sedarim*: (1) "Seeds," dealing with agricultural laws; (2) "Festivals," relating to the Sabbath and holidays; (3) "Women," including laws of marriage and divorce; (4) "Damages," which includes laws of inheritance, lost property, and usury; (5) "Holy Things," relating to laws of sacrifice and the Temple service; and (6) "Purities," laws pertaining to ritual cleanliness.

One of the Mishnah's sixty-three tractates contains no laws at all. It is one of my favorites, called Pirke Avot (Ethics of the Fathers), the Bartlett's of the rabbis, recording their most famous sayings and maxims. "If I am not for myself, who will be for me?" (1:4) is one of the most notable quotations in the book.

The Mishnah could neither encompass all the situations in any person's life nor cover new situations that were constantly developing. New situations and ambiguities in the Mishnah text often led to a discussion among the rabbis, and soon new rulings and decisions began to appear. Numerous life experiences, cases presented to the rabbis, and questions asked of them combined to expand and elaborate the Mishnah teachings. Scholars set these later teachings down in the Gemara, which was completed around 500 C.E. For the most part, these scholars lived in Babylonia, where the great academies were situated. The Mishnah and the Gemara together make up the Babylonian Talmud, the major compendium of the rabbis' discussions on Jewish law and the record of their decisions.

A second Talmud, the Palestinian or Jerusalem Talmud, was also composed. This one consists of all the discussions that took place among the scholars in the learning academies in Palestine. The Palestinian Talmud has always enjoyed a lesser status than the Babylonian Talmud because its academies were not equal in stature to those of Babylonia.

Because the Talmud is written in a mixture of Aramaic and Hebrew, it has remained inaccessible to the Jewish public. An incredible scholar by the name of Adin Steinsaltz has changed all of that. Within the next decade, he hopes to complete his modern commentary on the entire Talmud. In 1989 Random House began publishing his volumes of commentary, and they have sold very well.

For the first five hundred years following the final editing of the Talmud—from the years 500 to 1000 C.E., great scholars continued the process of interpreting the Bible. They also explained and commented on the Talmud and gained new insights from its teachings. This period is known as the gaonic period, and its scholars are called *geonim* (singular *gaon*, meaning "his eminence"). Among the better known *geonim* are Hai, Sherira, and Amram, each of whom headed a Babylonian learning academy. These scholars, as well as those who followed after them for approximately the next five centuries, until the midsixteenth century, were known as the *rishonim*, meaning "the early ones." In addition to analyzing and studying the Talmud, they wrote commentaries on it and answered questions that rabbis and teachers all over the world directed to them. Among the more celebrated scholars of the

postgaonic period (after the year 1000 C.E.) was Jacob Fez, known as
the Alfasi or the Rif; the French-born Solomon ben Yitzchak, better
known as Rashi; and Rabbi Moses ben Maimon of Spain, known as
Rambam or Maimonides.

What are the codes?

The Talmud never really served the Jewish people as a code of Jewish
traditions and rituals. The sea of Talmud was so vast that it was difficult for a person to locate all the specific references on any given subject. The situation led the rabbis to begin to codify the laws and set
them in order according to subject matter, so that one would be able
to find them more easily. Among the many famous codifiers was Maimonides (1135–1204). In his fourteen-volume code of law, called the
Mishneh Torah, Maimonides arranged in a methodical and logical
manner the established laws as set forth in the Talmud. The Mishneh
Torah is still studied today with great interest.

Other Jews also created their own codes of law. Rabbi Asher ben
Jechiel (1250–1320), the spiritual leader of the community of Toledo
in Spain, made an abstract of the material in the Talmud. His son,
Rabbi Jacob ben Asher, wrote another code, using a method similar
to that of Maimonides, arranging the laws by classification rather than
by location in the Talmud. He called his work Arba'ah Turim (The
Four Rows). This compendium of Jewish law consisted of four parts:

- Orach Chayim, dealing with laws of prayer and a person's daily
  conduct
- Yoreh Deah, dealing with the dietary laws, laws of ritual purity and
  mourning
- Even HaEzer, dealing with personal and family matters, including laws of marriage and divorce
- Choshen Mishpat, dealing with criminal and civil law

By far the most popular, respected, and authoritative code of Jewish law is the Shulchan Aruch (The Prepared Table), written by Joseph
Karo. The Shulchan Aruch is actually an abbreviated and simplified
form of the Arba'ah Turim, taking into account the views of previous

codifiers, including those of Alfasi and Maimonides. This code dealt with Jewish law and practice wherever the Jew might be: at home, synagogue, or business. The Shulchan Aruch was completed in approximately 1555 and together with subsequent commentaries on it became Judaism's most authoritative law code. Because Joseph Karo was a Sephardic scholar, he was charged with ignoring the views of Ashkenazic (French and German) legal authorities. As a result, Moses Isserles of Poland (1525–1572), a scholar known as Rama, wrote supplementary notes to the Shulchan Aruch called the Mappah (Tablecloth). The notes of Isserles set forth the views of Ashkenazic scholars and presented the customs of their communities. Whenever Karo and Isserles do not agree on a particular custom, the Sephardim generally follow Karo, whereas the Ashkenazim most often follow Isserles.

With the publication of the Shulchan Aruch, the period of the early scholars (*rishonim*) ended and the period of the *acharonim*, the later ones, began. From the end of the sixteenth century to the present, the *acharonim* have issued authoritative interpretations of the law. Among the most famous later scholars are the Polish sage Solomon Luria, known as Maharshal; the Hungarian Moses Sofer; and Rabbi Abraham Kook, the former chief rabbi of the Ashkenazic community in Palestine in 1921.

A very important late twentieth century interpreter of Jewish law for the Conservative movement was Rabbi Isaac Klein. His book, *Guide to Jewish Religious Practice*, serves as an important law code for many Conservative Jews today. The Reform movement remains committed to personal autonomy, provided a person uses the formula for personal choice based on knowledge. There are guide books and a responsa committee of the Central Conference of American Rabbis, the Reform Union of Rabbis. The leading *posek* (Jewish legal scholar) for the Reform movement is Mark Washovsky.

What are responsa?

Responsa are written replies that qualified authorities have given to questions about all aspects of Jewish law from the Talmudic period to the present. These authorities are referred to as *posekim* (singular *posek*). The questions that individuals asked their *posekim* were often based on some current situation that the codes did not deal with directly. For example, is it permissible to use a life-sustaining device to keep a patient alive? Is gambling permitted in synagogues? Is it permissible for a Jew to smoke cigarettes? The rabbi would give his responsum (answer), always basing his reasoning on supporting statements and earlier precedents found in the Bible, the Talmud, and later the Shulchan Aruch. In this way Jewish law continued to develop, change, and be modified in order to be in consonance with new times and new situations.

Is there one code of Jewish law for all Jews?

The Shulchan Aruch continues to remain the most authoritative law code for Orthodox Jews. For Conservative Jews, the *Guide to Jewish Religious Practice* presents both the so-called normative Jewish practice and the decisions that the Rabbinical Assembly's Committee on Law and Standards has reached. It deals with such contemporary issues as artificial insemination, organ transplants, and autopsies; and it reflects some of the most recent scientific advances of our day.

❧ Who's Who of Rabbinic ❧ Sages and Commentaries

Baal Shem Tov Israel ben Eliezer, the eighteenth-century founder of the Hasidic movement.

Epstein, Yechiel (1829–1907) Often called Aruch HaShulchan after his main work, he was one of the leading Lithuanian authorities in Jewish law.

Gaon, Hai The last and greatest of the Geonim immediately following the Talmud.

Gaon, Saadiah A tenth-century Babylonian scholar and teacher. He is considered the father of medieval philosophy and was head of the Sura academy in Babylon.

Gerondi, Nissim Fourteenth-century Spanish legal authority also known as the Ran.

Hinnuch Also called Aaron Ha-Levi, this fourteenth-century Spanish rabbi authored Sefer Ha-Hinnuch, which listed all 613 commandments as they occur in their weekly Torah portions.

Kagan, Israel Eighteenth-century rabbi and ethicist, known as the Chafetz Chayim, who wrote an important book called *Who Wants Life* (in Hebrew, *Chaftez Chayim*). The topics of the book are evil speech and gossip in Jewish law.

Kitzur Shulchan Aruch Condensed version of the Code of Jewish Law.

Kotzker Rebbe Eighteenth-century Hasidic rabbi, whose real name was Rabbi Menachem Mendel Heilprin.

Lubliner Rebbe Eighteenth-century rabbi, whose real name was Jacob Isaac Horowitz. His works emphasize joy in worship and humility in conduct.

Luzzatto, Moshe Chayim Eighteenth-century Italian commentator and ethicist.

Maimonides, Moses Eleventh-century medieval Jewish philosopher, author of the law code known as the Mishneh Torah.

Mechilta Name applied to certain midrashic works. For example, the oldest midrashic commentary to the book of Exodus is called the Mechilta.

Meiri Second-century Palestinian teacher and student of Rabbi Akiba. His Mishnah formed the basis of the accepted Mishnah of Judah the Prince.

Menorat HaMaor Midrashic work written by Isaac Abohav.

Midrash Refers to the nonlegal sections of the Talmud and the rabbinic books containing biblical interpretations in the spirit of legend.

Midrash Tanchuma Attributed to Rabbi Tanchuma bar Abba, the discourses center around the opening verse of the biblical portion designated for the week.

Nachman of Bratslav A leading Hasidic rabbi of the eighteenth-century. Also known as the Bratzlaver Rebbe, he was the grandson of the Baal Shem Tov.

Nachmanides Thirteenth-century Spanish biblical commentator, whose real name was Moses ben Nachman (also known as the Ramban).

Pakuda, Bachya ibn Eleventh-century Spanish philosopher who published *Duties of the Heart*, the first book on Jewish morals and ethics.

Peskita Rabbati Homilies included in the Midrash Rabbah.

Rabbenu Tam Jacob ben Meir, twelfth-century French scholar, grandson of the great commentator Rashi.

Salanter, Israel Eighteenth-century founder of the so-called *musar* ethical movement, his real name was Israel ben Ze'ev Wolf.

Tosefta A supplement to the Mishnah.

Yalkut Shimoni Midrashic collection relating to all the books of the Bible, compiled by Shimon Kayyara ha-Darshan in the thirteenth century.

Zohar The central work of the Kabbalah, containing much midrashic and homiletical material; composed in thirteenth-century Spain.

References

Artson, B. *It's a Mitzvah! Jewish Living Step-by-Step*. Springfield, N.J.:
Behrman House, 1995.

Boteach, S. *Kosher Sex*. New York: Doubleday, 1999.

Buber, M. *Tales of the Hasidim: The Later Masters*. New York: Schocken,
1948.

Bulka, R. P. *Judaism on Pleasure*. Northvale, N.J.: Jason Aronson, 1995.

Central Conference of Reform Rabbis. CCAR Response no. 33: "Reform
Attitude Toward Bar Mitzvah and Bat Mitzvah." 1979.

Chaimovitz, N. *Timeless Fashion*. Jerusalem: Feldheim, 1991.

Donin, H. *To Pray as a Jew*. New York: Basic Books, 1980.

Dorff, E. *Matters of Life and Death: A Jewish Approach to Modern Medical Ethics*. Philadelphia: Jewish Publication Society, 1998.

Eisenstein, J. D. *Otzar Dinim U'minhagim*. New York: Hebrew Publishing Company, 1917.

Etkes, I., and Chipman, J. (trans.). *Rabbi Israel Salanter and the Mussar Movement*. Philadelphia: Jewish Publication Society, 1993.

Finkel, A. (trans.). *Sefer Hasidim*. Northvale, N.J.: Jason Aronson, 1997.

Frank, A. *The Diary of a Young Girl*. New York: Globe, 1988.

Frankel, E. *The Classic Tales: Four Thousand Years of Jewish Lore*. Northvale, N.J.: Jason Aronson, 1989.

Freehof, S. *Reform Jewish Practice*. Cincinnati: Hebrew Union College
Press, 1944.

Friedman, M. *Capitalism and Freedom.* Chicago: University of Chicago Press, 2004.

Gold, M. *Does God Belong in the Bedroom?* Philadelphia: Jewish Publication Society, 1992.

Gordon, M. "Mezuzah: Protective Amulet or Religious Symbol?" *Tradition* 1977 (summer), 8.

Greenberg, S., and Levine, J. (eds.). *Likrat Shabbat.* Bridgeport, Conn.: Prayer Book Press, 1973.

Heschel, A. J. *The Insecurities of Freedom.* New York: Schocken, 1972.

Isaacs, L. N. "The Development of Children's Attitudes Toward the Aged." Doctoral dissertation, City University of New York, 1982.

Klein, I. *A Guide to Jewish Religious Practice.* New York: Jewish Theological Seminary, 1979.

Kushner, H. *To Life: A Celebration of Jewish Being and Thinking.* Boston: Little, Brown and Company, 1993.

Leder, S. Z. *More Money Than God: Living a Rich Life Without Losing Your Soul.* Chicago: Bonus Books, 2003.

Peli, P. *Torah Today.* Washington, D.C.: B'nai Brith Books, 1987.

Prager, D., and Telushkin, J. *Eight Questions People Ask About Judaism.* Simi Valley, CA: Tze Ulmad Press, 1975.

Rabbinical Assembly of America, Law Committee. "Statement on Suicide." 1998.

Riskin, S. *Jewish Week* (New York), Aug. 14, 1987, p. 21.

Salkin, J. *Putting God on the Guest List: How to Reclaim the Spiritual Meaning of Your Child's Bar or Bat Mitzvah.* Woodstock, Vt.: Jewish Lights, 1992.

Samet, R. *Aharas Yisrael.* Aish Audio Torah class. [http://www.aishaudio.com].

The Author

Rabbi Ron Isaacs is the spiritual leader of Temple Sholom in Bridgewater, New Jersey. Ordained at the Jewish Theological Seminary of America, he received his doctorate in education from Columbia University Teachers College.

A prolific author, his many books include the well-known *Every Person's Guide* series and *Ask the Rabbi: The Who, What, When, Where, Why, and How of Being Jewish.* Rabbi Isaacs was a founding member of the acclaimed Hebrew folk rock group Arbaah Kolote and served as host of Central New Jersey's popular radio program *The Jewish American Hour.* Rabbi Isaacs writes a monthly column called "Ask the Rabbi" that is featured in a number of New Jersey newspapers. His many students constantly visit his Web site, rabbiron.com.

Known as the teaching rabbi, Rabbi Isaacs has taught in the Graduate Rabbinical School of the Jewish Theological Seminary and has lectured throughout the United States at various synagogues and Jewish community centers. He has also chaired the Rabbinical Assembly's Publication Committee. For more than a decade, he and his wife, Dr. Leora Isaacs, have designed and coordinated the adult learning experience called Shabbat Plus as well as Family Camp at Camp Ramah in the Poconos.

Index